Law, Liberalism and Free Speech

Law, Liberalism and Free Speech

D. F. B. Tucker

Rowman & Allanheld
PUBLISHERS

ROWMAN & ALLANHELD

Published in the United States of America in 1985
by Rowman & Allanheld, Publishers
(a division of Littlefield, Adams & Company)
81 Adams Drive, Totowa, New Jersey 07512

Library of Congress Cataloging-in-Publication Data

Tucker, D. F. B.
  Law, liberalism, and free speech.

  Bibliography
  Includes index.
  1. Freedom of speech. 2. Liberalism. I. Title.
K3254.T83   1985   323.44′3   85-14449
ISBN 0-8476-7466-5

85 86 87 / 10 9 8 7 6 5 4 3 2 1
Printed in the United States of America

For Pam

Contents

Acknowledgments ix

Introduction 1

Part One: Political Theory and Freedom of Speech 9

1 Freedom of Speech and Functionalist Liberal Theories 11
   Utilitarian Functionalism   11
   Indirect Utilitarianism   18
   Democratic Functionalism   24

2 Freedom of Speech and Deontological Liberal Theories 31
   Lockean Liberalism   31
   A Rawlsian Alternative   34
   Identifying Rights   42

Part Two: Accommodating Rights and the Public Interest 57

3 Free Speech versus Access 65
   Gaining Access for Advertising and to Public Forums   66
   Access versus Editorial Autonomy   72
   Distinguishing Print and Broadcast Media   77

4 Free Speech versus Reputation 84
   The Functionalist Case for Defamation Law Reform   84
   A Deontological Approach to Defamation   93

5 Free Speech versus Privacy (Part One) 101
   Our Privacy Interests   102
   Privacy as a Right Not to Be Deceived   107
   Privacy as a Right to Political Liberty and Minimal Dignity 110

6 Free Speech versus Privacy (Part Two) 115
   Intrusions and the Press   116
   The Problem of Unwanted Publicity   123

7   Free Speech versus the Public Interest in Regulating
    Offensive Speech   126
        Liberal Theory and the Offense Problem   128
        Dealing with Offensive Speech in the Context of
            Demonstrations   136
8   Free Speech versus the Public Interest in Regulating
    Broadcasting   148
        Public Broadcasting   151
        Commercial Broadcasting   156
9   Freedom of Speech versus Democratic Authority   163
        Legal versus Democratic Authority   164
        John Hart Ely's Functionalism   171
        The Way Forward   177
        Concluding Remarks   182
10 General Conclusion   183

Notes   191
References   205
Index   209

Acknowledgments

Much of the research for this book was completed during a period of sabbatical leave spent in New York as a Visiting Scholar at Columbia University. I wish to thank the faculty of the Graduate School of Journalism for their hospitality, and John Chapman, who recommended me to them. I also need to mention Phillip Davison for the trouble he took to ensure that my stay was worth while, especially for phoning the housing officer at Butler Hall; Benno Schmidt and Floyd Abrams, who tolerated me as a participant in their weekly seminar "Current Problems in Communications Law"; and Kent Greenawalt for allowing me to attend his lectures on the First Amendment.

Some sections of the work have been presented to various conferences and seminars. In this regard, I wish to thank John Kleinig for his careful comments on a paper "Re-Reading Mill on Freedom of Speech," which I read to the Australasian Political Science Association. I also owe a debt to Denis Galligan, who encouraged me to participate in the staff seminars at the Law School at Melbourne University and for his comments on a paper "Liberal Theory and the Democratic State," which I read to a special conference on the theme "Law, Rights and the Welfare State." Of those who read my whole manuscript, I owe a special debt to Melinda Jones, who also helped me run a class on freedom of speech; and to Robert Ladenson, who identified a serious gap in the argument I present in chapter 2.

Finally, I wish to thank Neil Whitlock and the other administrative staff in the Department of Political Science at Melbourne University for allowing me to share their word-processing facilities. I hope I was not too much of a nuisance.

David Tucker
Melbourne University

Law, Liberalism and Free Speech

Introduction

Modern political philosophers usually distinguish two fundamentally different ways of approaching policy problems. We may postulate some goal (such as the maximization of happiness or the achievement of democratic accountability) and then review institutional arrangements or policy recommendations by asking whether they are functional to the realization of it; or we may recognize the existence of rights as placing limits on the ways in which governmental authorities may go about pursuing policy objectives. I will refer to the first approach as "functionalist" and to the second as "deontological."

Until very recently, the prevailing views with regard to policy concerning freedom of speech have been various forms of functionalism. The classical expression of such a liberal theory has been provided by John Stuart Mill in his essay *On Liberty*, and his way of reasoning has been followed by many subsequent writers. Indeed, functionalist ways of thinking have been well-represented in the United States Supreme Court, where such interpretations of the First Amendment protection of speech have been embraced by liberal-minded judges such as Holmes, Brandeis, and Brennan, as well as by conservatives such as Frankfurter and Harlan. In addition, many of the more significant commentators, including liberals such as Thomas Emerson and Alexander Meiklejohn, have embraced functionalism.

My purpose is to recommend an alternative deontological framework from which to construe "freedom of speech" which I believe offers significant advantages. I shall do this by reviewing a wide range of policy issues. My aim is to show, in each case, that the solutions I recommend in the light of my coordinating theory are sensible, reflecting an appropriate response (in the sense that it is not incongruent with our intuitive moral judgments), whilst providing coherence over all the different kinds of cases that arise. A good theory should not only enable us to reach satisfactory solutions when faced with hard policy choices but should illuminate, providing us with an understanding of why we make the judgments we do.

The work is divided into two distinct parts:

In Part One I am concerned to state my theoretical assumptions and to show how they differ from alternative approaches; in particular, from the much-favored functionalist framework derived from Mill.

In Part Two I test the theory by looking at dilemmas which arise when freedom of speech is in conflict with claims individuals make to have some interest (such as privacy or to be afforded the opportunity to reply when personally attacked) protected as a right. I shall show how the deontological approach I recommend helps us to see when freedom of speech must give way to allow for the fair treatment of individuals; and I claim that it has an advantage over alternative approaches in that it can provide a method for determining a priority when conflicting rights claims are being made. This is significant because, as I show, prevailing functionalist theories have led to a number of anomalies. I draw attention to the fact that (a) no acceptable rationale has been provided for treating broadcast speech differently from speech disseminated in other ways; also, (b) the United States Supreme Court has used a deontological argument in rejecting the claims of those who wish to establish a constitutional right of access to monopoly newspapers but relies on functionalist considerations in resolving most other policy dilemmas (for example, the interest which audiences have in getting informed is the rationale provided when the Court liberalized the law of defamation and when it allowed the Federal Communications Commission to force broadcasters to afford a right of reply to those who have been personally attacked in a program).

Here, I also review those policy problems which arise when freedom of speech seems to be in conflict with the public interest. The problem is to determine whether my recommended theory, which seems to work well when the problem is to establish a priority between conflicting rights claims, can also allow for sufficient flexibility to handle adequately cases when the general good may be compromised by the enjoyment of an unbridled right to freedom of speech. This is important because it is often assumed that deontological approaches, by committing us to an absolutist conception of rights, are unrealistic. I will demonstrate not only that sufficient flexibility can be accommodated to dispose of this objection, but that, unlike functionalist theories which tend towards a balancing of competing interests, a deontological approach can help us understand why we are inclined to defer when editors claim their autonomy as a right.

Finally, in chapter 9, I ask whether the deontological approach I recommend serves well or badly in providing an account of adjudication. This is important because most of us who value freedom of speech hope to see this liberty constitutionally protected. Thus we anticipate judicial review and suppose that it will be the judiciary rather than an elected parliament which will take primary responsibility for delineating the liberty. I argue that a deontological ethical theory offers significant advantages in achieving a successful defense of the practice of judicial review.

The orientation I adopt is derived from the work of two contemporary philosophers, John Rawls and Ronald Dworkin. Both writers develop a conception of rights and justice which is essentially egalitarian in its implications. Their coordinating assumption is that individuals have a right to equal respect and concern in the design of political institutions. This is the assumption that I call the "democratic commitment." Rawls and Dworkin are, of course, not the first moral philosophers to ground their theorizing on such a commitment. The idea that conduct is only moral if it exemplifies a universal rather than a particularistic point of view has served as a decisive critical standard from the very beginning of philosophical enquiry. For example, Christ's command that we do unto others as we would be done by which lies at the heart of Christian ethics embodies the ideal of treating others with equal concern and respect. By insisting that a person universalize his or her perspective, we impose an obligation which makes it illegitimate for that person to discriminate arbitrarily, and we make it very difficult to justify policies which favor those closely associated with him or her. Of the great moral philosophers who have used this device, the name of Immanuel Kant stands out, for he developed this meta-ethical position most forcefully, claiming that the obligation to universalize our judgments constitutes a categorical imperative; his views have since been refined and explored by many different thinkers, including many modern writers. Even utilitarians, whose most fundamental standard is the maximization of happiness by choosing policies which satisfy the desires of most people, often see the need to treat persons as equals by showing concern for each individual's claims to have his or her wants satisfied without prejudice. Thus, while there may be disagreement about how a commitment to a universal ethical standard can best be exemplified in practice, there is a significant consensus amongst those who have thought deeply about ethical issues that impartiality is a defining characteristic of "the moral point of view." This is a view which I share, and I take for granted throughout my discussion that the reader is willing to seek out its full implications.[1]

Rawls and Dworkin make a further, closely related, commitment that I have found significant: they think it important to distinguish approaches which accord a conception of rights a proper place, as providing the basis for claims which enable individuals legitimately to frustrate the policy objectives of the collectivity.[2] To illustrate this view, Rawls compares his own rights-based theory with utilitarianism:

The last contrast that I shall mention now is that utilitarianism is a teleological theory whereas justice as fairness is not. By definition, then, the latter is a deontological theory, one that either does not specify the good independently from the right, or does not interpret the right as maximizing the good.

And he goes on to describe the contrast:

In utilitarianism the satisfaction of any desire has some value in itself which must be taken into account in deciding what is right. In calculating the greater balance of satisfaction it does not matter, except indirectly, what the desires are for.

With regard to his own position he writes:

The principles of right, and so of justice, put limits on which satisfactions have value; they impose restrictions on what are reasonable conceptions of one's good. In drawing up plans and in deciding aspirations men are to take these constraints into account. Hence in justice as fairness one does not take men's propensities and inclinations as given, whatever they are, and seek the best way to fulfill them. Rather, their desires and aspirations are restricted from the outset by the principles of justice which specify the boundaries that men's systems of ends must respect. We can express this by saying that in justice as fairness the concept of the right is prior to that of the good.[3]

This analytic distinction provides the basis for the charge which Rawls and Dworkin direct at utilitarian writers—that they do not usually take rights seriously enough. If, for example, some polemicist claims to recognize the right to free speech but then qualifies his commitment by requiring that such a right should be ignored in circumstances in which a social goal may be frustrated or even those in which there may be great public inconvenience, his position is exhausted by the collective goal; the putative claim to a moral right adds nothing and there is no point in recognizing it at all. Similarly, those who hold to a religious conception of the role of the state (conceiving it to be the duty of governments to uphold certain moral ideals and to encourage citizens to live up to these, even if this requires that criminal law be used against nonconformists) can make no claim to take rights seriously, for they subordinate the claims of individuals to their religious conception of the point and purpose of social life. In general, Dworkin tells us: "The strength of a particular right within a particular theory is a function of the degree of disservice to the goals of the theory, beyond a mere disservice on the whole, that is necessary to justify refusing an act called for under the right."[4] In terms of this criterion, then, any theory which requires that rights claims always be considered subordinate to the goal of maximizing welfare, as most versions of utilitarianism do, can hardly be said to take rights seriously. Such theories, then, are not liberal.

Besides embracing the core commitments of the Rawlsian approach, in assessing institutions and practices, my procedure will be typically that which Rawls and Dworkin describe as establishing "reflective equilibrium":[5] I begin by selecting those orientations and governing principles which I take to be the most adequate. I then review problem cases to see if the solutions suggested in the light of my chosen coordinating criteria seem reasonable. The idea is to delineate a theory intuitively: in a good one, there should be a satisfactory fit between what we feel ought to be the case in a large number of cases and the resolutions I reach in the light of my chosen coordinating theory. We should be able to comprehend, in the light of principles generated by my chosen theory, why I reach the resolution of hard cases in the way that I do. If the theoretically informed judgments confirm our intuitive sense of justice, my approach will have proved itself illuminating and satisfactory. The purpose is not to treat intuitions as ultimate standards but to find a principled basis for accommodating many of our strongly felt judgments in given circumstances. It may be the case, of course, that some of the judgments I reach in the light of the principles allowed for within my chosen theory are counterintuitive. I will only abandon these anomalous judgments, however, if another theory is available which provides what appears in the light of intuition as a better trade-off of the competing interests. Of course, the fit between theoretically informed judgments and those arrived at intuitively will never be perfect, and there may be times when I feel uncomfortable about my commitments. However, I assume that it is better to be consistent in the light of articulated principles which can be justified in the light of some democratic liberal theory (that is, to have some understanding of why an outcome is chosen) than to have no publicly stated criteria at all.

The task which I set myself is very similar to that which the Supreme Court of the United States has actually had to confront in the free speech area. In that system, the justices have been expected to adjudicate in a way which provides some consistent reading of the requirements embodied in a constitution. In this regard, they have had to articulate what they take to be the significance of the First Amendment (which states that Congress shall make no law "abridging freedom of speech, or of the press, or the right of the people peaceably to assemble, and to petition the government for a redress of grievances"), and the Fourteenth Amendment (which states that no State shall make or enforce any law "which shall abridge the privileges or immunities of citizens of the United States," nor "deprive any person of life, liberty, or property without due process of law"); and they have had to do this in a way which provides consistency in dealing with a range of problems. I do not imply that the justices have found it necessary to agree on theoretical matters. Rather, in making determinations, each has had to articulate some guiding criteria or accept the prevailing wisdom of the Court. For example, even Chief Justice Burger, whose critical assessment of the leadership of Earl Warren was the very reason President Nixon appointed him, felt obliged to go along, in a surprisingly large number of cases, with a good part of the liberal legacy he inherited from his predecessor.

I have found this work of the Court extremely interesting. This is partly because it has dealt with policy issues in a quite different way from courts in other democracies; also, the reasoning of the justices is often illuminating. However, my use of American cases is sufficiently idiosyncratic to warrant a few words of caution and amplification. First, cases are selected not because their resolution illuminates the law in a given area (by helping lawyers anticipate the likely reasoning of judges in similar cases) but because they serve as good examples to tease our intuitive responses. Here, I make use of history (taking the facts of a case and the reflection upon it by a court) in much the same way a philosopher of science may make use of examples from the history of science. It is not merely that the problems that have actually been confronted are often difficult and puzzling—often more so than those that we can construct with made-up examples—but the fact that they have been addressed by practical men and women gives us some objective evidence of common intuitive responses. What is interesting for me, here, about the work of the United States courts, is that it provides a first attempt at establishing a "reflective equilibrium" in dealing with speech problems, and it is with this focus in mind that the cases are reported. When I do state the law in an area, then, my motive is usually that of showing the kinds of accommodation reasonable and conscientious persons are inclined to reach when dealing with hard cases. I shall of course be critical of some of the accommodations made. However, if the resolutions I reach in the light of my coordinating deontological approach are too far out of step with the prevailing wisdom about what should be done (reflected in the law rather than the legitimating arguments provided by the courts), this must count against my suggestion. A theory gains in plausibility when it accommodates our intuitive judgments as to how problems should be resolved. What I hope to show is (1) that my approach offers greater consistency and can account better for the accommodations actually reached than its main rivals; (2) that when I do recommend changes to improve consistency, these do not provoke a conflict with strongly held moral convictions.

This methodological program is likely to give rise to the charge that I am seeking to legitimate the status quo in the United States. There is some truth in this charge, but it is also misleading. If what is meant by "status quo" is the whole social system known in Marxist literature as the capitalist mode of production, the charge is grossly misleading. First, freedom of speech is a significant universal value and has application in all societies including those which may be described as socialist. Second, the fact that a capitalist system such as the United States has exemplified fairly progressive policies by offering its citizens a constitutionally protected right (judged by our intuitive responses) is a good point to be made in favor of that system. Moreover, it is a standing embarrassment that no known socialist society has been able to sustain freedom of speech in a meaningful way for very long. Socialists need to recognize the problem and articulate the principles they believe ought to be binding in this area. In this latter regard, they can perhaps benefit from an attempt to comprehend a system which does seem to work reasonably well. Third, to say that the United States provides a progressive lead in that freedom of speech is recognized in that system as a basic political right is in no way equivalent to supposing that it is a model democracy. In fact I believe that despite its flourishing liberal culture the United States is a very badly functioning democracy. Indeed, it barely qualifies for inclusion in the list of what Robert Dahl has described as polyarchies.[6] My point here is simply that this work is neither a defense of the United States system of government or a defense of capitalism. I merely use American cases to tease my own (and I hope the reader's) intuitions in confronting hard policy problems relating to communications and, when I have stated the law, my purpose is to assist the process of "reflective equilibrium" rather than to claim that the accommodations actually reached in the United States are the best possible.

In reviewing the work of the United States Supreme Court I have found it useful to make certain comparisons to the law and the policy recommendations of various commissions of inquiry in the United Kingdom. My intention in undertaking this task is to test my own sense of the restraints which may legitimately be imposed on our claim to communicate freely. I am interested in delineating the profile of a basic political right in the light of what I take to be the most adequate understanding of the democratic commitment which has been provided by contemporary philosophers, judges, and political commentators.

PART ONE

Political Theory and Freedom of Speech

I wish to present a deontological theory to account for our fundamental right to communicate.

As the novelty of such an approach and its significance can best be appreciated by way of a contrast with the main alternatives, I will begin by providing a brief statement of the central difficulties with functionalism and a very brief account of some problems with a Lockean approach. I will focus on the contributions of J. S. Mill and Alexander Meiklejohn, the functionalist writers who have had most influence. After reviewing these alternatives (the task of chapter 1) I develop the Rawlsian position I recommend by addressing the three tasks which any adequate liberal theory of freedom of speech must accomplish if it is to succeed: these are the problems of (1) establishing which forms of communication fall within the protected zone of liberty, (2) providing general justificatory arguments for establishing freedom of speech, (3) identifying the priority which must hold between any putative right to speak and other claimed rights. These tasks are all interrelated. How "speech" is defined greatly influences the kinds of argument which may be relevant to deploy in justifying liberty, and how we justify liberty will not only influence how we demarcate the protected category "speech" but will be decisive when we determine whether the liberty to speak should have priority over competing claims. Nevertheless, I shall deal with each of the issues in turn.

1

Freedom of Speech and Functionalist Liberal Theories

The best-known school of liberal theorists are the utilitarian writers. Despite the simplicity of their critical principle that we should always maximize pleasure (or the variant that we should maximize general average utility), utilitarians have made a substantial contribution to liberal political thought. Liberty is important to utilitarians primarily because their orientation tends to be want-regarding; thus, although Bentham conceived of pleasure as a psychological feeling of well-being, this commitment has usually been interpreted as giving individuals what they actually do desire.[1] It follows from this that we should generally allow people to choose what they wish to do, and for this reason utilitarians have usually been suspicious of moral paternalism. (Some paternalism is allowed for but only when it can be shown to maximize want-satisfaction.) In economics, as is well known, the utilitarian concern with want-satisfaction was linked by Adam Smith with the idea that markets, if allowed to operate freely, will provide a mechanism for allocating resources most efficiently. An analogous model of the political process in democratic systems was worked out by James Mill and Bentham, who saw the aim of the systems of representation as that of ensuring that the interests of the rulers would be congruent with those of the electors.

UTILITARIAN FUNCTIONALISM

Although there are problems with the utilitarian analysis of market mechanisms, there is no doubt that this legacy has had a considerable impact, especially on liberal political theorizing. Nevertheless, because they do not take rights claims seriously enough, neither Bentham nor James Mill should be regarded as a liberal. The great tradition of utilitarian liberal theorizing actually begins with the publication of John Stuart Mill's essay,

On Liberty, for it is in that work that an attempt is made to give rights claims an independent weight in moral and political argument. The younger Mill wanted to place limits on the kinds of harm which governments may legitimately prevent, and in doing this he was eschewing the pure balancing approach advocated by Bentham and his father. He claimed that, in the long run, more good than harm is likely to follow from recognizing a general principle limiting political authority than if we allow governments to deal with problem cases on an ad hoc basis.

Many of the elements of Mill's liberalism which have had a lasting significance relate to his individualism. We can distinguish his critical rationalism, his optimism and humanism and his "harm principle." Consider his rationalism. By this I mean his belief that individual actors are able critically to assess social institutions and by persuading others successfully bring about social change. The idea is not that any particular individual can affect change on his own but that each of us somehow makes a difference and that by increasing our various capacities, especially by developing our ability to think clearly, we are able to improve our life's circumstances. Also involved in this conception is the notion that we can distinguish objective critical standards and are not bound by the norms which are largely taken for granted within particular cultures. As Mill sees the human predicament, individuals are not so shaped and motivated by their socialization that it becomes impossible for them to reflect critically upon the values they have been taught to respect and which are widely endorsed in their community. What Mill values is the questioning individual who seeks out reasons for affording deference to social norms. It is in his view always better to have reasons other than simple dogmatic acceptance of positive morality for what one thinks is good than to simply conform out of habit or lazinesss. This commitment reflects Mill's humanism, which, in turn, is closely linked with his optimism about human nature.

Given these assumptions, it is easy to see why Mill should have defended his harm principle, which reads:

> the only purpose for which power can be rightfully exercised over any member of a civilized community, against his will, is to prevent harm to others . . .
> He cannot rightfully be compelled to do or forbear because it will be better for him to do so, because it will make him happier, because, in the opinions of others, to do so would be wise, or even right.[2]

What Mill hoped to ensure was the maximum area of liberty for the individual so that, in taking responsibility for our own lives, we would come to develop ourselves and contribute more to enrich the lives of others. Societies benefit from the quality of their citizens and, in this regard, a free society, by expecting more from its members, has a definite advantage in securing the good life over those which simply illicit unquestioning conformity.

I regard Mill's idea of demarcating a private realm into which it is illegitimate for governments or other collective agencies to intrude as the fundamental coordinating assumption of all subsequent liberal theory. All liberals accept that individuals enjoy certain rights which enable them to demand an area of autonomy for themselves. Disagreements simply reflect various assessments of what privileges are to be included in this zone of freedom, particularly whether we should regard individuals as the owners of their capacities.

As I have said, Mill attempts to demarcate the realm of liberty using his "harm principle," which embodies his distinction between "self-regarding" and "other-regarding" actions. A problem with this approach is, however, that what is to count as "harming others" is never made clear by Mill. As he acknowledges that all our actions have some effect for good or ill, we must necessarily make judgments about what is to count as "harm" for the purposes of applying his principle. Even actions which are predominantly "self-regarding" can harm others by virtue of the example that is set or because offense to others may be caused. Although it is clear that Mill wishes to exclude these forms of harm from being counted as "harming others" for the purposes of applying his principle, it is not clear why we should allow this.

Another problem with Mill's conception is that as soon as it is allowed that communities depend crucially on some process of socialization by means of which values come to be integrated socially and internalized individually, the idea that liberty can promote the good life looks questionable. How can there be value integration where liberty allows for experimentation and competition? Once we proceed, as for example Lord Devlin does in his Maccabaean Lecture, from the premise that society is entitled by means of its laws to protect itself from dangers which threaten its existence, and if we include also the assumption that value integration is necessary in this sense, then, by a process of deductive reasoning, we may conclude that society is entitled to uphold the base values of its culture—enforcement of morality is justified because this is functional to social existence.[3] Thus, in his critical discussion of arguments supporting discrimination against women, Mill allows that the real views of his opponents seem to be:

1. that it is necessary to society that women should marry and produce children,
2. that they will not do so unless compelled (socialized),
3. therefore it is necessary to compel (socialize them).

But he dismisses this kind of argument too lightly by treating it as equivalent to the argument of slavers who may have put forward a case for slavery as follows:

1. it is necessary for society that people labor in plantations,

2. without slaves no one would labor in plantations,
3. therefore, slavery is justifiable because it is necessary.

Clearly what is fallacious about this argument is the factual claim that no one would labor in plantations without slavery. What is really implied here is that no one would be prepared to work at the wages the plantation owners would offer, and Mill is quite right when he argues that a market price should be paid to attract labor if the system of plantation production is itself to be justified. However, he should not be allowed to extend his argument, by parity of reasoning, to cover the case of mothering. Mill's claim seems to be that if women need an incentive to be mothers, then they should be paid. But how much? As much as is required to get them to do it? But suppose women think it wrong that they be delegated the nurturing roles and are not prepared to accept any price that society can afford to pay. Are we to say that mothering itself is now no longer justifiable? What Mill fails to take into account here are the complex sentiments and values which are associated with mothering. Some people, for example, would seriously argue that every effort must be made to uphold the family as a viable institution because only within the family can one generate a nurturing environment based on love. Those who adopt such a view would not be likely to endorse a view of mothering which comprehends the role in terms of purely material incentives. For, unless women are morally motivated and are taught to want to be mothers whether with or without pay, as a fulfillment of duty and their own nature, they will surely not be successful at the task of caring for and loving the very young. But, where women are so motivated and accept the role because they are brought up to see their fulfillment in these terms, the material incentives would count for very little.

This is one reason why the demarcation of a private realm which Mill hoped to achieve by recommending his "harm principle" fails. Unfortunately, no other major utilitarian writer has been able to provide a more adequate principle.

If we leave aside for the moment the problem of whether utilitarian liberals can successfully define a realm of liberty and turn to consider the general justificatory arguments which they have been able to provide for placing a priority on liberty, we are faced by a wide range of considerations. For example, Justice Brandeis, in his famous dissenting opinion in *Whitney v. California*, writes (referring to the American democratic tradition):

> Those who won our independence believed that the final end of the state was to make men free to develop their faculties. . . . They valued liberty both as an end and as a means. They believed liberty to be the secret of happiness. . . . They believed that freedom to think as you will and to speak as you will are means indispensable to the discovery and spread of political truth; and without free speech and assembly discussion would be futile; that with them,

discussion affords ordinarily an adequate protection against the dissemination of noxious doctrines.[4]

If liberty is conceived narrowly, as embracing no more than a right to
freedom of expression, further considerations are relevant. The legal
scholar Thomas Emerson tells us that speech needs to be specially protected because "thought and communication are the fountainhead and
expression of the individual personality," because speech "is correctly
perceived as doing less injury to other social goals than actions," because
the harm speech may cause is not often irremedial and, finally, because

> the power of society and the state over the individual is so pervasive and the
> construction of doctrines, institutions and administrative practices to limit
> this power so difficult, that only by drawing [such] a protective line between
> expression and action is it possible to strike a safe balance between authority
> and freedom.[5]

Emerson's and Brandeis's lists overlap to some extent but their emphasis is different: Brandeis stresses that liberty is an indispensable instrument for the attainment of certain widely accepted goods (happiness, the
spread of political truth, and protection against the dissemination of noxious doctrines); Emerson stresses that liberty protects society from the
ever-present possibility of tyranny. These concerns are, of course, shared
by Mill, whose essay, *On Liberty*, has been a reference for most utilitarian
discussions.

When taken together, these considerations provide good reasons why
we should be inclined to recognize political liberty as a right. However,
the weight which each carries depends very much on how the area of liberty is conceived. I shall mention a few of the problems.

Consider the notion that the preservation of liberty tends to assist us in
the advance of knowledge. A problem with this view is that we are no
longer so sure that there are "true" answers to all questions. Indeed, it
may be suggested that when it comes to rival conceptions about the nature of the good life most of us remain agnostic, preferring to tolerate
culture-relativism rather than assume the burden of demonstrating the
superiority of our own. That the problem has implications which bring
Mill's case against censorship into question is illustrated by the ferocity of
contemporary debates about so-called media imperialism. One argument
often put against allowing a free flow of communications between na-
tions is that a consequence of such liberty has been the flow into poorer
countries of the cultural product of more technically advanced societies.[6]
This is thought harmful in that ideals and conceptions of the good life
which are often projected are inappropriate. For example, it is suggested
that the constant portrayals of patterns of life reflecting Western individu-
alist values such as self-reliance and consumerism are having a deleterious effect on traditional communities who cannot hope to share in

Western affluence at this stage of the world's economic development. Yet if a country is poor, it is virtually powerless to prevent this consequence unless it resorts to censorship discriminating against the cultural products of the international media conglomerates. Because only a few countries have the technical skills or the means for producing high quality programs, and because those who do have shown a willingness to "dump" their programs on other markets at very low rates (after they have reaped profits from domestic consumption) the flow of communications between countries is likely to be one way. Thus, unless a strong case can be made showing that free competition for the minds of the people of the world is bringing us all closer to the truth (that is, unless we can claim that Western conceptions of the good, particularly those reflecting American values, are morally superior to rival conceptions), we must concede that the case for censorship as a form of cultural protectionism is a strong one.

Another problem is that it may produce bad consequences to publish correct information, so censorship may often seem justifiable in circumstances where truth is not in question. There are, first of all, those problems which arise where the liberty to publish is in conflict with some other value such as privacy, security, or economic efficiency. In cases of this kind it is not easy to see how the solution a utilitarian reaches in striking a particular balance can be anything other than arbitrary, reflecting his or her personal priorities. Consider the possible conflict between freedom of speech and the protection of privacy. In thinking about this dilemma, the utilitarian must often trade off the harm caused to an individual through public exposure with any good that publicity may be likely to bring, and in many circumstances an individual's privacy may seem the more significant good of the two. Once we ask whether the public gains by learning of private scandals, we must see that the case for censorship is strong. But even if we accept the view that knowledge of private facts is rarely useful, we must concede that there are exceptions which will have to be taken into account (for example, should public figures be required to disclose their tax returns? Does the public have a legitimate interest in learning about Prince Andrew's love affairs? What about those of John Kennedy when he was in office?) Also, the balancing process may be complicated by other concerns such as the goal of rehabilitation for those who have served periods in prison or of encouraging victims to report crimes of sexual assault.

A final difficulty for utilitarians occurs when there is a legitimate fear some citizens will respond badly if certain information is made public. For example, consider the dilemma faced by those psychologists who believe that their research into the relationship between IQ and race demonstrates that the lower intelligence of some groups can be accounted for as a genetic endowment.[7] Surely the publication of this finding led to an increase of racial prejudice. If this result was anticipated, were the psychologists justified in publishing their finding? The philosopher John McCloskey explores this dilemma by asking whether it would be expedient to publish the true figures concerning the incidence of murder and rape in a community if these show that blacks are substantially more violent than whites. He suggests, in response, that in some circumstances publishing such facts would be so destructive of good race relations that temporary censorship would be expedient and, therefore, justifiable on utilitarian grounds.[8]

The most persuasive utilitarian argument for recognizing liberty is the claim that the freedom to associate, communicate, and travel is a necessary prerequisite for democratic politics. The weight which can be placed on this consideration will, however, depend on the kinds of reasons which are provided for believing that democratic procedures are more likely to result in better consequences than would be the case if other decision-procedures were followed. But utilitarian democrats are faced with a paradox when they say they are in favor of democratic decision-procedures. For example, if they commit themselves to "majority rule" they must face the fact that the policy likely to produce the most beneficial results may not be the policy chosen by the majority.[9] What they have to show is why we should accept the popular choice even when we think it is foolish. After all, knowledge and wisdom are not easily acquired, and we must expect that most people, precisely because they do not apply themselves conscientiously to the task of becoming informed, will be neither wise or knowledgeable. Utilitarian democrats must, then, explain why majority-rule decision-procedures as well as a commitment to liberty of expression should carry the weight that democrats place upon them. This would seem to be impossible, however, because utilitarians embrace elitism in holding that policy dilemmas should be resolved by a process of calculation.

In facing this dilemma some utilitarians have advanced a revised concept of democracy which avoids the notion of popular sovereignty. For example, John Stuart Mill distinguishes between "governing" and "controlling," holding that the representative process should be understood as a means for ensuring that the most competent are chosen as policy-makers. Similarly, Joseph Schumpeter tells us that "the democratic method is that institutional arrangement for arriving at political decisions in which individuals acquire the power to decide by means of a competitive struggle for the people's vote."[10] These conceptions deliberately leave the power to decide in the hands of an elite who have the expertise, time, and resources to make well-considered decisions. The democratic vote merely serves to determine which set of elites is going to have political authority for a given period. Thus, Mill, Schumpeter, and those utilitarians who embrace an elitist conception of democracy need only show why it is better to have a system which provides for liberty of speech and periodic elections, forcing elites to compete for office. They do not need to assume that the people know better when it comes to deciding specific policy. This way of avoiding the democratic paradox has had a considerable influence. In justifying their revised conception of democracy, utilitarian writers tend to rely on the claim that great harm (resulting from tyranny) will be likely to follow, in the long term, if democratic procedures (of the kind reflected in Schumpeter's definition) are not respected. These elite theorists also insist that arguments about whether democracy is the best form of government are quite different from arguments about whether a government should adopt a particular course of action in dealing with the issues of the day. What they insist is that so long as we distinguish questions about the best form of procedure for reaching public decisions from questions about public policy, we must necessarily recognize that it is possible to argue, without any contradiction at all, that one's own judgment about policy should not be implemented if it is not supported by the majority party in a parliament (that is, by the ruling elite).[11]

Utilitarians should not be allowed to resolve the democratic paradox so easily. If we allow that elites are more likely to make better choices because they have greater skills of analysis and capacity to recognize sound advice, we must face the fact that they may be inhibited in achieving this good service by the democratic requirement that they seek election. The best policies to promote may not be the best policies to advocate in an election campaign. Thus, unless general hypocrisy prevails so that the promises made by politicians become meaningless, we must acknowledge that the decisions made by the public at election time will limit the range of policy options which the successful governing elite will be able to impose. Yet these democratically imposed choices may not be wise. (Mill worries about this problem, arguing that representatives should not be regarded as mere delegates. Although this suggestion is well-taken, it is hard to see how moral exhortation is going to solve the dilemma.)

INDIRECT UTILITARIANISM

Although classical utilitarianism and the more sophisticated version provided by John Stuart Mill appear to provide an inadequate theoretical orientation from which a convincing defense of freedom of speech can be constructed, modern interpretors and revisors of the tradition offer better possibilities. David Lyons, for example, in a controversial reading of Mill's work, tells us that we need to distinguish a number of different questions which may be asked by anyone contemplating a course of action. He or she may ask, first, whether the act in question is expedient; second, whether it is the kind of action which should be regarded as morally wrong; third, whether it is the kind of action which should be proscribed or compelled by way of the law.[12] The point of distinguishing these questions is that we need to highlight the costs of moral or legal enforcement as factors which any consistent utilitarian may take into account. Thus, in a given case, it may seem expedient to pursue a course of conduct (for example, breaking a promise), yet we may recognize that what we propose is immoral (in that we believe that more good than harm will be produced if people accept that trustworthiness is a moral virtue). As to whether it is useful to use the law to enforce some course of action (for example, prohibition of the viewing and sale of pornographic videos), the cost of administration, pain of punishment, and difficulties of enforcement may well counsel against making use of such an instrumentality. Thus, in many cases a course of action may be regarded as inexpedient (going for a swim shortly after drinking alcohol), but we may not regard those who indulge as immoral or support proposals which would make such actions illegal.

These distinctions provide a way of reading Mill's proposals in *On Liberty*, for we may interpret his "harm principle" (which holds illegitimate attempts by governments to regulate conduct which causes no significant harm to other people) as delineating a category of behavior (that which is self-regarding) which should not be regulated by legal instrumentalities. Thus, even though we may regard someone's behavior as inexpedient or even immoral, we may (as utilitarians) nevertheless oppose attempts by governments to regulate it. Many reasons may be given for identifying a self-denying principle of this kind, but the most plausible concerns the difficulties of identifying the harmful acts which may fall under such a principle. Consider, for example, the institution of a film censor. We may contemplate a censorship system because we are persuaded that some films are likely to have little social value as well as proving harmful to particular individuals who may view them. However, even conceding this, we may consistently oppose a government's proposal to authorize a censor because we believe that the censor will not easily be able to distinguish harmful from beneficial films. We may argue that, if a censor is established, numerous mistakes will be made so that many films of cultural significance will be proscribed; and we may conclude that it is better overall to embrace freedom, even allowing that some harm will follow because people may abuse it.

Mill's principle is, of course, wide ranging and, as a consequence, his arguments for inhibiting governments do not seem plausible. The problem he faces is that it is relatively easy to identify purely self-regarding actions which are clearly harmful (for example, the taking of drugs or the practice of riding cycles without a protective helmet). Thus, when we seek principles which delineate a private realm we must proceed more cautiously by identifying a less inclusive category than that protected under his proposal, such as that embraced by freedom of speech. Alternatively, we may wish to qualify Mill's liberalism by articulating a theory of paternalism to allow for the identifiable cases that fall under his principle, but I will not pursue this strategy here.

Perhaps the most successful attempt to defend a free speech principle along these lines is Thomas Emerson's argument, which I have already presented (see the quotation on page 15). He contends that it is possible and desirable to distinguish "speech" from the more general category of actions which governments may legitimately regulate because (1) it is difficult to distinguish harmful speech, (2) the harm caused by speech is usually remediable by correcting or evaluating a speaker's claims, (3) it is dangerous to allow governments the right to identify harmful speech because they will be tempted to abuse this power by censoring any opinions which they dislike.

Emerson's indirect consequentialism is plausible and goes a long way towards establishing a utilitarian defense of a right to freedom of speech. However, his account is vulnerable to the charge that the category "speech" which he delineates like the category "self-regarding act," which Mill includes under his harm principle, may be over-inclusive. After all, there is a long-standing belief that certain categories of communication, such as speech that is defamatory, insulting, obscene, blasphemous, or dangerous, should not be protected under freedom of speech. Emerson must explain why these categories should or should not be included under his definition of speech. In fact, Emerson tries to avoid this problem by distinguishing "speech" as one of two possible strategies we may adopt in our attempts to affect others (for good or for the worse): first, we may try to give them reasons through the communication of information or by argument and appeals to emotion; second, we may physically manipulate the environment in which they act or threaten to do so (unless you do X, I will pull the trigger of the gun I have pointed at your head). He calls the first strategy "speech" and the second "action" even though this does not conform to common usage (attempts to communicate are usually described as forms of action). Emerson's effort takes us in the right direction, but it is doubtful whether he remains a consistent utilitarian for, as I show below, his definition of speech embodies the Kantian notion that an individual be treated as an autonomous agent — that is, as responsible for harm caused when it results from his or her own decisions. Thus, Emerson is claiming that although people are sometimes likely to make bad choices when they are provided with reasons for acting by others, it is dangerous to allow governments to identify and prevent this (doing so involves paternalism, isolating some citizens as unworthy of responsibility or identifying some opinions as unworthy of a hearing). Put simply, the claim is that more harm than good is likely to result if we allow governments to violate personal autonomy by censoring opinions.

I hope that Emerson is correct in his factual claim. However, I do not think it will convince many people. Take, for example, the debate going on at the present time in the United Kingdom and other democracies about the propriety of censoring racist speech when this is likely to produce hatred or heighten tension within communities. It does not seem such a difficult task to frame a carefully worded statute identifying the communications which are likely to prove harmful. Moreover, there is wide consensus that racism, whether lawful or not, is unlikely to have any redeeming social value, so many believe that there is very little at risk when we allow governments to enact such a censorship law. Of course, Emerson may still be right. Contemporary judgments are unhelpful in the long-term, and the institutionalization of a censorship right is a dangerous practice (as should be clear to anyone who cares to substitute "communist," "male-chauvinist," or "feminist" in the above example). Nevertheless, the point remains that the utilitarian case Emerson has made out, however reasonable it may seem to some, is not convincing enough to persuade parliamentary majorities, commissions of inquiry, and many other sensible and cautious commentators. The problem, then, with even the most coherent utilitarian argument for recognizing a right is that we fall back on the issue of whether the factual assumptions embodied in the theory are plausible and very often they are not sufficiently so.

John Stuart Mill and Thomas Emerson are liberal functionalists who attempt to defend a strong conception of freedom of speech. By "strong" in this context I mean that the principle of freedom they articulate allows little or no scope for a balancing of competing interests by those who are applying it. All the balancing allowed for is embodied in the definition of the delineated protected realm—and this task is accomplished by the theorist. We can say they defend an absolutist conception of free speech. The opposite of an absolutist conception is a pure balancing approach. Here, speech would be regarded no differently from other conduct, and governments would be entitled to censor whenever they could demonstrate that a reasonable evaluation of the public interest had been made. On such a conception of free speech, the presumption most liberals make in favor of liberty would carry very little weight, although an onus of justification would be placed on those who censor to give reasons for their judgments.

The Balancing Approach

In practice, when parliaments, courts or commentators discuss freedom of speech, neither the absolutist nor a pure balancing approach is the most popular. Much more common are intermediate conceptions in which freedom of speech is supposed to serve as a warning device which can be cited to draw attention to the fact that a fundamental shared value is in question. The regulation of speech, it is widely assumed, places a special onus on governments, for they must provide convincing evidence that any censorship they indulge in is necessary to avoid some widely acknowledged evil. Here, there is a strong presumption in favor of the liberty to speak, but it does not always claim priority. The difficult theoretical problem is, however, to articulate the balance which needs to be struck between categories of speech and competing values. Another difficulty is to decide who should have authority to strike the balance (for example, should a court be authorized to review the judgments made by a representative parliament about matters as varied as what is to count as "obscene," "offensive," or "defamatory" speech or whether a journalist's claim to a privilege should be upheld).

I shall postpone my discussion of the last issue to a later chapter in which I propose to compare functionalist and deontological accounts of adjudication. Here, it is necessary to look more closely at the balancing approach to freedom of speech, not so much because it is as theoretically interesting as the previous functionalist theories I have discussed but because it has been far more influential.

The best defense of balancing has been provided by Frederick Schauer in his recent book *Free Speech: A Philosophical Analysis.*[13] According to Schauer, freedom of speech should be characterized as an independent political principle which must be balanced against other principles such as those identifiable in terms of some conception of due process, privacy, or justice. Schauer tells us that, when a free speech principle is recognized, it serves to indicate that the regulation of the domain delineated by "speech" requires a stronger justification than would be acceptable for regulating other forms of conduct. "Speech," then, is protected by the existence of freedom of speech because it enables us to put administrators on notice that a special, higher than normal, threshold of justification must be forthcoming when communications which qualify under the principle are regulated. Many different reasons are provided by Schauer for disabling the state from regulating speech as though it were regulating any other form of action, and each of these contributes to what he calls the "weight" and "scope" of the freedom identified. The "weight," for Schauer, is the burden of justification that must be met by a government seeking to regulate; "scope" consists of the forms of communicative and other actions that may be deemed to fall under the principle. To illustrate his conception, he tells us that some speech, such as fair criticism of public officials, falls into the core of what he delineates as the liberty protected under freedom of speech. When the regulation of such speech is in question, the citation of the principle disposes of the case. Other speech falls further from the core (for example, a defamatory attack against a private individual) and Schauer tells us that it is, consequently, less deserving of protection. In this kind of case—that is, when the "speech" in question falls nearer to the periphery of the circumscribed liberty – the citation of freedom of speech carries little weight. Of course, some speech (such as attempts at fraudulent misrepresentation) fall outside the ambit of freedom of speech altogether.

How, according to Schauer, are we to determine the weight and scope of a free speech principle in any context? Schauer tells us that there is no easy method and warns us against the dangers of the oversimplification of supposing that it is possible to defend an absolutist conception: "If there is a Free Speech Principle, it means that Free Speech is a good card to hold. It does not mean that Free Speech is the ace of trumps." But how are we to know whether it can trump at all? Schauer's answer is complex and defies summary. Each new set of circumstances requires not only that we have to remind ourselves of the general justificatory arguments he provides for thinking that freedom of speech is an important value (so that we can establish the weight which must be attached to the principle when dealing with a problematic category of communication), but we also have to determine the weight of the countervailing interest or principles. What Schauer commits us to, then, is a difficult evaluative task which clearly has no determined outcome, for people are likely to weigh the competing considerations in different ways. For example, in reviewing proposals for defamation law reform, he writes:

> It may be that the harm to reputation is so serious that is is sufficient to meet the higher burden of justification established by the Free Speech principle. The value of reputation may be so great that its protection outbalances even the added weight of the interest in Freedom of Speech.

And in reviewing the problems associated with the enjoyment of a right to public assembly, he tells us that "the legitimacy of the countervailing interest in order, traffic flow and the like" weakens the free speech interest.[14] It would seem, then, that in applying Schauer's free speech principle, we not only have to remind ourselves of the general justificatory arguments he provides (so that we can establish the weight which must be attached to the principle in a given case), but we must also determine the weight of the countervailing considerations against which it must be balanced.

The indeterminacy characteristic of Schauer's balancing approach makes it virtually useless. Moreover, Schauer is clearly hoping that a court will be authorized to review the actions of a parliament to uphold freedom of speech. But if the theory the judges are provided with involves their evaluating every set of circumstances in the way that Schauer recommends, their claim to frustrate democratic representatives will be grounded in rather sandy soil. We may well ask why a few unrepresentative officials should be allowed to make policy in the speech area. I shall return to this difficulty with balancing approaches. Here, I merely note that other functionalists are less vulnerable to this line of attack and that writers such as Mill, Emerson, and Meiklejohn (whose work I discuss in the next section) allow that their position may be vitiated if too indeterminate. Thus in terms of their accounts, once a problem is identified as involving freedom of speech, liberty must be afforded priority. In adopting an absolutist approach, these writers implicitly recognize that fundamental political principles indicate the points at which individuals have special claims which ought to be accommodated or afforded even at considerable social cost. And in doing this they also acknowledge that such principles are not general rules of thumb which serve to remind policy-makers to be cautious (for example, the rule that a parliament should have very good reasons when restricting speech) but must be regarded in such a way that they may not be abridged.

Schauer's steps in the direction of pure balancing indicate that he is not greatly worried by these concerns. However, the likely effect of his analysis may well be to lend force to the growing prejudice that it may be necessary to abandon consequentialism or at least to find very indirect strategies (embodied in the recognition of principles disallowing balancing) for pursuing our goals.

DEMOCRATIC FUNCTIONALISM

A useful functionalist theory attempting to provide a liberal account which avoids the problems associated with utilitarianism has been put forward by Alexander Meiklejohn. He agrees with Mill that liberty must be justified by its consequences and that what is important is not any abstract right of a speaker but the interests of his or her audience. However, he does not wish to rely on general utilitarian arguments of the kind that Mill deploys in *On Liberty* to justify his liberalism. Rather, he identifies popular sovereignty as a fundamental democratic commitment and justifies recognizing a right to communicate on the grounds that it is functional to the realization of this ideal. Thus, although Meiklejohn uses functional arguments, his orientation is not utilitarian but is founded on a conception of the democratic commitment.[15]

By embracing self-government as an ideal, Meiklejohn avoids the serious problem of elitism, which vitiates the utilitarian commitment to democratic procedures. He does not have to consider the democratic paradox I identified because the goal which he makes overriding is that the people decide even if what they choose is bad policy. Nevertheless, Meiklejohn cannot avoid all the difficulties endemic to a consequentialist way of arguing, and many of the problems that I raised regarding utilitarian functionalism are relevant in assessing his position.

Although Meiklejohn's focus is on the interest an audience has in being exposed to a wide-range of ideas, he is, of course, sensitive to the fact that the democratic commitment to freedom has also protected speakers. Thus, he allows that speakers do have a significant right in that, as he puts it:

> the vital point, as stated negatively is that no suggestion of policy shall be denied a hearing because it is on one side rather than another. And this means that although citizens may, on other grounds be prevented from speaking, they may not be barred because they are thought to be false or dangerous. Action shall not be outlawed because someone thinks that it is unwise, unfair, unamerican. No speaker may be declared out of order merely because some officials disagree with what he intends to say.[16]

In terms of Meiklejohn's framework, then, policies regulating speech are evaluated by asking whether they assist democratic debate. As I have said, the crucial issue for him is not that everyone should be free to speak but that everything that people need to hear in order to exercise their democratic sovereignty is communicated. The government or some other authorized body must take on the role of chairing the proceedings and has an obligation to ensure that every group has a chance to put their point of view. This could mean that where a line of argument has already been sufficiently well-stated, it may have to be censored in order that others can obtain a hearing. Thus, we can see how regulations such as those which place limitations on the amount that can be spent on advertizing candidates during elections, or those which restrict how much money any single person or organization can donate for political causes, could be compatible with Meiklejohn's view. His framework allows governments to prevent some points of view from monopolizing the public forum. Also, although it is not clear how far Meiklejohn himself would be prepared to go in allowing governments to discriminate positively by subsidizing some speech, his framework allows them to support programs which enable the otherwise inarticulate to learn the skills of effective communication and to obtain media access (for example, providing skilled technicians and advice about how best to produce material for modern media such as television).

We can see, then, that Meiklejohn defends a citizen's right to speak only because it is necessary for us (the collective of other citizens) in exercising our democratic sovereignty to hear him or her. In arguing in this way his position is very similar to that of a utilitarian like Mill, for a central part of the utilitarian case for protecting a right to expression relates to the importance of speech as a prerequisite of democratic politics. Utilitarians who defend the idea that liberty be afforded a priority argue in two stages. First, they suggest that democratic systems of government are likely to be better at producing happiness in the long run than any other form of government. Second, they deduce from this that freedom must be respected as a right. Meiklejohn's argument is similar although he makes no attempt to justify democratic accountability, taking for granted his reader's commitment to the ideal of popular sovereignty, which he claims is embodied in the Constitution of the United States. His argument is that if the American contract embraces a commitment to government by the people, then the First Amendment should be read as embracing a right to be informed.[17]

I turn now to consider some criticisms that have been made of Meiklejohn's approach.

A first problem is the narrow range of communications which Meiklejohn's argument legitimating the protection of liberty establishes within the privileged category. In terms of his reasoning, our speech would only be protected if it can be regarded as contributing to the political life of our community, and it would not necessarily be protected if it has some other purpose (for example, as entertainment or as a contribution to science or art). We can see, then, that the notion that what establishes the communication right is our need as citizens to gain information which might help us to assess our government's fitness to hold office places a heavy burden on those who claim such a right, for they must show that what they have to say has political relevance. Inevitably, then, those who are persuaded by Meiklejohn will be drawn into a process of evaluation and balancing for some types of speech, because they fall less clearly into the protected category, may warrant censoring in order to promote other worthy social interests. It has been argued, for example, that negligent journalism is unworthy of privileged status and that obscene speech contributes so little to public debate that it should not be tolerated. In each case the legitimacy of censoring will depend on whether the category of speech in question can be said to be useful. Thus, Meiklejohn's arguments are far less liberal and are closer to a utilitarian balancing approach in their implications than many would find desirable.[18]

Besides cases in which a category of communication is clearly irrelevant to political life, liberals who follow Meiklejohn's line of reasoning face a problem in providing reasons for protecting those forms of speech which are of value mainly because of their cathartic effect, where the message is not as important as the fact that it is conveyed (for example, abuse directed at a public official). Many communications, widely regarded as political, are of this category in that they are important because they allow individuals to display the concern and emotion they feel about public issues rather than because they communicate any fresh information. Often the feelings of the communicators are already well-known and the message they convey is confused or simple. Moreover, this kind of expressive political speech is often offensive. Nevertheless, most liberals would require that it be protected. What they wish to avoid is the very possibility of there being a dispute of this kind. They hold that it is inappropriate for any authority to make an evaluation about the worthiness of speech and, more particularly, that a government may not take its judgment about the significance of what a speaker is communicating into account as part of its justification for censoring him or her. But Meiklejohn's line of reasoning legitimates this kind of evaluation and points the way towards a balancing approach.[19]

Ronald Dworkin has made a further related criticism of Meiklejohn's approach. He worries that theorists who focus on audience interests (as Meiklejohn and Mill clearly do) may easily confuse arguments recommending a policy as useful or good (in that it produces an informed electorate or the promotion of true beliefs) with arguments appealing to political principle.[20] Thus, Dworkin tells us, Meiklejohn is asking "How much freedom do we need to enjoy in order to make democracy (rule by the people) possible?" whereas, he should be asking "What liberties must be guaranteed to an individual if we are to respect fundamental rights?" Dworkin's concern is that in aiming to achieve a system of communication ensuring that citizens are effectively informed so that they can make responsible judgments, Meiklejohn loses sight of the rights of speakers (in that his theory does not include any concern about whether a censored individual suffers some special affront to his or her dignity). What we need, in Dworkin's view, if we are to make the case for political freedom complete, is support for the notion that citizens are entitled to express their point of view, whether this is conducive to the democratic process or not.

At the heart of Dworkin's worry is the problem of delineating the boundaries of a citizen's right to information, for, in his view, it is implausible to construe our commitment to freedom as a right to know (that is, as a right which is justified by way of a reference to our audience interest where what is thought important and central is that citizen voters are fully informed). The reason why this is not a good strategy is that we are immediately faced with problem cases which cannot be resolved in a satisfactory way so long as we use the concept of a right significantly. To illustrate this point, Dworkin asks us whether any limits would have to be placed on such a putative "right to know" in order to promote other competing social interests; also, what our attitude will be to those who have access to confidential sources (whether, for example, we would claim a right that they inform us even if they do not wish to).

If we consider the problem relating to access to information, we see how inclined most of us are to adopt a balancing approach weighing the social benefit of public disclosure against any costs to other interests (such as health or efficient funding for research) that this might involve. This has been the approach generally adopted by those responsible for drawing up legislation providing a right of access to government files, and most "freedom of information" statutes include provisions exempting certain categories of speech to protect important competing social interests which would be deleteriously affected if complete access to information were to be insisted upon as a right. (For example, communications affecting national security, public safety, law enforcement, diplomatic relations, and the deliberations of courts as well as important executive committees making policy are usually exempted). Dworkin argues that a balancing approach to the issue of deciding how open a government ought to be is not only the usual practice but desirable, for even if we wished to protect the public's interest in being informed, we could not easily specify in advance, once and for all, the precise nature of the categories of communication which we would wish to be made available. As Dworkin points out, there have been problems in the United States with the *Public Information Act* (amended 1974). He cites some recent complaints to illustrate the point: The United States National Disease Control Center has asked that the "freedom of information" statute be amended so that it does not have to make its reports public arguing that hospitals will not seek its aid in locating infections so long as journalists can make its findings available to potential litigants. Doctors have pointed out that their attempts to test drugs using double-blind experiments are complicated when reporters disclose information that makes their sampling less reliable. Scientific funding agencies complain that researchers are vulnerable to plagiarism when grant applications listing research in progress and planned experiments are made public. Dworkin's claim is that the many problem cases make it clear that our interest in being informed must usually be balanced against the social costs involved and cannot be asserted as a right. (There are some exceptions to this generalization, for example, the right of the public to have access to criminal trials; the interest of an accused person in hearing the evidence brought against him or her and in enjoying a legal right to have witnesses subpoenaed; our interest in knowing the law and having legal resource materials publicly available; our interest in enjoying an effective right of discovery when pursuing legitimate civil actions; our interest in learning what facts about us are available in files held by various agencies and in learning when and to whom any of that information may have been passed; our interest in learning what others wish to communicate.)

The public discussion which greeted some recent court decisions dealing with speech problems in the United States provoked Dworkin into articulating his worries. The cases which interest him most are: *United States v. Progressive*, involving an attempt to prevent by way of prior restraint the dissemination of the magazine article "The H-Bomb Secret: How We Got It—Why We're Telling It" and providing the occasion for a preliminary injunction restraining a publication; *Herbert v. Landau*, in which the United States Supreme Court held that when a public figure sues in an action for defamation, reporters may be examined about their methods of investigation and editorial judgment in an effort to show whether they were malicious or reckless; a case before the New Jersey Court in which a reporter, Myron Farber, was held to be in contempt of court and liable to imprisonment for not handing over his files (which may have contained information useful to a defendant on a murder charge); *United States v. Snepp,* in which an author (writing about the CIA) was ordered to turn over his profits to the government because he had broken an agreement made with the agency allowing it a right of prior review so that matters of a security-sensitive nature could be censored.[21] Dworkin claims that an important difference between these cases has been overlooked in the public discussion of them, in that commentators fail to distinguish cases in which the right to speak is centrally involved from those in which it is not. In this regard, he tells us that the issue of the so-called "newsman's privilege" (claimed in both the Farber and Herbert cases) does not involve any matter of principle because a government is not asking, in these cases, for an injunction imposing a restraint on a potential speaker. Further, Dworkin argues, there is no right to silence when what we know may be vital for the defense of an accused person or relevant in other circumstances of central importance to an individual. The *Progressive* and Snepp cases, on the other hand, involve censorship because in each a speaker is imposed upon. Dworkin suggests that the failure of liberal writers to notice this difference can be traced to the influence of those who orientate from the citizens' need to know. In his view, these approaches discourage us from noticing that a government which balances our interest in learning the truth against competing considerations (such as a person's interest in not being convicted when innocent of a crime or in vindicating his or her reputation when the subject of a malicious libel) does less violence to our liberty than one which prevents a potential speaker from communicating. What Dworkin wishes to recommend is a return to the notion that it is the speaker's right to inform which is crucial.

The issue of the "newsman's privilege," which both Herbert and Farber claim, is close to the problem dealt with in *New York Times v. Sullivan.*[22] In Sullivan's case, the court protected publishers from the fear of damages when they published defamatory material about public officials in good faith. The rationale provided for this involved balancing the competing interest of the public (in having access to information which it needed to make proper evaluations of those who it elects to office) and those of the official defamed. Those who support the claim to privilege made by the investigative reporters Herbert and Farber wish to take this reasoning a step further: As they correctly point out, journalists rely heavily upon confidential sources in gathering material, and their capacity to protect these sources will affect their ability to inform the public. Thus, if it is worth protecting publishers against libel damages to serve the public interest in being informed, it should also be worth offering newsmen a protection against having to reveal their sources and methods of investigation.

According to Dworkin, the central question we are faced with in assessing this argument for a "newsman's privilege" is to determine whether the claim of the press not to be subjected to interrogation about their sources can be justified as a right. As he shows, however, anyone who claims this must convince us that the privilege be protected as a matter of principle and not merely as an expedient or good policy. But when we examine the argument put forward in support of Farber or Herbert we find that no principle is cited; the claim rests on the public's interest in information, and this, as we have seen, is a consideration which is mostly balanced against other competing social interests. Thus, Dworkin argues that Myron Farber's claim to privilege must give way because it is in conflict with the right of an individual accused of a serious crime not to be convicted if innocent. Herbert's case is more difficult for it is questionable whether public officials who are defamed have a moral right to recover damages. But if we hold that they do, then the court would be correct to rule, as it did, that a journalist may be subjected to interrogation even if this violates editorial autonomy. In any event, Dworkin is correct to see that the Court's refusal to recognize that the press have a privilege with regard to their sources does not represent a serious threat to freedom of speech.

On the other hand, both Snepp's case and that of the *Progressive* represent unacceptable forms of censorship for, in both, individuals who wished to speak out were hindered from doing so.

2

Freedom of Speech and Deontological Liberal Theories

If we abandon Meiklejohn's functionalist approach for the reasons that Dworkin and others have provided, is there another more adequate liberal theory available?

LOCKEAN LIBERALISM

The main alternative to functionalist theories has traditionally been Lockean liberalism. In this tradition we start from the assumption that any coercion of an individual requires justification. Lockean liberals conceive of people as autonomous and hold that they are often in conflict with their communities. If states wish to establish authority, it follows that they must be able to legitimate such a claim. Lockeans insist that any collective judgment imposed upon an individual which forecloses on the ability to choose for himself or herself must be presumed illegitimate unless it can be accounted for as one that would have been agreed to on a presumption that the individual in question would have acted rationally. Thus, in the Lockean tradition, any challenge to a limiting imposition can be met by recounting how it could have come to be freely chosen by a rational agent; we are concerned with origins for we are interested to know how—that is, by what processes—political association came about or could have come about. If it can be shown that rational individuals would have freely chosen to accept the imposition (perhaps, to realize some undeniable communal interest such as the maintenance of good order), then the claim to authority must be regarded as legitimate; if this cannot be shown, on the other hand, the imposition will be regarded as coercive.

As I have said, the focus of the Lockean theorist is on the transformation problem: how did mankind pass from a situation where there was no political authority to one in which we recognize some authority claims as legitimate? This focus on process and origins reflects the fact that once it is assumed that persons have rights (such as the rights to life, to liberty, and to property) which do not arise out of any association with others but are held prior to any such political involvement, it becomes difficult to show how any political association could arise without transgressing these rights. By requiring an explanation of origins, the Lockean approach establishes a test for demarcating between acceptable and unacceptable institutional demands. Only those which can conceivably be said to respect individual rights are tolerable; and Lockean theorists, therefore, require apologists to show how a political authority's claim to regulate the behavior of citizens could have arisen from the state of nature without having transgressed their rights. Unless a story can be constructed to show how the political realm emerges out of the nonpolitical by processes which respect everyone's natural entitlements, we, as Lockeans, have to acknowledge that government involves illegitimate coercion.

In assessing the Lockean contract approach, it is important to stress that a hypothetical history of the transformation from a state of nature to civil society does not necessarily reflect the real origins of existing institutions. Most of us admit that the history of mankind has been barbarous and that so-called civilization has often involved conquest and enslavement of one kind or another. Hypothetical histories designed to show what can and what cannot be justified in the light of a commitment to the notion that individuals have rights should not be taken, then, as descriptions of what actually happened. The point of such a hypothetical reconstruction of the origins of civil society is to show how a given set of institutional practices could have come into being in a way which does not violate rights. The legitimate functions of the state are prescribed, for Lockeans, by the possibility of providing some outline of the origins of the kind suggested. Unless an acceptable story of this kind is forthcoming, we must assume that our rights are being violated by the coercive instrumentality whose legitimacy is being questioned. On the other hand, Lockeans think that if we can show how a given set of institutions could have evolved without violating rights, then we would have provided some reason for valuing them in preference to those which embody processes which do.

There are two main objections which are raised against Lockean approaches. First, the notion of an abstract individual, standing apart from society (the assumed starting point of the orientation) is an absurdity. It follows from this that the rights which we attribute to such individuals (for example, that he or she is the natural owner of any personal capacity and is entitled to claim the fruit of any use made of such skills) appears arbitrary. The second objection is rather different in that the focus is on the consequences of the commitment to take Lockean rights seriously (rather than upon the assumptions of such a theory). Because Lockean liberals are committed to conceive of political society as a contrivance for the maintenance of orderly exchanges between persons (regarded as the owners of their own capacities) and for the protection of the property which each of them may acquire, it is argued that their theory justifies unbridled capitalism and is, consequently, unacceptable to those who believe that the results of capitalism for many would include economic poverty. The point put simply is that anyone who hopes governments will ensure that adequate welfare support is provided must challenge the Lockean approach precisely because it denies authority to coercively redistribute wealth, even out of a concern for the plight of the poor. This is because Lockeans hold that any attempt to reallocate wealth against the wishes of the owners of resources involves a violation of the owners' rights.

Lockean theorists mostly deny that the consequences of free market competition are severe, and they often suppose that private benefactors will be generous in their support of charities. However, these responses do not dispose of the fact that their theory allows the possibility that the poorer sections of society will not be provided with sufficient help to lift them out of a situation of degrading poverty. It should be noted, also, that is is not merely material needs which are in question. If Lockeans had their way, we could face a situation in which private owners could monopolize significant aspects of life, such as educational facilities and the mass media. While most of us are horrified by the notion that the market system should be the sole determinant of what is taught or communicated, this is a consequence which those who accept Lockean assumptions must be prepared to accept.

As I have said, the consequences of taking Lockean assumptions about political rights seriously has been unacceptable to many liberals, and the approach has never enjoyed a significant following. Most theorists and judges have preferred utilitarianism and have been suspicious of the doctrine that there are natural rights. (The most significant Lockean liberal who has had an influence on the United States Supreme Court is Justice Hugo Black. Some of Chief Justice Burger's judgments also reflect Lockean assumptions, although on a few issues – for example in treating obscene speech as an unprotected category – he uses functionalist arguments.)

Rawlsian liberalism now offers an alternative which has been gaining some support. The significance of *A Theory of Justice* lies partly in the fact that Rawls provides us with a rights-based theory which makes none of the Lockean assumptions thought to be questionable. His approach has the further advantage of not ruling illegitimate attempts to redistribute wealth in the form of welfare payments to the poor. Instead of assuming an abstract individual facing his or her community as naturally autonomous, Rawls concedes the social basis of our human characteristics. His individualism is premised on the very different assumption that we are all the product of a process of socialization, owing everything we are to others. Thus, far from being illegitimate, collective coordination of an institutional kind is accepted by Rawls as part of the human predicament. He poses the central issue of normative political theory as that of finding principles to guide our social interactions which reflect our dependence on others. "Justice" replaces "liberty from coercion" as the central coordinating value, and Rawls takes it as given that persons of good will would be disposed towards democratic solutions, reflecting our sense of fairness.

A RAWLSIAN ALTERNATIVE

In this section I will attempt to show that Rawls's answer to the question he poses—If our society is to call itself a democracy, what requirements have to be met?—is reasonable, at least with regard to the dilemmas we confront in evaluating communications policy. My purpose, then, is to provide what I take to be Rawlsian answers to the main tasks identified earlier, that is, the problem of defining "speech," the problem of justifying liberty, and the problem of identifying the priority which must hold between any putative right to speak and other claimed rights.

Defining Speech

With regard to the problem of demarcation, it is worth noting at this point that liberals in the United States have been forced to confront the problem more squarely than those in other democracies, for the wording of the First Amendment uses the term "speech" to indicate a protected category of actions which may not be regulated by the Congress. I do not mean to imply that there has been any agreement amongst American writers as to how to demarcate this protected zone of freedom. Some have attempted to distinguish between "speech" and "action," adopting what has come to be known as an absolutist approach. In terms of this account, so long as a communication can be shown to be "speech," it automatically falls under the First Amendment. Justice Black, for example, does not allow for exceptions, but he defines "speech" in such a way that actions such as demonstrating in streets or symbolically burning flags, which most of us regard as forms of political communication, are not protected.[1] A more common approach is for theorists to delineate what they take to be the central meaning of the First Amendment (usually thought to protect a right to criticize government). Thus, on this account, speech which falls clearly into the category of actions which the framers of the constitution hoped to keep free from government intervention is entitled to more protection than forms of speech such as obscenity and libel, which are traditionally regarded as having no social value. Justices who adopt this kind of approach go in for a considerable amount of balancing, and their liberalism is often difficult to sustain. However, because they weight the scales in favor of their chosen reading of the central meaning of the amendment, they cannot avoid the definitional problem. Controversies over delineating the scope of the amendment's protection have involved debate about who is to be counted as a "public figure," what is a matter of "significant public interest," and what constitutes "commercial," "obscene," or "dangerous" speech.

Most of the difficulties in reaching a satisfactory definition of the protected realm of liberty arise out of the functionalist framework in which the problem has usually been posed. When one's justification of freedom of speech is that open debate is conducive to the realization of some significant and desirable social goals, there will be a tendency to narrow the scope of the principle to eliminate those categories of speech which are widely regarded as serving no purpose. Thus, functionalists have tended to identify forms of communication which—perhaps because they are specially intrusive or involve the use of resources which are scarce (as in broadcast speech or public assemblies)—are deemed less worthy of protection. And if it can be shown that some form of communication (for example, speech involving racial abuse) is likely to produce bad consequences, they have tended to argue that such speech should be forbidden.[2]

Deontological approaches (those which proceed from a strong conception of rights) avoid these tendencies, for the protected sphere of liberty is delineated by interpreting an understanding of the democratic commitment. For example, if we accept that such a commitment involves treating others with equal concern and respect, we ask what liberties have to be afforded to satisfy this requirement. Of course, a question of this kind does not allow for an easy answer—as Rawls's six hundred pages testify. With regard to the problem of delineating a right to liberty of speech, however, a more specific answer can be provided.

A good start has been made by the philosopher Thomas Scanlon, who tells us that, given a commitment to recognize the equal autonomy of citizens, a government would not be justified in restricting speech if the purpose is to avoid:

a) harms to certain individuals which consist in their coming to have false beliefs as a result of those acts of expression; b) harmful consequences of acts performed as a result of those acts of expression, where the connection between the acts of expression and the subsequent harmful acts consists merely in the fact that the act of expression led the agents to believe (or increased their tendency to believe) these acts to be worth performing.[3]

These principles place emphasis on the idea of establishing citizens as sovereign in deciding what to believe and embody a commitment to respect their dignity. However, in formulating the principles, Scanlon fails to take sufficient account of the fact that we are often vulnerable as the recipients of communications. For example, we surely would agree that fraudulent and deliberately misleading speech should not be protected.

Taken without qualification, then, Scanlon's principles cannot be accepted. Nevertheless, because they place emphasis on the idea of establishing citizens as sovereign, they point in the right direction. What we have to allow for is the fact that we are not always in a position to assess what we are told nor to do everything that may be necessary to get better informed. Of course we may nevertheless choose to disregard what we have been asked to believe; however, we would have no rational reason for making such a judgment so, unless we have good grounds for distrusting our informant, the more prudent course would be to take his or her word on trust. In this kind'of circumstance we can say that a speaker is in authority, for those who act in the light of what he or she leads them to believe are vulnerable. Moreover, as the well-known example of the person who falsely shouts "fire!" in a crowded cinema illustrates, this is the kind of circumstance in which it makes sense to hold a speaker responsible for the subsequent actions of his or her audience. This case should be contrasted with the situation which would have arisen were he or she to have put forward the proposition that the cinema management were such swindlers that their property ought to be burnt. In the latter case, there is time for further discussion and reflection before the recommended action is contemplated—the audience can choose to inform themselves more adequately. Similarly, with speech which maliciously misleads, we can hardly claim that attempts to manipulate by way of the propagation of what is known to be false information is a form of dialogue, so it surely makes sense to hold a speaker responsible. What we have to allow for, then, is a measure of paternalism to accommodate circumstances in which an audience is not in a position to assess what it is told.[4]

A government would also be justified in restraining speakers where the harm that follows from a communication cannot be remedied by further debate. For example, the harm caused through the publication of pamphlets which explain how to construct suitcase bombs cannot be ameliorated by any official counter-manual. Censorship of this kind of speech is not paternalistic, however, for the objective is not to protect vulnerable recipients but to prevent those who may have criminal intentions from successfully accomplishing their plans.

Of course, the mere fact that an audience is assured of being in a position to evaluate properly what a speaker is claiming is no guarantee that the majority of its members will do so. People are often gullible and take little trouble to get themselves informed even when information is available; also, unwarranted deference is often afforded to certain speakers. Nevertheless, under Scanlon's principle a governmental authority may not protect individuals from any harm which results because of audience failures by censoring speakers. It may take action against those who act precipitously on the advice of others, but it may not anticipate this likelihood by preventing speakers from seeking to persuade. If there were no limit to legitimate paternalism, there would be no scope for the autonomy which Scanlon thinks so important.

I would also suggest that in allowing for paternalism when the objective is to ensure that audiences are not vulnerable because of circumstances beyond their control, we can still impose limits on the manner in which a government may act to protect an audience from being manipulated by speakers and in this way secure its autonomy. We should insist, for example, that audiences should normally be left to make up their own minds about what and who to believe and that a government, seeking to protect them from an unscrupulous speaker, ought to confine itself to persuasion, the dissemination of warnings and to providing further information (through government-sponsored scientific reports, for example). This should be the extent of the paternalism so long as there is opportunity for all points of view to be heard and assessed. Of course, in some circumstances there may be no time for protracted public debate. Here the recipients of a communication are more vulnerable, for they have no capacity to evaluate the claim or warning and are forced to act on trust. In this circumstance, more intrusive forms of paternalism may be necessary and the law used to restrain those who would cause harm through the propagation of information that is false or misleading. What a government may not do, on this account, is to protect audiences when the vulnerability of members results from their personal failings, such as laziness or gullibility.

What reasons can be given for insisting that governments respect the equal autonomy of citizens even when this results in harm (when individuals who are unwary take too much notice of bad advice)?

Here I can only say that the principles I have taken over from Scanlon follow as an implication of the commitment to treat others in a way which respects their dignity as persons; further, that no utilitarian reasons can be nor need be provided for making such a commitment. (I elaborate on this point in the next section when I outline a Rawlsian approach to the justificatory problem.)

Before concluding this section, it is worth mentioning the special case of advertising, for this is a category of communication which is legitimately regulated. The justification for this arises out of the considerations I have been advancing in discussing Scanlon's principles—although the problem is not that there is not enough time for a response but that the advertiser provides such a constant barrage of the same message that it is not possible to put an alternative view. The point is that advertising does not usually form part of a public dialogue. Also, we know that advertisers are usually self-interested and that they hope through their communication to sell commodities. They do not engage in speech because they have some sincerely held beliefs which they wish to disseminate. And although many people have strongly held views about widely advertised products (for example, that packaged foods are often bad for one's health, that big cars are unnecessary and cause avoidable pollution, that certain forms of entertainment are trash, that alcohol is a dangerous drug), no one is usually motivated to establish these views by making the significant economic sacrifices that would be necessary to propagate them through an advertising campaign.

Another feature of advertising distinguishing it as a form of speech which should not be protected under Scanlon's principles is that advertisers often aim to influence not merely by appealing to reason but subliminally. They do this by repeating their message and by making associations which may or may not be misleading. Of course, we are affected subliminally all of the time as we go about our lives, for we are never fully aware of those features in our environment which affect the way we behave and the kinds of people we become. However, we would worry about such influences in our lives if we were to learn that other people were in control of our attitudes and habits, and a government which acted to protect us from such manipulation would not be resented. As I have said, advertising is a form of communication which sometimes falls into this category. The case of cigarette commercials may serve as an illustration, for most of us would agree that smoking is a thoroughly harmful practice—we can assume that most of us would prefer not to experience the desire to smoke. Suppose, then, that it is possible, using subliminal methods, to make us feel a strong impulse to take up the habit. Surely we would want our government to protect us from this harm? But if we agree that harmful subliminal advertising should be banned, we may also wish to see regulations placed on the more familiar techniques of commercial promotion where these affect us in ways we are not conscious of. After all, the appeal of the advertiser exploits our vulnerability to suggestion and associations (for example, that people who smoke are successful, sophisticated, enjoy outdoor sports, and have great sex appeal). Of course, we do have some defense against these messages so long as we are conscious of the attempt to influence us. We can reflect on the associations made (for example, we know that smoking does not improve our enjoyment of sport); and luckily most people can see through advertising when they bother to make judgments of this kind. But we are not always vigilant, and the advertiser hopes to influence us in the long run by exposing us to a constant repetition of the same message. Even the methods of advertising with which we are all familiar may, then, have a subliminal influence. Because there is nothing much we can do about this as individuals, we need the help of our governments to protect us from this potential harm. Whether they ought to help or not must depend, of course, on how serious this harm is. All I suggest here is that commercial speech, when this involves advertising, should not be entitled to the same protection against government regulation as other forms of communication.

What I suggest, then, is that Scanlon's principles should normally provide the criteria for demarcating the forms of speech which fall into the area of a protected liberty. However, in some cases a government may legitimately regulate such speech when it can justify this as a form of paternalism and provided it acknowledges that individuals should normally make up their own minds about what to believe and when they are properly informed.

Justifying Liberty

The novelty of the approach developed by Rawls and Dworkin lies in the fact that they reconceptualize the liberal commitment to allow for regulations of a democratic kind and so avoid the dilemmas of Lockean liberalism, which overemphasizes the importance of liberty as a fundamental value. In their view, the Kantian ideal of treating persons as ends embraces a commitment to justice, conceived as the right which citizens may claim to be treated with equal concern and respect. Thus, Rawls justifies his understanding of the democratic ideal by way of an assertion that a commitment to justice lies at the heart of any adequate conception of political legitimacy, and he suggests that this entails that citizens be entitled to the most extensive liberty compatible with a like liberty for others. In terms of this commitment, he would also have us maximize the capacity of poorer groups in any society, providing them with a capacity to make use of political rights, and he argues that inequalities in social life should not exceed the point at which an effective value of equal political liberty is assured.[5] (So, a government agency would sometimes be justified in subsidizing political campaigns, providing funds for public access television, or establishing standards of fairness in broadcasting, so long as its actions were impartial.)

In this respect, then, the implications of Rawls's commitment to "fairness" are similar to those we can derive from reflecting on some functionalist considerations. For example, Alexander Meiklejohn has justified regulation of the press because he claims, given the short time usually available for political debate and the fact that modern media are usually cluttered with entertainment, it is only when governments act to regulate discussion— so that it is focused and so that all opinions are heard—that citizens will become properly informed. It is this interest of the audience which a government is justified in protecting, according to Meiklejohn. Rawls differs from functionalists like Meiklejohn in claiming that the right to expression is a personal right to speak, albeit an equal one in that one may claim no more than a fair opportunity. This difference of focus is significant, for it enables a Rawlsian liberal to avoid some problems which the notion that a government act as the chairman of a meeting of the whole society gives rise to. In terms of a Rawlsian conception, for example, it would be inappropriate for a government to make any judgments about the significance of what a speaker is communicating; nor may it decide questions of relevance. Its regulative role is restricted to that of ensuring speaker rights and it has no authority to regulate on behalf of any putative audience interest. For Meiklejohn, on the other hand, what is most important is not so much that we have a fair chance to express ourselves as individuals but that all important opinions are disseminated.[6]

This does not mean that Rawlsian liberals would not recognize a right to be informed in some special circumstances. One special problem area occurs when information is protected from public scrutiny by a shield of secrecy for, in a few cases, an individual may have a special need which justifies their claiming access to it as a right, even if the agency holding it is reluctant to disclose it (for example, someone accused of wrong-doing may have a moral right to hear the evidence that is brought against him). Another problem area occurs when potential speakers are physically prevented from communicating (for example, criminals often lose much of their ability to communicate when convicted, and foreigners may not be granted visas which allow them to address meetings), or a person may have contracted to keep confidences (for example, Snepp is alleged to have accepted a limitation on his right to speak when he joined the Central Intelligence Agency as an agent). In these rather complex circumstances, when no right to speak is available although a speaker is willing, Rawls's orientation may enable us to claim that we have a right to learn what others wish to communicate. Thus, in the case of a government refusing a visa on the grounds that a speaker will have an undesirable influence, we can argue that this constitutes a form of paternalism which denies us, as the individuals who constitute his potential audience, the right to assess what he has to say for ourselves. In Snepp's case, we could argue that the contract which he signed with the CIA (by means of which he is alleged to have forfeited his right to speak) is invidious, for it prevents him from informing us about an area of life which is of great political significance. Similar considerations apply to the case of prisoners: we can claim that any attempt on the part of an authority to censor them prevents each of us from making a proper assessment of what is taking place in the prisons. I do not mean to imply that a government may not prohibit the disclosure of specific information which has been properly classified, only that it may not usually establish secrecy by imposing restraints on its servants (or anyone else), for this constitutes a form of unjustifiable paternalism. Finally, it would also be necessary to acknowledge that election campaigns give rise to special problems which may justify regulating the press, for they impose special burdens on citizens. We may say that the audience interest in hearing a fair presentation of all sides during elections may legitimate our treating party political messages as a special category of speech by limiting some speakers and facilitating others.

A final point to make about the Rawlsian conception of the democratic commitment is that it marks a shift in the way that liberals have thought about the nature of political rights. Whether they follow the philosophies of Mill or Locke, liberals have tended to suppose that liberty, conceived as a right to be left alone (which includes the right to think about any topic and to state opinions), is the central democratic commitment. The latter see no conflict between the utilitarian goal of maximizing happiness and their belief that liberty is a primary value. And the former assume a conception of the individual as the owner of his or her capacities, claiming that people have a natural right not to be coerced into relations with others which are not freely chosen. On the other hand, Rawls allows much more weight to be placed on justice conceived as fairness. Indeed, it would be correct to say that the leading value which informs his discussion is not liberty but equity.

Dworkin marks this shift in liberal theory even more clearly than Rawls when he declares quite firmly that the "idea of a right to liberty is a misconceived concept that does a disservice to political thought . . ."[7] In his view, traditional liberals are inconsistent in that nearly all of them concede that governments may legitimately place a great many restraints on liberty. For example, they do not complain if told that only licensed drivers may be in charge of a vehicle or may only proceed one-way down a specified street. Nor do they necessarily complain if governments regulate markets paternalistically by requiring goods to be packaged and labeled, or if they insist that hire-purchase agreements contain provisions to protect the innocent. Even extreme libertarians are prepared to allow that governments may sometimes restrain citizens in these kinds of ways to achieve acceptable social goals. But if we are prepared to allow governments to restrict liberty in pursuit of our common interests, it becomes difficult to see what point there might be in asserting, as Locke and Mill do, that we have a fundamental right not to be coerced. Yet most liberals do want to claim that there is some sort of political right to liberty. They are, consequently, caught up in a paradox.

Dworkin suggests that we can best avoid this apparent contradiction by comprehending that our commitment to liberty is a corollary of the even more fundamental commitment which most of us make to equality. This is shown, he believes, by the fact that liberal political ideals can be stated without mentioning liberty: the fundamental liberal commitment, he tells us, is to the view that governments ought not to discriminate on the grounds that some citizens are more worthy of concern than others; and he goes on to claim that this commitment "might be called a liberal conception of equality," for it does not assume liberty as a right.[8]

This way of stating the democratic commitment is a plausible one. It is also far-reaching, embodying a conception of justice which has egalitarian implications and allows the implementation of strict procedural standards of neutrality. Thus, in treating citizens with equal respect, a government may not promote any particular conception of the good life and must eschew any claim to knowledge of what constitutes human excellence by refusing to set the agenda of public debate.

IDENTIFYING RIGHTS

Theorists who embrace what I have called the democratic commitment (what Dworkin refers to as the liberal conception of equality) as their starting point have devised various ways of teasing out precisely what is required of us if we are to treat others with equal concern and respect their dignity as persons. It is necessary for me to look at some of these before considering the rights which may be identified in the light of them.

Rawls's technique for reaching a consensus is the most famous. He asks us to perform a thought experiment by imagining how a discussion over disputed claims would proceed if the individuals concerned were asked to negotiate from a position of complete equality. He calls the hypothetical circumstances which he regards as setting up the conditions for a fully equitable negotiation the "original position." Rawls claims that if we can show that a right would be acknowledged by negotiators who have no predetermined advantages, then we would have established a critical standard which can provide a moral basis for dialogue in more realistic political circumstances. Those who refuse to recognize such a right as a guide in their relations with others could be said to be taking advantage and would stand as necessarily condemned in terms of the justificatory theory. For example, suppose we are unsure whether individuals have a right to religious freedom. We imagine our negotiators discussing the problem. Each will know how important deeply held religious convictions are to believers, but they will not know (because in terms of Rawls's method we impose a "veil of ignorance" about particular characteristics which can prejudice judgment) whether they themselves are religious. In this case, it is easy to see why the negotiators will decide to recognize the right in question.

One difficulty with Rawls's account is that if individuals are too ignorant about their circumstances, they may not be able to reach any reasoned judgments at all. This is why Rawls allows us to lift what he calls the veil of ignorance, making more and more general information about the future society available to the negotiators. A problem, here, is that we may define the circumstances of the negotiation in such a way that only our own favored principles are likely to be chosen. Thus, it has been claimed that the hypothetical negotiation adds no moral force to the reasons we may already be able to provide for endorsing our chosen principles. This problem has, I believe, been exaggerated, as can be illustrated by the following example.

Suppose that negotiators representing a number of football clubs, forming a league, meet to articulate principles of justice relating to matters such as how players may be recruited or transferred between clubs, how tickets for final matches are to be allocated, and so on. Our negotiators may fail to reach consensus because each will have the interest of his own club in mind. Moreover, there may be a conflict between those clubs with strong neighborhood roots and those with supporters in many parts of the territory in which the league operates, or between those which are rich and able to pay high sums for players to transfer and those which are struggling financially. One thing these league negotiators could do is establish a dialogue under a veil of ignorance. They could pay for a number of experienced sports administrators to come from other countries, allow them a week or two to familiarize themselves with the problems of the league in question, and then let them negotiate the guiding principles. These informed outsiders are likely to reach impartial decisions, for they will not be representing particular clubs. Yet it does not seem unrealistic to suppose that they could reach agreement.

A different account of a neutral dialogue, though modelled on Rawls's contribution, is put forward by Bruce Ackerman.[9] His project is to avoid having to conjecture a dialogue between individuals who have no idea who they are. Thus, he does not impose a veil of ignorance on the participants; instead he lays down rules of debate which are enforced by an umpire whom we are to suppose has a perfect technology of justice at his or her disposal. The rules which Ackerman would have such an umpire enforce are that no participant in the dialogue may assert:

> a) that his conception of the good is better than that asserted by any of his fellow citizens, or b) that, regardless of his conception of the good, he is intrinsically superior to one or more of his fellow citizens.[10]

The method of imaginatively reconstructing a hypothetical dialogue of the kind that Rawls and Ackerman envisage is a useful one and allows us to establish some agreement about rights. For example, although we may disagree about the precise profile of various rights, most of us will endorse a right to a fair trial; a right to be protected against the hazards of disorder; a right to be free from intrusion into our privacy; a right to reply when personally defamed; and a right not be threatened, physically violated, or personally insulted. We would also endorse Rawls's principle that each person is to have a fully adequate total system of equal basic liberties which are compatible with a similar scheme of liberties for all. Some people may demur: there may be a sense of unease about the recognition of a right to privacy, even in the limited way I have stated it, and there may be objections to the idea that individuals should be afforded a right of reply when personally attacked. On the other hand, some liberals will argue that my list is too limited and that it should include a right to take civil action and obtain compensation when one is defamed, as well as a right to similar redress if embarrassing private facts about one have been published. (I will not try to resolve possible differences here, since I discuss the more controversial rights fully when I deal with problem cases). It is, however, important to reiterate that the test I am using is whether negotiators under a veil of ignorance in the Rawlsian "original position," or operating under the rules imposed by Ackerman, will be inclined to endorse a specific right—that is, whether the rights we claim are entailed by our fundamental commitment to treat others with equal concern and to respect their dignity as persons.

Dworkin's way of teasing out the implications of the democratic commitment is rather different. He tries to trace out the parameters of neutral dialogue by way of a careful analysis of competing arguments about particular issues such as the debate which followed the publication of the Wolfenden Report (which recommended that homosexual practices in private between consenting adults no longer be criminal), the debate about the right to view pornography, and the debate about affirmative action programs in the United States.[11] Dworkin argues that if he can show that the reasons put forward in support of a particular policy take a given set of values for granted, merely citing conventionally held moral standards in a dogmatic way (for example by resting the case on the claim "homosexuality is immoral, degrading, and wicked"), he is entitled to declare that they are unacceptable. He tells us that the reason why this is so is that arguments of this kind deny equality to competing points of view in that they are not neutral between the various conceptions of the good which might be held by individuals. By carefully attending to argument in this way, Dworkin attempts to lay bare the anatomy of principled moral dialogue. His aim is to see whether our differences involve matters of principle, rest on factual disagreements, rely on citing the beliefs of others, or are merely emotional rationalization reflecting prejudices.

The approach Dworkin has developed owes much to the work of H. L. A. Hart, who, in his debate with Lord Devlin about whether morality may be legitimately enforced by way of the criminal law, asks us to distinguish between what he calls "positive morality" and "critical morality."[12] The former he describes as "the morality actually accepted and shared by a given social group" whereas the latter includes "the general moral principles used in the criticism of actual social institutions including positive morality." The main point which both Dworkin and Hart insist upon is that the mere citation of the standards embodied in positive morality cannot serve as justificatory standards within our critical morality, for the latter depends on the possibility of framing principles which are general or in citing values which are universally held to be important and in terms of which we coordinate our thinking over a wide range of different issues.

Another way a claim that we have a right to some benefit can be tested is to see whether we are inclined, in practice, to recognize exceptions. For example, if we claim that an individual has a right to a civil remedy when defamatory attacks have been made against him, we would not be consistent if we also allow for a special privilege in circumstances when the public interest seems to demand it. Thus, we cannot consistently also justify protecting those who write references or even witnesses giving evidence to a court or tribunal. Similarly, someone who argues that we have a privacy right to control how we are presented to others by preventing the dissemination of embarrassing private facts cannot also allow for the exceptional cases when a disclosure would be in the public interest (for example, the disclosure of medical reports assessing the health of a prime minister or the disclosure of his or her tax return). The requirement that we coordinate our intuitive moral judgments so that they form a coherent program of action provides a useful regulative standard. In terms of such a standard, we are required to reflect upon our commitments, applying our standards to similar cases or accounting for those in which we are inclined to make anomalous judgments. In this way, that is, by articulating our standards and by testing them in the light of possible problems which might confront us, we impose on ourselves a burden of principled argument. The aim is somehow to shape our intuitive judgments into a coherent package which is adequately coordinated in the light of fundamental principles.

But which rights ought we to acknowledge? Also which putative claims ought to be afforded priority when there are conflicts?

We can usefully begin answering these questions by getting clearer what it means to assert the existence of a right. One suggestion which I believe to be the most cogent is that we refer to rights when we wish to indicate those circumstances in which a person's choices must be respected. If I claim a right, I am saying either (a) that an area of liberty must be respected so that I am able to do X if I choose to—that is, that I should be afforded an immunity to the attempts made by others (particularly governmental authorities) to impose various obligations upon me; or (b) because of some special circumstances giving rise to the existence of the right, that my choices to waive or extinguish or to enforce or leave unenforced another person's obligation to provide some benefit should be determining. The view of "a right" which I am recommending has been defended by H. L. A. Hart, who holds that moral rights belong to a branch of morality which is specifically concerned with determining when one person's freedom may be limited by others.[13] On this view, any putative claim to the enjoyment of a right immediately raises two fundamental and closely related issues: the question of liberty or immunity and the nature of authority. What is relevant to the first concern is the existence or nonexistence of obligations. Thus, I am at liberty to do X (I have a right to do X) if it can be shown that I have no duty not to do X. And the question of whether such a duty exists is usually settled by reference to whether anyone with the appropriate authority has placed me under an obligation. (I say "usually" because there are some natural duties which are widely recognized as giving rise to legitimate rights claims.) We can establish our liberty to do X, on this account, by denying the authority of those who wish to regulate our behavior (that is, by claiming an immunity) or by establishing our own authority (as the owner of this car I am at liberty to transfer it to you).

The above characterization of the point of rights claims in political, moral, and legal discourse does not cover all the circumstances in which the concept of a right may be significantly used.[14] Political rights provide the main category of exceptional case for we do often talk of rights in referring to benefits or privileges when we assume that these must be afforded to every individual. For example, the right to a fair trial when accused of a crime or pursuing a civil action, or the right to security of the person, or the right to enjoy privacy. These are not purely rhetorical uses of the concept of a right, for although we elaborate our claim to such rights without reference to any acts of authorization, the point of claiming this kind of interest as a right is to insist that particular individuals are entitled to claim the benefit. By referring to rights in this context we are delineating when one person's interests (as opposed to his or her choices) must take priority over those of others. Further, the justification of such rights arises out of an acknowledgment that political association gives rise to a special relationship. In claiming this, I am again indebted to Hart, who in an early paper had noticed that an

> important source of special rights and obligations which we recognize in many spheres of life is what may be termed mutuality of restrictions, and I think political obligation is intelligible only if we see what precisely this is and how it differs from other right-creating transactions (consent, promising) to which philosophers have assimilated it. In its bare schematic outline it is this: when a number of persons conduct any joint enterprise according to rules and thus restrict their liberty, those who have submitted to these restrictions when required have a right to a similar submission from those who have benefited from their submission.[15]

My claim is that the "mutuality of restrictions" entailed by political association establishes more than this, for each participant has a legitimate expectation that he or she will not be required to shoulder disproportionate burdens. It is this consideration of fairness which gives rise to political rights, and it is by elaborating upon Hart's insight that Rawls and Dworkin have developed their theories.

In identifying political rights, we must ask ourselves what interests of an individual are fundamental, in the sense that he could legitimately complain of a disproportionate burden if it were not acknowledged that he should have it satisfied prior to any collective pursuit of other benefits. In answering this question, however, we have to bear in mind that most of the interests which an individual may himself regard as fundamental to his life's plans (the satisfaction of a desire to study at Harvard University, to become a wealthy businessman, or to enjoy an annual beach holiday) would not fall into this category. Thus, we cannot determine whether an interest is "fundamental" in the requisite sense by only considering whether a particular person cares deeply that it be afforded. To successfully establish a right, we have to universalize our perspective, trying to determine whether there are some primary goods (Rawls uses "primary" to indicate those goods which every rational person is presumed to want whatever his or her plan of life, and I have his meaning in mind here) which all individuals would recognize if they were to make a considered judgment; and we have to decide whether the realization of an equal enjoyment of such "primary goods" could be said to be required by our general obligation to honor the mutuality of restrictions — the claim of each person to equal concern and respect.

As indicated above, a problem we confront when we think of rights in this way is that of subjectivity — we cannot really comprehend how other people are likely to feel about the realization of any interest because it depends on who they are. People's notions of dignity, for example, are often very different, so that exposures which one person may regard as embarrassing another may rather enjoy. These differences make it difficult to delineate particular rights, such as, the profile of our right to privacy (see my discussion in chapter 5). A second difficulty is that some goals (such as a share in the determining of collective decisions) will seem more or less significant depending on what we can assume about the nature of society and the character of our fellow citizens. Liberal theorists usually agree in identifying certain minimum realistic limitations on what should be assumed in this regard. For my purposes I shall accept these as providing a framework for discussion. Thus, regarding human nature, I will suppose (a) that most people will not always act altruistically and that some may well seek to dominate others by claiming unfair privileges or by controlling coercion; (b) that most people are unlikely to be highly competent social theorists, economists, or lawyers, and that even when they agree on ends, they may not agree on the most appropriate means for their realization; (c) that citizens are likely to care very much about the welfare of those in their immediate family but not so deeply about those with whom they have little daily contact; (d) that some people will hold beliefs about what is right or wrong and about religious matters which will strongly influence their judgments about the behavior of others. With regard to the assumptions I make about the nature of society, I suppose (1) that it is large and characterized by a modern industrial system involving a complex division of labor requiring specialization of skills; (2) that scarcity of resources gives rise to many disputes about distribution; (3) that the population is divided into a plurality of communities although strongly integrated by a common economic system and a centralized political authority. The question I ask, then, is what basic rights should be recognized as fundamental, given these assumptions.

If we adopt the heuristic device (which Rawls recommends), imagining negotiators who have to agree upon constitutional principles under a "veil of ignorance," we will be able to identify arguments for recognizing rights. For, given the way that the negotiating position is constructed by Rawls, we can see why we have good reasons for supposing that the rights implied by such a principle ought to be acknowledged. Moreover, we would hold that any person or any government who fails to respect such rights acts illegitimately. What individual interests, then, would negotiators operating under a "veil of ignorance" agree to protect as a matter of principle?

A full answer to this question cannot be given here for it would require a book in itself to view all the considerations which might be canvassed. Thus, although I believe that there are good reasons for accepting Rawls's proposal that each person is to have "a fully adequate scheme of equal basic liberties which is compatible with a similar scheme of liberties for all," I shall review only those considerations which may be significant in establishing freedom of speech as a constitutionally protected interest. Of course, these lines of argument will often be relevant to the wider question of when individuals should be let alone by governments but my focus, here, will be on the narrow issue of freedom of speech.[16]

In considering whether a free speech principle ought to be acknowledged, Rawlsian negotiators would reflect on the four pessimistic assumptions listed above as a, b, c, and d, and on the general characteristics of the future society which they are asked to think about (listed as 1, 2, and 3 above). These considerations are, of course, deliberately introduced to disallow utopian speculations, and they counsel strongly in favor of a cautious, defensive approach. Thus, the negotiators are likely to follow Thomas Hobbes in seeing the necessity for establishing some form of political authority (for otherwise they would leave themselves vulnerable to the limited altruism of others in the struggle for scarce resources). They would go beyond him in their distrust by also acknowledging that its establishment poses a danger (for whoever can control such authority would be placed in a good position to exploit others or to impose his, her, or their will). For this reason, the negotiators would seek out democratic solutions to the problem of controlling political power; and, in this latter regard they will be impressed by Meiklejohn's functionalist argument that freedom of speech, particularly the right to hear and express political points of view, is a necessary prerequisite for such a system of government. Other functionalist claims supporting freedom of speech will also impress the negotiators. For example, they will acknowledge Emerson's claim that because harmful speech is often difficult to identify, whereas the damage it causes may be easy to remedy, very good reasons must be provided before censorship ought to be tolerated. Also, they will be likely to find Mill's views about the importance of criticism for the advance of knowledge convincing.

Of course, as we saw in chapter 1, utilitarian arguments do not allow us to adopt freedom of speech as an absolute commitment and are compatible with the adoption of a variety of strategies in resolving difficult communications policy dilemmas. Thus, if the Rawlsian negotiators restrict themselves to utilitarian and other functionalist forms of argument, they would feel free to seek to define categories of speech (such as defamatory claims made about private individuals, or obscene or racist speech) which are deemed to have no redeeming social value. They may also agree to follow the general practice of most contemporary liberal societies by allowing for two and perhaps even three different systems of communication to operate simultaneously (for example, by allowing the regulation of broadcast speech and advertising but protecting the print media).

But Rawlsian negotiators are not restricted in the kinds of argument they may review in determining whether freedom of speech is desirable or about how to conceive of such a commitment. Moreover, they will be wary of utilitarianism for they will realize that the collective pursuit of common goals (such as knowledge or effective democratic accountability) may well place some fundamental interests of particular individuals in jeopardy (for example, an individual's interest in privacy or in obtaining a fair trial when accused of committing a criminal offense). Thus, the negotiators would realize that they should be less concerned with the general impact any principle of free speech they adopt is likely to have, overall, than with its likely consequences for the future individuals whose interests they have a responsibility to protect. Moreover, negotiators operating under a "veil of ignorance" are likely to be more attracted to neutrality as an ideal than are those philosophers whose thinking is purely consequentialist, and they will be likely to endorse Ackerman's rules for neutral dialogue as a general social principle; that is, they would require a communications system to be so structured that nobody—especially no government official—is able to justify imposing his or her conception of the good by holding that it is better than that asserted by other citizens. The argument, here, is not that as a matter of fact one person's conception of the good cannot rationally be judged better than that asserted by others but that within "the veil of ignorance" it is not easy to make judgments of this kind, and that the negotiators should consequently endorse neutrality as a defensive strategy.

Ironically, one of the strongest arguments for neutrality arises out of what little the negotiators are able to say about the nature of the good. For, insofar as they are able to reflect coherently upon this topic within the "veil of ignorance," they will be impressed by a line of argument which derives from Aristotle and, in part at least, from the liberal tradition inspired by Immanuel Kant. What these writers emphasize in their different ways is the importance of developing our rationality (that is, the human faculty which enables us to question, make discriminating judgments, calculate, and perceive anomalies as well as analogies) as an ingredient of the good life. In terms of the humanistic conception which their work has inspired, the doing of good acts and the living of life according to sound precepts are not thought to be the only matters of significance for individual wellbeing. What is equally important, if not more so, is that each individual chooses to live the good life for himself or herself and that he or she takes such choices seriously, providing good reasons in support of the choices made. A commitment to liberty follows, then, for Kantian humanists, precisely because it is the choosing for oneself which distinguishes us as persons. Thus, in their view, a policy of moral paternalism (supposing this were to be adopted by a benevolent political authority) would be self-defeating, for by enforcing worthy standards our dictator would encourage people to uphold them for the wrong kind of reason; moreover, such a policy of paternalistic intervention would violate the dignity of the persons whose considered choices are restrained.

How far the Rawlsian negotiators would be able to go in reaching agreement over the implications of Kantian humanism is difficult to say. At one extreme, some could support a view of human nature which takes autonomy and freedom as the primary ingredients of the good life. In terms of this conception, we would hold that of the various ways in which future individuals could live, those which involve self-discipline, planning, and the development of a capacity for accomplishing complex tasks are inherently better than those which result in purely physical or largely passive pleasures. Other delegates may demur, holding that there are no good reasons for supposing that one way of life is inherently superior. But whichever position particular negotiators take here, each will anticipate the possibility that some citizens in the future society may embrace Kantian humanism and will understand why such individuals would care deeply about freedom and autonomy. Thus Kantian negotiators will argue that censorship by governmental authorities should be banned as a matter of principle because it constitutes a violation of the dignity of persons. They would hold that even a benevolent ruler who restrains communications to ensure that his or her subjects are prevented from acquiring bad habits or a poor sensibility, as a result of laziness or indulgence, should be regarded as acting illegitimately. Those negotiators who are relativists will support this suggestion, for they will deny that there can be good reasons for preventing anyone from doing what he or she chooses so long as they are not harming others in a serious way.

It is instructive to observe that this latter conclusion does not necessarily follow if the argument about personal self-fulfilment is posed within a wider utilitarian discussion, in the way that it is by John Stuart Mill in his essay *On Liberty*.[17] For unlike Rawlsian negotiators, who are able to endorse the neutrality principle as a protective device, so that future governments may not legitimately prevent any individual from deciding what to believe or from articulating his or her own reasons for acting in the way chosen, Mill is obliged to show that the enjoyment of such a liberty would be conducive to the development of his favored form of individuality. But this latter consequence is a contingent matter and it may well be that the characteristics of individuality which he favors are more likely to be developed in a disciplined rather than libertarian environment (for example, this is often the assumption when a policy requiring broadcasting stations to carry current affairs commentary is enforced). Thus, many commentators (especially churchmen) argue that in choosing liberty as a basic principle, Mill fails to acknowledge how susceptible most people are to morally depraved suggestions. What those who support Mill's ideal have to acknowledge is that if people are likely to make a bad use of their liberties, they may develop characters more inclined towards indulgence than the pursuit of excellence; and that if we envisage this contingency, we must allow that the utilitarian argument put forward by him will be undermined. Rawlsian negotiators would, however, be unimpressed by this latter consideration, for their focus would be individuated: they would ask (each supposing that he or she as a future citizen cares about moral autonomy and that his or her own conception of the good is Kantian) whether censorship would constitute a violation of a fundamental interest. And the answer they will give must clearly be affirmative, for they will see that censorship would deprive citizens of the ability to choose for themselves what they wish to believe or commit themselves to.

I think it should be clear why Rawlsian negotiators are likely to favor freedom of speech and would regard the possibility of censorship as highly threatening. But how are they to conceive of the freedom to speak? Here, we must acknowledge the serious difficulties which arise when other values seem to conflict with liberty. Nevertheless, two points can be made in a preliminary way before we explore particular problems in detail. First, Rawlsian negotiators would be inclined to define what is to count as "speech" in the manner recommended by Thomas Scanlon (also embracing the revisions to his position which I have recommended). Thus, they would hold that, if a commitment to freedom of speech is to govern a particular case, this means that an authority may legitimately regulate communications only in those circumstances when audiences are clearly vulnerable because of circumstances beyond their control (when, for example, there is insufficient time for considered judgment) and that they may never restrain speakers because they think that their message will have an undesirable influence. Second, the negotiators are likely to agree that freedom of speech ought to be regarded as no more than a residual right, that is, as the immunity from collectively imposed obligations which we have left to us after we have done our part in ensuring that everyone else is treated fairly. On this conception, then, although we may in general assume freedom of speech, it would nevertheless be appropriate for a government to regulate speakers to ensure that somebody's right to a fair trial or to security (supposing that these interests are deemed fundamental) is not placed in jeopardy.

Of the widely recognized moral rights which seem reasonably uncontroversial (and I do not take much trouble to defend my own acknowledgment of them) are those which protect us from the aggression or foolishness of other individuals. We would be likely to establish, among other things, that each of us should enjoy a moral right to obtain compensation when our interests (whatever these may turn out to be) are significantly harmed by others (the qualifications I add below about what is to count as a "significant harm" in this context are controversial); and that other persons (including any political authorities) should be severely limited in the manner they may intrude upon or coerce us. Apart from these protections we would also seek to ensure that there is no anomalous discrimination preventing anyone from participating on an equal basis in the processes of collective decision-making or in enjoying an equal claim to the goods provided through such a political instrumentality.

With regard to the issue of political participation, it is clear that entitlements and liberties such as the right to vote, to join political associations, and to communicate opinions would be given a high priority by negotiators. They will know that the life of all individuals in any future society could be affected through collective decision-making and will want to ensure that each person will have a fair chance to recommend and have implemented what he takes to be the best policies. Besides providing protection against the possibility of tyranny, a widely enjoyed effective right to participate in the political process is a necessary expression of the commitment to ensure that every individual's dignity is respected, and this would be acknowledged by the negotiators. However, the negotiators will have difficulty determining the precise profile of such a right to participate. For example, does freedom of speech require that individuals be afforded access to forums when they seek to communicate? And, if so, how can such an access right be reconciled with our commitment to respect editorial autonomy? (I deal with these issues in chapter 3). Another difficult dilemma worth considering arises when individuals seek to respond when personally attacked in the media; they may claim a right to have their opinions afforded exposure of a kind which allows them a reasonable chance of vindication. We find that the case which can be made for establishing such a right is a strong one. At issue is whether a person's interest in vindicating his reputation is of a kind which deserves to be protected even at some cost to other social interests. More particularly, whether it should be given a priority when there is a conflict with the public interest in "uninhibited, robust and wide-open" debate. We clearly accept that an individual's interests do sometimes have a priority over any public benefit that may result from liberty of expression. For example, we regard certain privacy interests as fundamental in this sense, and most of us would acknowledge that a person's right to a fair trial should normally be afforded a priority over the right to speak. Do we have a similar right to secure our reputations?

Would individuals in a state-of-nature negotiation, ignorant of their particular circumstances (such as whether they are more likely to suffer from attacks than to disseminate them) be likely to recognize that some mechanism facilitating the vindication of reputation for those falsely accused should be constitutionally protected? The argument advanced in these circumstances would be similar to the case that Rawls makes for the recognition of religious freedom. Our negotiators will know enough about human nature to realize how intensely an individual is likely to feel when his reputation is called into question. They will readily concede that each of them could suffer public accusations, and will know what it would be like to feel a sense of frustration and outrage if they were not afforded some reasonable opportunity to reply. Our negotiators will also notice that when we secure the dissemination of an alternative view of the facts, we act in the spirit of the democratic commitment. The very point of freedom of speech is to safeguard a right to participate in democratic life, and the interest of other citizens in learning the truth weighs in favor of establishing a right of reply.

Would the establishment of such a right to attempt vindication necessarily violate any competing right of speakers to autonomy? If so, should the former right take priority?

I have already indicated that our right to freedom of speech falls into a residual category. On this conception, the more specific claims of individuals (such as any that are grounded in their interest in securing their reputations) must usually be held to take priority when these are recognized as matters of moral right. Moreover, it is significant in this context that the claim of a speaker to autonomy is sometimes weak. For example, if we take the case of malicious deception (supposing that the harm to someone's reputation has been caused by the dissemination of a known falsehood), it is clear that the publisher or broadcaster involved would forfeit any claim to editorial autonomy. The deliberate propagation of a falsehood is not the kind of speech which qualifies for protection under any conception of freedom of speech in that the disseminator attempts to manipulate rather than persuade. Thus, anyone who suffers from a libel of this kind would have a moral claim to full vindication, as would be the case had the harm been caused through a deliberate physical act (such as by planting incriminating evidence).

Once we allow that the "good faith" of a disseminator is relevant to the claim to editorial autonomy, it becomes clear that we can sometimes require the disseminator to ensure an opportunity for those who are defamed to vindicate themselves. For example, suppose that a libel had been disseminated in good faith but that a publisher or broadcaster refuses to correct the error when this is pointed out. In this case, the decision not to correct has the same consequence as would a determination to publish or broadcast material known to be misleading. What distinguishes the cases is that the latter is an omission rather than a commission. From a moral point of view, however, the status of the two is similar. Surely we may legitimately impose on publishers and broadcasters the requirement that they correct acknowledged errors when these have harmed an individual. The situation is, of course, more problematic when there is genuine disagreement about the facts. But even here, the "good faith" of the publisher or broadcaster is evidenced by a willingness to allow a reasonable opportunity for the person under attack to reply. The crucial question is whether there is open discussion or whether only the accuser's opinion is deemed relevant.

Another difficult decision which negotiators in a Rawlsian dialogue will confront is whether a person's interest in obtaining compensation when his interests are damaged by others should be regarded as more fundamental than the interest we all share in the enjoyment of the liberty to communicate. Here, judgments about the significance of the kind of damage in question may have to be made. For example, communications which are likely to damage a person's chance of obtaining a fair trial clearly threaten a fundamental interest. However, some interests which may be damaged by unbridled communicators are less important. A dilemma that I will be considering in Part Two is whether a person's interest in controlling how he is presented to others to ensure that he is not unnecessarily embarrassed should be afforded as a right. (By this I mean that it should take priority over Rawls's general liberty principle in terms of which we justify our right to speak.) We can state the problem by asking whether we should afford individuals the possibility to claim damages by way of amelioration when they have been harmed by unsought publicity.

Negotiators discussing constitutional principles under Rawls's "veil of ignorance" (where they have no particular knowledge about themselves) would have difficulty deciding whether this interest is likely to be fundamental to them; as they would deciding about the obverse problem of whether the revulsion people sometimes feel when they find the behavior of others offensive is a significant harm. How deeply we feel about not being confronted by others or not being presented to others depends on who we are, and this in turn is influenced by the importance attached to privacy in particular cultures. It follows that were subjective feelings the sole criterion for what is to count as "significant," the principle that individuals be afforded a right to compensation when seriously harmed by the actions of others would be indeterminate.

The very fact that this issue cannot be easily addressed within a Rawlsian state-of-nature dialogue indicates that the interest under consideration may not be suitable for classification as a "primary good." Whether a person cares deeply, or is likely to, about the enjoyment of some privilege would only be relevant when reviewing the legitimacy of a rights claim if one can presume that a large number of individuals will feel in a similar way. For example, Rawls makes a case for claiming religious freedom as a right on the grounds that negotiators will know enough about human nature to realize how intensely an individual is likely to feel about his or her fundamental religious practices and beliefs.[18]

We may ask, then, whether our negotiatiors could make any progress in deciding whether a person's interest in avoiding serious embarrassment should be regarded as fundamental, given only their general knowledge about human nature (informed by the "real world" assumptions we have allowed them to acknowledge as a reasonable basis for their discussion). They will know that children sometimes suffer excruciating anguish when their names are called in school, that people differ considerably in their responses to public exposure, and that some are so sensitive that they even resent favorable public references to themselves. From general observations such as these, the negotiators would be able to see that limits to the control individuals enjoy over how they are presented will have to be imposed if social life is to be possible at all, but they will have great difficulty deciding what these should be without some specific knowledge of the kind of society they anticipate. However, given the asumptions we have provided as common ground (that is, that the future society will be large, complex, and modern, with an advanced division of labor and that it is to be served by a communications system which includes mass circulation print and broadcast media), we may be sure that they would be reluctant to count embarrassment as a fundamental harm. The reason for this is that they will know that social life in such a society could not proceed without frequent public scrutiny of the private realm.

PART TWO

Accommodating Rights and the Public Interest

In Part One I was concerned to elaborate a theory of rights. I now turn to consider hard cases when freedom of speech is in conflict with other competing claims in the light of that theory. The idea is to test the theory (a) by seeing whether the kinds of anomalies which functionalist theories tend to give rise to can be avoided; (b) whether the theory offers a coherent approach; (c) whether it can accommodate all categories of communication (in particular, whether broadcasters and those who disseminate messages through mass circulation newspapers can be accommodated under the same principles); and (d) whether the policy outcomes recommended in the light of the theory are intuitively acceptable.

We can distinguish two different kinds of problem case:

The first arises when individuals make claims to special rights. Here, I have allowed that the general immunity from regulation which speakers may claim in the name of freedom of speech must give way. Our liberties can only be enjoyed in a democracy after everything reasonable has been done to ensure that the legitimate rights which have been claimed by individuals are honored. I begin by discussing access problems, asking when a person who seeks to communicate ought to be afforded the facilities of some desired forum. I then turn to evaluate various claims made by individuals to control what is commmunicated about them. There is controversy over whether (a) individuals who have been publicly accused of committing crimes or other strongly disapproved of acts or whose character has been brought into question enjoy a moral right to be facilitated in answering their critics; (b) individuals ought to enjoy a right to compensation in circumstances when their reputations have been called into question, especially if the evidence indicates that this might have been done unfairly; and (c) individuals should enjoy a right to compensation when subjected to publicity relating to matters of a private nature. (These tasks will occupy chapters 3, 4, 5, and 6.)

The second kind of problem which I need to confront if I am properly to assess my chosen liberal theory occurs when freedom of speech creates or is likely to create a significant nuisance: How ought we to accommodate the competing claims of liberty and the common good? This latter problem is complex because it is clear that no one in a democracy has a right not to be inconvenienced. Thus, a policy may be legitimate even if it imposes some difficulties in the way of the pursuit by a private individual of a right, so long as the restraints do not make enjoyment of it impossible. For example, a person may be asked to contribute to legal costs in securing a right to a fair trial, and this would be legitimate so long as the burden is not so great that the possibility of such a debt functions as a form of repression. The problem is, of course, that it is not easy also to determine when a burden has become repressive.

What we confront here is the indirect effect which a government pursuing a legitimate interest may have on the enjoyment of a right. For example, a municipal decision to control the distribution of pamphlets in parks may be directed at solving a litter problem but it may make it more difficult to organize political meetings. This is a problem which we will come across time and again when dealing with free speech cases, for a government intent on censoring speech will almost always pretend to be doing something else. Thus, it is likely to restrain communications indirectly by pursuing some other more respectable objective. Governments do, of course, often have very good reasons for imposing restraints on speakers (for example, to protect patients in a hospital from the noise of loud-speakers or even a rowdy crowd) and this is a problem which any viable theory must provide a solution to.

A way of resolving the dilemma has been worked out by Justice Hugo Black.[1] He tells us that when confronted by such a case we must ask: first, whether the restraint on a speaker is a mere inconvenience or involves total or partial censorship. If it prevents a speaker from successful communication, the government must be regarded as acting illegitimately. Second, we must ask whether the impact of the indirect restraint is fair (that is, whether it is administered in a way which shows an equal concern for the person whose right to comunicate is affected). Here we must recognize that democratic governments are often tempted to abuse the trust placed in them, and they may withhold privileges from some groups while favoring others. Third, we must ask whether there is some other available remedy for achieveing the objective which does not affect the right of expression. And, if this is the case, we must ask whether the cost involved is such that it would be reasonable to seek this other course of action. Besides these considerations, which allow a limited amount of balancing of the competing interests, we must require governments to proceed with the utmost care in framing laws which affect liberty so that they are not overly broad in their impact.

I

All liberal theories, whether functionalist or deontological, share some core commitments. First they all hold to the view that governments may not discriminate between speakers imposing an official view of what needs to be heard, read, or seen. From this basic commitment, most liberals deduce that a government which places prior restraints on a speaker would not normally be justified. This would be the case unless the restraint was necessary to secure some basic right (thus, if there was an immediate danger that people could be physically injured, restraints on a potential speaker may be justified). Also, because liberals regard freedom of speech as a right, they share the burden of delineating the boundaries of the privilege. Thus every liberal theory must provide some criterion for demarcating what is to count as "speech."

Most of the disagreements between liberal writers emerge at the level of justification, for they often provide different reasons for placing a priority on liberty amongst our values. It is precisely because disagreements emerge at this point that theorists also differ over the weight which they are willing to place on the claims of fairness in moral arguments about rights. Thus, those who regard liberty as their coordinating value do not recognize equity as a consideration which can establish rights claims. On the other hand, those whose orientation is essentially utilitarian also have difficulty accommodating fairness standards, and their commitment to liberty may be more qualified than that of most other liberals. I have provided some reasons for thinking these approaches are less adequate than the Rawlsian orientation, in which a right of every citizen to equal concern and respect in the design of political institutions is taken as fundamental. There is, of course, no easy way to show why it is rational to make the democratic commitment which I have endorsed. However, those who refuse to make it eschew neutral dialogue, and we may accuse them of force, fraud, or a desire to impose their metaphysical beliefs. As for those who are well-meaning but remain skeptical, I must ask their indulgence, for (if I am to vindicate my decision to embrace the commitment to treat others with equal concern and respect and to demand this standard of behavior from those in authority) I must be allowed a license to persuade the reader not only that Rawlsian liberalism provides a basis for reaching the most satisfactory resolution of hard cases when reviewing communications policy, but that it provides us with the best available understanding of why we are inclined to resolve them in these ways.

II

Some preliminary points about the capacity of the competing theories to handle the two kinds of problem cases I identify are worth noting:

Cases Involving Conflicts When Basic Rights are Claimed

Theorists who adopt a Lockean deontological approach find themselves in difficulties when handling hard cases of this kind, for, in delineating basic rights, they place so much emphasis on property claims and on liberty that little regulation of the media to accommodate the public interest in a fair and vigorous public discussion can be legitimized. Suppose, for example, that a prime minister wishes to address the nation. According to Lockean values, this should not be accomplished in ways which violate property rights. Thus, unless media owners voluntarily provide access for him or her, it would not be possible to obtain access; moreover, it would be illegitimate (in the light of Lockean values) to seek to impose a duty to provide access through legislation. Similarly, consider a person's Lockean right to gain compensation when harmed by another. The recognition of such a right makes it difficult to justify allowing a privilege to speakers against liability (so as to encourage uninhibited discussion, as is the case in the United States law of defamation, which protects those who attack public officials) or the privilege afforded to parliamentary discussion in the United Kingdom.

If one test of a theory is that it enables us to reach policy recommendations which are intuitively acceptable, the tough-minded Lockean approach must be regarded as a failure. In any event, I shall not take much trouble to demonstrate its inadequacies, for I have chosen to focus on the competing claims of the two more plausible liberal approaches outlined: the functionalist (whether along the lines recommended by Meiklejohn or utilitarian writers) and the Rawlsian. The former recommends itself precisely because, by avoiding a strong commitment to the recognition of absolute political rights, it allows the kind of flexibility which Lockean liberals have difficulty accommodating. Thus, in dealing with the issue of defamation law reform or the issue of whether governments should regulate forums to ensure access for significant speech, a functionalist can place considerable weight on public interest concerns such as the establishment of circumstances conducive to vigorous, uninhibited public debate.

In recommending a Rawlsian approach I shall suggest that the flexibility exhibited by functionalist approaches is acquired at some theoretical cost for, while the theory often generates solutions which seem satisfactory when no rights claims are involved (for example, when discussing the kinds of information which citizens should be allowed to obtain access to), it is less satisfactory when rights claims are made out. For example, in dealing with cases in which there is a conflict between freedom of speech and the right of an individual to enjoy privacy or his or her right to vindication when unfairly attacked on the media, insufficient protection is offered those who may have been harmed. Consider the case of privacy protection: if we balance this interest against the public interest in unfettered discussion, it will often seem the lesser in importance (as when the person whose privacy is harmed is an important political leader). The same is true with regard to the claim to a good reputation when this has been unfairly brought into question on the media, for it is often clear that the public interest is best served by allowing false accusations to be disseminated (for example, during debates in parliament or when an individual is standing for election to a public office).

Freedom of Speech Versus the Common Good

Cases where there seems to be a clash between the public interest and freedom of speech provide a challenging test for my claim that a Rawlsian deontological approach has definite advantages over functionalism. It may be argued that it does not provide enough flexibility to permit a satisfactory resolution of this kind of issue because, once we are committed to the cognition of a right, no balancing of competing interests is allowed for. Functionalist approaches, in contrast, because they allow us to weigh the force we attach to any putative claim to "freedom" in the light of our assessment of the general justificatory arguments we see as relevant, provide for flexibility. If the consequence of regulating a particular category of speech is likely to result in more good than harm, a functionalist can allow for this, whereas a Lockean or Rawlsian liberal cannot. The problem for functionalists is, however, that they find it difficult to place sufficient weight (to satisfy our intuitive sense of the importance of the value) on the recognition of editorial autonomy.

My purpose is to show that what appears to be a weakness is actually a strength. I shall hold, first, that Rawlsian liberalism is not as inflexible as is often suggested. In this regard I draw attention to the fact that even though a government bound by the principles of Rawlsian liberalism would not be entitled to balance liberty against any competing interest, it could legitimately place even significant burdens on speakers. Thus it may require speakers to acquire a license or to refrain from causing a nuisance to others. The proviso it must honor when imposing burdens of this kind is to make sure that they are not so severe as to vitiate the enjoyment of the right. For example, in the analogous case of our right to a fair trial when accused of a crime, governments may require defendants to contribute substantially towards the costs of enjoying the privilege. However, when a defendant is incapable of meeting this requirment, he or she has a right to expect that the state will itself bear the costs. A second point which I wish to emphasize is that Rawlsian liberals are able, better than those who embrace functionalist approaches, to explain why we intuitively place such a heavy weight on editorial and speaker autonomy when reviewing communications policy.

Usually when access is provided through compulsion, editorial autonomy is threatened. Whether policies violating autonomy in the name of fairness are desirable or not is, however, an issue badly handled by functionalists. The reason for this is that they tend to simplify the issues so that we identify the public interest without fully comprehending the significance of the various claims in contest. If access is likely to serve a good purpose (for example, a requirement that politicians be provided with time by broadcasters in order that they may more effectively campaign for office) then, prima facie at least, a strong functionalist case is made for regulating the media to ensure such access. But if we allow for access in this case, what about other deserving claims—for example, is campaigning for an election more important than campaigning to stop a war? Moreover, whenever we have a rule requiring that access be provided, hard cases will arise which functionalists will find difficult to resolve. For example, suppose we impose a duty on newspaper editors to publish representative letters which criticize their editorials. One problem we may have with this rule is that the question of whether or not access will serve a good purpose is one that can hardly be resolved without taking into account the content of the communication in question; and there is also the issue of the quality of the communication in question. For example, one letter complaining about a newspaper's editorial support of a local municipality's decision to rebuild the local library may be misinformed about the costs of the various alternatives; yet another letter, less deserving of dissemination because it is more supportive of the editorial, may be accurate. Which letter should the editor publish on the issue, supposing there is only enough space for one of them? Of course, one could argue, even on utililitarian grounds, that discretion about what should be published should be placed in the unbridled hands of editors; and once a commitment to uphold editorial autonomy is made, the dilemmas become more manageable. But this option is not easy for functionalists to justify.

Perhaps the most serious weakness of the functionalist approach to the problems of access is that it is indeterminate. Moreover, given certain factual claims about monopolies or media imperialism it can lead to conclusions which countenance extensive regulation of the media. This is forcefully illustrated by the arguments and conclusions of the recent UNESCO MacBride Report, *Many Voices One World*. This document is premised on the claim that a coherent understanding of freedom of speech should proceed in two stages: first we should list audience interests and, second, we must ask what freedoms are conducive to the realization of these interests. One claim made in the report is that because of the complexity of modern media and the economics of message production, there exists a one-way flow of information from the developed to the developing world which is not serving any good purpose. The commission sees the world as a vast public meeting in which only the wealthy can get a hearing, and it advocates interventions in the free flow of communications to ensure greater national sovereignty for poorer countries so as to create an international environment in which more voices are heard. Less extreme conclusions are derived using a similar line of argument by Justice White in the important United States Supreme Court case *Red Lion Broadcasting v. FCC*; and by the legal scholar Jerome Barron in his book *Freedom of the Press for Whom?*, in which he extends the reasoning of the *Red Lion Broadcasting* judgment to argue for the recognition of a constitutional right of access to all the mass media in the United States.

I do not claim here that functionalists must necessarily endorse illiberal conclusions; merely, first, that the use of Meiklejohnian arguments may, given certain factual claims, lead to such conclusions; and, second, that the position is inherently indeterminate because people disagree about whether editorial autonomy is a fundamental right, about the dangers attached to governmental regulation, and about the benefits which can be anticipated when the press are imposed upon.

III

As we shall see, the deontological approach I adopt leads to more libertarian conclusions than those inclined to be reached by the balancing of competing interests. This is because, first, I have embraced the principle that an evaluation of the content of a communication (whether it is likely to make any significant contribution to debate about public policy or to art or science) must not be taken into account in formulating policy. This commitment clearly follows from the ideal of treating other persons with equal respect and is embodied in Ackerman's neutrality principle, which I quoted above. Second, I have placed the onus on those who wish to censor a speaker to show that some person has a moral right which would otherwise be compromised. In most circumstances, this is not easy to do, for a rights claim can only be established when we are prepared to recognize that an interest is so fundamental to a particular person that it is necessary to afford it to him even at considerable social cost. The liberal bias of the theory is, however, a reason for recommending it and confirms my own intuitive judgment.

3

Free Speech versus Access

Anyone who wishes to communicate must first gain access to an audience. It follows that effective censorship can take place by those who control access to the most desirable forums. Examples spring to mind. A local council may refuse to allow a political group to use its hall for a meeting or refuse to issue a permit allowing it to march in public places such as streets, a square, or parks. A newspaper editor may refuse to publish a letter on a matter of controversy because it expresses a viewpoint critical of his own editorial. A broadcaster may find it profitable to restrict programming so that no news or public affairs commentary is put to air.

Different kinds of situation of this kind, giving rise to distinct problems, are worth distinguishing. First, there are those cases where the size and nature of audiences are determined by what is said. People voluntarily gather to listen, deliberately tune in, or go out of their way to read because they are interested. Does a speaker have a moral right to monopolize his or her audience, or do hecklers, applauders, and others who may wish to address it have a legitimate claim to gain access? Clearly, if we recognize a right to speak as a fundamental part of the democratic commitment we cannot tolerate policies which impose on speakers, forcing them to convey messages which they do not wish to communicate. But does this mean that they have a right to exclude other speakers from obtaining access to the audience which their skills have gathered? When a prime minister demands the right to address the nation in prime time on a commercial television station, he or she is imposing on the autonomy of program makers. This may be desirable (in that it may be very useful to the community for the prime minister to be able to address a much wider viewing audience than would be the case were such a broadcast to have been transmitted on an official government station). But does the imposition constitute an abuse of power? Second, there are cases where those who control a forum are not in the business of communicating. Their claim to control a particular forum derives from the fact that they are the managers or owners of it. The most significant of the public forums owned in this way is advertising space (available on modern media and in places like subway stations, where large numbers of people will be exposed to the messages displayed). We must decide whether the owners of this space should be able to control access to it. A closely related issue concerns the power of editorial writers. Most of us do not read newspapers or listen to the radio to be preached at by the owners of these facilities. Once we tune in or purchase our paper, however, we become a captive audience and are vulnerable to those of the management who wish to tell us a few things. Should an owner be allowed to take advantage of this circumstance without any obligation to be fair, or ought he or she be made vulnerable to a right of reply? Finally, it is worth distinguishing those access problems which involve claims made by particular individuals who assert that they have a right to be afforded access to a given forum. Here, the person may claim that unless such access is afforded, he or she will suffer some harm to a fundamental interest.

The question I wish to address in this chapter is whether a Rawlsian liberal approach, in terms of which we seek out neutral principles to coordinate policy so that core rights are respected and identified, is capable of providing a more plausible resolution of the dilemmas which the problem of how to provide reasonable access for speakers gives rise to.

GAINING ACCESS FOR ADVERTISING AND TO PUBLIC FORUMS

A first issue is the proper scope which should be afforded to those who claim a right of editorial autonomy when confronted by the demands of others for access to a forum, when this latter demand is grounded in a claim to the enjoyment of a right. Let me begin by considering a case in which the proper scope of editorial autonomy is clearly called into question, that is, where a speaker demands access to the audience of some other communicator in a way that seems clearly illegitimate. (One has to rely on intuition to determine this, and there may be disagreement). An example is the United States case *Avins v. Rutgers Law Review*.[1] Alfred Avins asserted that because the *Rutgers Law Review* was funded with public money, it should be forced to provide access to all significant points of view. (This should not be an unfamiliar line of argument to Australian or British readers, for in these systems the state-funded broadcasting services operate under a "public interest" obligation requiring them to present all serious contending views on matters of controversy.) Avins was hoping to make use of the fact that, in the United States, the Bill of Rights makes it illegitimate for a government to discriminate between speakers. Thus, he did not challenge the right of the privately funded law journals to have an editorial policy favoring particular points of view. His focus was only upon those outlets which are government-funded, and his specific complaint was that an article he submitted to a state-funded journal was rejected because of his conservative opinions.

From the perspective of a more general assessment of the right to communicate, the fact that a journal is funded by a private patron or by the state should not make any significant difference. Government publishers, like every other, need to be free to disseminate any materials they choose (indeed, municipal, state, and provincial authorities are often important contributors to public debate, setting forth opinions on a wide range of issues) and, so long as the total system of communication allows other independent points of view to be heard, there is no reason why this should be regarded as illegitimate.

The *Rutgers Law Review* is merely one of a large number of significant law journals; moreover, it is not a mere mouthpiece of the funding agency, but a credible independent voice. Thus, unless one is prepared to accept Avin's claim that a government may never support speakers in pursuing its conception of the general good, it is difficult to find any basis for questioning the editorial autonomy claimed by the *Rutgers Law Review*. Freedom of speech implies that those who have a point of view should have the right to put it forward without fear of censorship.

Not surprisingly, the New Jersey court of appeals found in favor of the editorial rights of the *Rutgers Law Review*. Not all situations in which governments have been involved in a particular form of communication have been so easy to resolve, however, and there are harder cases to consider. In particular, it is more difficult to support claims to editorial autonomy in situations where access to a forum is regulated by a government. As the use of the broadcast spectrum was not freely available to the highest bidder for very long, because governments took upon themselves the task of allocating the forum among speakers, those responsible for articulating the standards which need to be applied in regulating broadcasters have been faced by the most difficult cases. Indeed, the problem of spectrum scarcity (if such a claim can be plausibly asserted) and the supervisory role of governments over the broadcasting medium of communication are complicating factors which have led many liberals to qualify their commitment to the ideal of speaker autonomy.

It is, of course, not only broadcasters who may control significant, scarce forums. Publishing companies may enjoy monopolies in particular areas when they control the only newspaper. The dilemma posed by private ownership of a scarce forum is, of course, compounded when government licensing is implicated. Nevertheless, publishers who control markets because competition would not be viable may need to have an obligation to neutrality and to fairness imposed upon them.

I shall discuss these issues shortly when I consider the response of the United States Supreme Court in the two leading (and contradictory) cases

Miami Herald Publishing v. Tornillo and *Red Lion Broadcasting v. FCC*.[2] At this stage I wish to look at cases in which someone claims a right to control a significant forum even though she is not grounding that claim on the assertion of a right to editorial autonomy but for other reasons (such as that she is the owner or manager of the resource or because the communications to be carried have some impact on a legitimate activity she is pursuing).

Let us begin with cases in which the owner of a forum (whether a private individual, a governmental authority, or a privately owned corporation) claims to enjoy a discretion to exclude the spokesman of particular points of view from gaining access to it. The typical kind of case I have in mind occurs when institutions (such as hospitals, universities, and corporations) open their property to the public (for example, as part of a shopping center, a bus station, or a university campus). Areas of this kind often attract those who wish to use it as a forum for public displays, marches, and other forms of demonstration; and because these are often directed against the interests of the owner of the property (for example, demonstrators on a campus may voice disapproval about the investments made by the university in South Africa or complain about its discriminatory housing policies) conflicts are frequent. If the owner tries to regulate the use of designated public places to exclude those whose views he deems unacceptable, some judgment about the legitimacy of this behavior is needed.

One part of the answer seems straightforward: we must allow that once the public are admitted on an indiscriminate basis, whatever right to communicate they would enjoy in a public place controlled by a governmental authority ought also to be enjoyed when the property is privately owned. Of course, in most democracies there is no legal right to demonstrate in public places. However, as liberals, we would say that some such right ought to be afforded. My only point here is that whatever moral claim can be made to establish a right to make use of publicly owned streets and parks can be used to establish a claim to use similar resources which are privately owned and when they have been opened to the public. Thus, the fact that a bus station is owned by a municipality and not by the Greyhound company is not relevant when considering the rights the public enjoy within it.

The point I make in the last paragraph is understated, for democratically elected officials have a stronger moral claim to make evaluative judgments in the name of the public than private authorities. Thus, in most democracies, government agencies are often authorized to regulate advertising, imposing judgments about whether particular communications are misleading or otherwise undesirable (for example, they have often decided that the advertising of tobacco products by broadcasters is undesirable and have also placed limits on political advertising).[3] If we are to suppose that these forms of regulation are justifiable (perhaps, because we think commercial speech is a category which does not deserve full protection), it does not follow that we cannot object if private owners make this evaluation in regulating privately owned forums that have been opened to the public. Experience in running a bus, train, or taxi service, or even experience as a broadcaster, in no way qualifies one to legislate public morality or determine what is in the public interest.

Of course, the controllers of a resource which serves indirectly as a forum in which communications can be brought before a target audience (such as the walls of a bus terminal's waiting room) clearly have an interest in ensuring that its use as a forum does not undermine the other primary uses for which it has been reserved. Thus, a bus company would have a legitimate interest in ensuring that the public do not suffer aesthetically from poster advertising and may also wish to protect passengers from exposure to material they find indecent. Interests of this kind, which are functionally related to the uses which the owner of a resource makes of a property, justify the imposition of controls on communicators. On the other hand, once a decision has been made to open a space to the public (on whatever terms are set forth), those who seek access must be treated impartially. The owners of a forum have no business censoring speakers, and their discretion to control should be no greater than that which would be allowed a governmental authority.

Deciding whether a regulation is functionally necessary may not always be easy, and some deference to the judgments of the owners of a forum may be wise. Nevertheless, private companies have shown an eagerness to act as censors by imposing restrictions which are clearly not functionally relevant in the way described. (For example, some transit companies have refused to carry advertisements providing the address and contact number of medical clinics which offer teenagers confidential contraceptive advice and treatment for venereal diseases. Some newspapers have refused to carry advertisements for R rated movies, and many have also discriminated for political reasons). Thus, adjudication may be necessary.

The following principles seem appropriate: (a) No owner (not even a governmental authority) is obliged to make a resource available for use as a forum. Governments do, of course, have a general obligation to ensure that a sufficient number of forums are available, and streets and parks have usually been put to such a use. This general obligation does not fall upon every government agency, however, and in some circumstances there may be good reasons for not making a forum available for public use. (Thus, if a government-funded broadcasting station or transit authority refused to carry advertising, they would be clearly entitled to take this stand.) (b) Functionally relevant regulations may be imposed.

Finally, (c) discriminations which are content-specific should not be imposed. Thus, a broadcaster who sells advertising spots ought not to control the messages carried and—apart from setting functionally relevant administrative standards, allowed for under (b)—must accept the advertising of all who are willing to pay for it on an equal basis.

Perhaps the most serious challenge to these principles calls (c) into question, for it has been held (by no less an authority than the United States Supreme Court) that discriminations which are not content-neutral may, nevertheless, be functionally relevant to the purposes for which a forum is used, and are sometimes tolerable as an insignificant abridgment of the right to communicate under principle (b). The occasion for this judgment concerned an appeal seeking a declaratory judgment and injunctive relief by a politician, Harry J. Lehman, after the Ohio Rapid Transit System (which was owned by the City of Shaker Heights) refused to carry his political advertisements in its buses.[4] Lehman, who was standing as a candidate in an election for the State Assembly, argued that because the transit authority already carried commercial and public service advertising its rejection of his material was discriminatory. Of course, if the authority's buses already carried political advertising, the case would have been perfectly straightforward. However, it had rejected all advertising of a political nature and not just Lehman's posters, treating all the contesting candidates in a similar way.

In his judgment for the majority, Justice Blackmun concedes that "the policies and practices governing access to the transit system's advertising space must not be arbitrary, capricious or invidious." However, he goes on to argue that the managerial decison to limit the car card space to commercial and service-oriented advertising "does not rise to the dignity of a First Amendment violation" of this kind. According to Blackmun, administrative interests informed the managerial decision to discriminate against those who wish to convey political messages. He tells us,

> Revenue earned from long-term commercial advertising could be jeopardized by a requirement that short-term candidacy or issue-orientated advertisements be displayed on car cards. Users would be subjected to the blare of political propaganda. There could be lurking doubts about favoritism, and sticky administrative problems might arise in parceling out limited space to eager politicians.

And he goes on to claim, "These are reasonable legislative objectives advanced by the city in a proprietary capacity."[5]

Bus cards are not a very significant forum, and perhaps an issue of such trivial dimensions should not be considered worthy of principled and considered adjudication. But what if every advertising forum were closed to political advertisers? A possibility which Blackmun's judgment does not exclude is that radio stations and television companies may well decide (because political campaigns are a nuisance and entail extra administrative burdens) to give commercial advertisers preference. This is a problem with the *Lehman v. City of Shaker Heights* judgment for, in recognizing someone's claim to a discretionary power, it is not a good practice to assume that he is going to use it in a particular way. We need to find a principled basis for deciding whether he should be afforded the authority claimed. In this regard, Blackmun's reasoning not only calls my principle of content neutrality into question but departs from the approach developed by the United States Supreme Court in previous public forum cases, where the tendency has been to insist that administrative discretions be very narrowly defined.[6]

Another difficulty with Blackmun's judgment is that the list of administrative problems which he cites are not substantial enough to justify the conclusion that the exclusion of Lehman's poster was not invidious. Justice Brennan, who vigorously dissented, is clearly right when he points out that the principle of neutrality should only be abandoned if serious interests are in conflict and that mere administrative convenience cannot be convincingly presented as such a countervailing consideration.[7] In the light of free speech principles (embodied in the First and Fourteenth Amendments to the United States Constitution), authorities may not select which issues are worth discussing. This requires the court to make sure that any restraints placed on a speaker are narrowly tailored to facilitate some significant purposes for which the forum is legitimately used. In Lehman's case, neither the efficiency of the transport system nor any special interests of the passengers would have been harmed by the inclusion of his political advertising amongst the messages displayed in the buses. Of course, Blackmun is right when he asserts that the administration of a forum which allows controversial speech may be more difficult than would be the case were such messages excluded. But this is part of the cost we pay for freedom. Furthermore, these costs can be anticipated before the forum is opened. For example, if a hall is hired out to members of the public, it must be anticipated that some groups who hold meetings will be likely to attract a hostile audience and that this could lead to some disruption and property damage. The manager of the hall may decide that this possibility is so serious a threat that the hall ought not to be hired out. On the other hand, he could calculate the costs beforehand and set the charges appropriately. What he may not do, in a democracy, is to restrict the use of the hall so that only groups whose activities are uncontroversial can make use of it.

As I have said, bus cards are not a very significant forum, and it is not surprising that no great fuss was made when political advertisers were excluded from obtaining access to the buses used in the Ohio Rapid Transit System. More important forums such as mass circulation newspapers and broadcasting stations have been the subject of greater legislative attention, and some efforts have been made to ensure access to politicians who wish to advertise during election campaigns. However, it is only broadcasters who have been imposed upon. (For example, Section 315 of the Communications Act, 1934, and the Federal Election Campaign Act, 1971, in the United States, both ensure that advertising time will be provided by broadcasters to legally qualified candidates for federal office who are willing to pay the regular commercial rate, and to do so on an equal basis. The right of local candidates is more problematical.[8])

The singling out of broadcasting as a category of speech deserving less protection than print media is a matter of controversy, and I shall address and reject the main arguments supporting this different treatment in a later section. At this stage, I must articulate the principles which need to be applied in dealing with claims to autonomy when the size and nature of the audience are a product of editorial skill.

ACCESS VERSUS EDITORIAL AUTONOMY

A stronger argument justifying private control over a forum can be made out when the owner of a particular forum is vitally interested in cultivating the audience that may be attracted to view or hear the messages conveyed. This is the circumstance of most advertising forums, in that messages are carried by those who are in the business of delivering audiences by capturing the attention of large numbers of people. The contrast with the simpler situation discussed above can be easily made by way of an example. Suppose a tobacco company sells poster space visible from the highway which runs adjacent to their very long, high wall. They do this to cash in on the commercial value of their extensive property and the fact that so many people pass by. The company cannot claim to have generated the audience, nor that the numbers of passers-by will be determined by the messages on the posters displayed. The public just happens to pass that wall and this is what makes it valuable as a forum. In terms of the neutrality principle I have articulated, the company would have no legitimate authority to regulate the content of the advertising messages. Thus, if anti-smoking lobbies are first in line, their messages must be carried.[9]

Contrast this case to the situation faced by, say, the editors of *Reader's Digest*. This is a magazine which carries articles which are carefully selected so that they will be likely to appeal to a poorly educated but significantly large audience who seek a simplified, easy-to-understand presentation of conservative opinions on matters of general interest (such as health, religion, family life, developments in science, communism, and so on). It can be argued that the magazine's audience is a product of editorial skill and, thus, that the owners of the *Reader's Digest* have a right to deliver it to whomever they choose and for whatever consideration they decide is appropriate (subject to advertising standards); moreover, that it is legitimate for the editor of the magazine to vet the content of advertising because the expression of some opinions, by offending the target audience, could affect the composition of the readers. The crucial issue we need to decide is whether this alleged relationship justifies our recognizing the autonomy of editors over the advertising space carried by a magazine, newspaper, or broadcast show; or, whether we ought to enforce access rights to such media for the purposes of advertising.

Although the principles I articulated in the last section cannot be applied without modification to the advertising forums attached to modern communications media, I shall argue that only minor revisions are required. Specifically, my principle (c) (requiring regulations to meet the requirement of content neutrality) must be replaced with a set of guidelines setting out how content-based discriminations, which exclude an advertiser from gaining access to an audience, may be evaluated so that we can judge them legitimate or illegitimate.

Let us begin analyzing the problem by considering a hypothetical case. Consider a magazine which attracts an audience of motorbike enthusiasts by providing racing news and consumer-oriented assessments of the comparative advantages of various makes and models of machine. Most of us would concede that the editor of such a magazine had a legitimate interest in selecting advertising so that it was of interest to his or her target audience (for example, communications by bike dealers and manufacturers listing what they have for sale, by bike clubs listing meetings, or by clothing manufacturers listing accessories would be relevant; grocery advertisements would not be). Our deference to editorial autonomy here, and our concession that in this case discriminations based on content are acceptable, sharply distinguishes this type of situation from the cases discussed earlier, when the forum in question was not a product of editorial skill. This case is much closer to *Avin v. Rutgers Law Review* in which, as we saw, there were good reasons for upholding the principle of editorial autonomy.

Even if we allow that editorial autonomy may include some right to regulate the content of advertising forums, we do not thereby concede that an absolute discretion is available to editors. The scope of the discretion we would be prepared to allow is likely to depend on the character of the host program, magazine, or paper, on the nature of the message which a prospective advertiser wishes to have carried and on the significance of the forum in question. For example, because newspapers carry material of a wider ranging nature, because their audiences are diverse, and because the significance of their forum is so substantial, their editors have a weak claim to determine the content of the messages that are carried as paid advertisements. Although some editorial judgments affecting the content of a newspaper's advertising would be justifiable (for example, an editor could make a strong case against carrying messages which lowered the tone of the paper, making it offensive to a large number of potential readers), the functional relevance of the discrimination would need to be shown. Even the discretion of those who edit material carried in forums with a focus on a special audience such as the *Reader's Digest* is not an absolute one. For example, suppose the editor of our motor sports magazine refused to carry advertising marketing a particular bike because its rival (a big spender on advertising) objected or because the company wishing to place the advertisements had helped to sponsor a rival magazine. Or, suppose a public interest group who desperately wished to warn teenagers against the dangers of riding without helmets was refused access. I shall argue that discrimination in each of these cases would be illegitimate.

Let us take the first case. Here the argument that the content of the proposed advertisement would have a deleterious effect on the marketability of the magazine is without merit. The advertisement of a particular motorcycle is definitely relevant to the concerns of the target audience and the fact that the magazine carries similar messages makes it clear that the motives of the editor, in censoring the advertisement, are commercial (in that they relate to his wish to please a more significant client or to ensure that pressure is placed on companies so that they do not patronize a rival). This, then, is a discrimination which constitutes a restraint on the freedom to trade and should be dealt with under different principles from those which are applicable to the issue of editorial autonomy. (In my view, then, the United States Supreme Court was perfectly correct when it ruled that newspapers which enjoy monopoly power and refuse to accept advertisements, with the aim of protecting or extending market power, were vulnerable under antitrust law.[10])

The second case of discrimination involving the claims of a public interest group to advertising space is more controversial. One can understand why the editors of a magazine promoting an activity would resist carrying advertisements which focus attention on any severe dangers it involves. Such messages would be against the interests of those whose livelihoods depend on the popularity of the practice, and this group would include not only the owner of the magazine but most of its major clients. On the other hand, such a warning is directed specifically at the audience which the magazine attracts, so the editor will have some difficulty finding a functional reason for excluding it.

The strongest case for excluding such an advertisement proceeds by extending the notion of editorial autonomy to include a discretion over the content of advertising. Our editor could attempt to justify excluding the material (put forward to warn readers of some hazards associated with the riding of motorcycles) on the grounds that it will be resented by most of the readers of the magazine. As the manager of a business, our editor cannot be expected to act in the public interest. (We do not expect every bar to carry notices warning drinkers about the bad effects of liquor, nor do we require those who market high calorie foodstuffs to warn consumers about obesity[11]). One role of an editor is to exclude any materials which could have a negative impact on sales. And, it may be argued, his authority to take decisions to achieve this goal is grounded on the same considerations which would legitimate the rejection of an article which analyzed the dangers involved in motorcycle transportation or sports. If the democratic commitment requires that the editors of the *Rutgers Law Review* be afforded a right to select articles, then our editor could claim by parity of reasoning, that he enjoys the same right to autonomy when determining the content of the motor sports magazine. If this point is granted, excluding advertisements which carry messages running contrary to the spirit of the magazine's promotion of motor sport would simply count as a legitimate exercise of editorial judgment.

This argument carries significant weight for, in the light of democratic ideals, the autonomy of an editor should not be imposed upon without very good reason. However, the claim is weakened by the fact that an editor's right to control the content of advertising is not nearly as strong as his or her claim to determine the nature of other materials which make up the program, magazine, or newspaper. The reason for this is that advertising is carried alongside other material and so constitutes a separate forum. In many cases, it will not even be under the control of the editor (this is most often the case in broadcasting, for those who organize the advertising normally fall under the authority of the marketing manager, rather than the program producer, who exercises the editorial role). As I have argued, once a forum is open to the public, the manager of such a forum (whether he is the editor of the adjacent material or not) must refrain from arbitrary discriminations. Thus, the principles I articulated earlier do have some relevance even in the complex situations in which the audience is gathered by another speaker. However, in this kind of situation the requirement of content neutrality will need modification because categories of messages may be irrelevant to the concerns of the target audience. For example, it would be ridiculous to require a magazine whose target audience is motorbike enthusiasts to carry messages advertising groceries. Sometimes the manager of a forum will rule a message irrelevant even though it is directed at the target audience (for example, political advertising may be excluded from *The Reader's Digest*). In this kind of case, we need to assess the judgment to see whether it is supportable. Factors which need to be taken into account include (a) the burden of carrying such a message—that is, whether it will have a deleterious effect on the size of the audience; (b) the availability of alternative forums for reaching the same audience; (c) the importance of conveying the message to the prospective advertiser (for example, whether the advertiser needs to vindicate a reputation after suffering a libel, needs to reply to criticism, or wishes to accomplish some special purpose of great personal importance such as the conducting of an election campaign).

If I were asked to adjudicate given the facts in the hypothetical example I discussed above (involving the exclusion of public interest advertising from a motor sports magazine), I would rule that the alleged "wet-blanket" effect of carrying a warning concerning the dangers associated with motorcycling are too speculative to justify a claim that the magazine's discrimination was functionally relevant (this is a matter of fact, and if strong evidence to the contrary were produced, my judgment would have to be reviewed); and, second, that the importance of the forum to the potential speaker was significant because there is no other obvious means for addressing the fraternity of motorcycle enthusiasts. I would not hold that the interest group had a special reason for conveying the warning (it had not been the subject of an attack in the magazine nor had it suffered a defamation). Taken together, these considerations show that it would not be wrong to require the magazine to carry the controversial advertisement.

I conclude that access to advertising forums can be legitimately denied only in those circumstances when a close integral connection is shown between the content of the message a communicator wishes to convey and the likely size of the audience, that is, in situations when by carrying a particular kind of advertising a speaker will stand to lose a significant number of the audience. Denial may also be justified when some other functional connection is established, for example, that the message is irrelevant to the audience's interest, that it is offensive to numbers of them, or that it is aesthetically displeasing. Short of some such argument, a media owner has a moral obligation to administer advertising forums fairly.

In practice, the right to obtain access to advertising forums falls far short of this standard. If we look at the policy adopted in the United States, we find that the Supreme Court has ruled that freedom of speech must be understood as including an editor's right to control advertising forums. Thus, it has held that any attempt by Congress or state legislatures to impose an obligation on media companies to carry issue-oriented messages in the form of paid advertising (apart from special obligations which occur during election campaigns) violates their constitutional right to freedom. The issue which occasioned this judgment arose out of the efforts of the Democratic National Committee and a group calling itself Business Executives' Movement for Peace to purchase advertising time on television to solicit funds for their protest against the Vietnam War. When they were rebuffed, putatively because this kind of advertising was controversial and would have evoked an obligation to facilitate the dissemination of contrary views, the matter made its way to the Supreme Court, where Chief Justice Burger provided the media companies with one of their most significant victories, rejecting all arguments which questioned an editor's right to control advertising:

> For better or worse, editing is what editors are for; and editing is the selection and choice of material. That editors—newspaper or broadcast—can and do abuse the power is beyond doubt, but . . . [c]alculated risks of abuse are taken in order to preserve high values.[12]

The legal situation in other democracies is usually no different, although more emphasis is placed on self-regulation as a means of preventing abuse. For example, apart from special obligations which arise during election campaigns, commercial broadcasters in the United Kingdom have complete autonomy to exclude any public interest advertising they choose. As for newspapers in the United Kingdom, they have no obligation to afford access to anyone at all, whether for the purposes of advertising or for any other reason.

DISTINGUISHING PRINT AND BROADCAST MEDIA

I argued in an earlier section that publishers and broadcasters have no moral right to monopolize advertising forums, and that it would be perfectly proper to treat them as common carriers in establishing a right of access to advertise. Many liberals would be willing to go along with this proposal so long as it applied only to broadcasters. Indeed, most would go further in regulating broadcasters to promote fairness, requiring that they avoid bias by presenting all significant points of view on any matter of controversy discussed in their programs.

This notion that we should impose upon broadcasters in the name of fairness but not regulate publishers is very widespread. For example, recent British committees which have looked into matters affecting the media (the Annan Committee on the Future of Broadcasting and the Williams Commission on Pornography and Film Censorship) assume that because the influence of the broadcasting media is so significant and because broadcast programs are (it is alleged) more pervasive than materials disseminated in other ways, regulation of their content in the public interest is necessary and legitimate. In the United States two quite different interpretations of the First Amendment have been developed by the Supreme Court, which has chosen to uphold "fairness" standards when these are imposed on broadcasters but has ruled all attempts to regulate publishers unconstitutional. As I show, the reasons which the court provides for proceeding in this way are not convincing; however, they do illuminate the central dilemmas we must face in balancing the claims of an individual to fairness against the liberal ideal of speaker autonomy. I shall explore the problems by contrasting the arguments put forward in the two leading cases, *Red Lion Broadcasting v. FCC* and *Miami Herald Publishing v. Tornillo.*

In the *Red Lion Broadcasting v. FCC* case (and the companion case *Radio and Television News Directors' Association v. U.S.*) the central issue was whether the Federal Communications Commission (the body authorized by the American Congress to allocate broadcasting frequencies amongst competing applicants, and to regulate broadcasting in a manner responsive to the public "convenience, interest, or necessity"[13]) could legitimately require broadcasters to carry messages they did not wish to disseminate. Congress clearly intended the FCC to assume regulative functions but, because freedom of the press is constitutionally protected in the United States, the broadcasters had a strong case when they claimed that Congress (through its surrogate the FCC) exceeded its authority when it imposed on editorial judgments about what to broadcast. What they demanded, in effect, was that the court recognize that they enjoy the same right to autonomy as was afforded to the *Rutgers Law Review* (in the case discussed above).

Surprisingly, the court found that editorial autonomy must give way when reasonable standards "in the public interest" are imposed by Congress. Justice White wrote the unanimous judgment claiming, first, that there is such a scarcity of spectrum space that, without governmental regulation of the use of frequencies, there would be chaos:

> Not everyone can be allowed to use any frequency at whatever power level he wishes . . . if there is to be any effective communication by radio, only a few can be licensed and the rest must be barred from the airwaves. It would be strange if the First Amendment, aimed at protecting and furthering communications, prevented the government from making radio communication possible by requiring licenses to broadcast and by limiting the number of licenses so as not to overcrowd the spectrum.[14]

Second, having established that some form of government regulation is necessary to enable speech to take place at all, Justice White argues that this fact justifies the Congressional decisions to allocate licenses to those who will best serve the public interest, and to regulate those licensees by imposing "public interest" standards.

Justice White's conclusion is not a logical deduction from his premise: it does not follow from the fact that governments need to allocate broadcasting frequencies that they are justified in evaluating the worth of various speakers and in setting standards. Why not use a lottery system for the initial allocation of the license and so avoid the necessity of choosing between speakers? Why not sell the licenses to the highest bidder? Provided certain technical qualifications are imposed on those who seek the right to use a frequency, either of these options could be employed. Furthermore, they would be more in keeping with traditional liberal theory, for Congress (through its surrogate the FCC) would not have to evaluate prospective speakers.[15] What Justice White fails to notice is that scarcity is a matter of degree. Clearly, short of utopia, any communications system will embody serious inequalities. Not everyone who wishes to have access to a source which may be needed to communicate effectively can expect to obtain it. Thus, those who own or control printing presses (and broadcast stations) will be able to serve as gatekeepers, effectively determining who will gain access to these important public forums. This lack of fairness is not normally regarded by liberals as vitiating the point and purpose of preserving liberty (the freedom of speakers from government control). It is only some utopian Marxists who take such a view. Traditional liberal theory only countenances the restriction of liberty when the scarcity of a vital source is so severe that those who have a control over it can establish a virtual monopoly. Justice White does not take this point into account. He thinks that so long as he is convinced that the broadcast forum is one "for which there are more immediate and potential users than can be accommodated, and for which wise planning is essential," he is justified in holding that government regulation in the "public interest" is legitimate.

Another troubling aspect of White's judgment is the use he makes of a functionalist reading of the significance of the First Amendment. He tells us, "the purpose of the First Amendment [is] to preserve an uninhibited marketplace of ideas in which truth will ultimately prevail," and "it is the right of the public to receive suitable access to social, political, esthetic, moral and other ideas and experiences which is crucial [here]." These views indicate that the analogy which informs White's reasoning is that of Alexander Meiklejohn's small town meeting, in which the chairman legitimately intervenes in order to ensure that discussion proceeds in an orderly, relevant way. Justice White seems to be holding that Congress may authorize the FCC to take on the role of neutral umpire, excluding points of view which an audience has little need to hear from the airwaves.

I have already drawn attention to some of the problems associated with the Meiklejohnian position. Justice White's reasoning is vulnerable on two counts:[16] first, we normally endeavor to prevent governments from controlling the agenda of public debate, and the right to freedom of speech has been understood as protecting this interest; second, the claim that we can best ensure that the public are well informed by authorizing a neutral umpire is vulnerable to empirical refutation.[17]

In *Red Lion Broadcasting v. FCC* the Supreme Court did not directly address the issue of whether it was legitimate to treat broadcasters differently from publishers. This led to a good deal of speculation, for commentators, sensing the influence of Meiklejohn on the court, concluded that it would favor audience interests over editorial autonomy when dealing with all the media and not just with cases involving broadcasters.[18] In

1972 an ideal case for testing this speculation emerged. It involved a dispute between the politician Pat Tornillo and *The Miami Herald Tribune*. The newspaper's editors had behaved in a grossly unfair way by attacking Tornillo in two editorials and by refusing to publish the letters he wrote as a response. The harm this caused Tornillo was considerable, because the accusations made against him were published while he was conducting a campaign for election to the Florida House of Representatives and were clearly intended to persuade the electors to vote for a rival candidate. The case was particularly relevant as a test of how far the Supreme Court was willing to go in applying Meiklejohn's reading of the First Amendment, for the citizens of Florida had a significant interest in reading Tornillo's reply to the editor critic. Furthermore, *The Miami Herald Tribune* enjoyed a virtual monopoly.[19]

Tornillo requested an injunction enforcing his claim to a right of reply, and, in this regard, his case was greatly strengthened by the fact that there was a Florida statute which afforded candidates who were running for office the right to demand that a newspaper print any reply that he or she made to charges it had printed. The issue before the Court was whether in enacting this legislation the state legislature had violated the First Amendment constitutional guarantee of freedom.

Chief Justice Burger, writing the majority opinion, firmly rejects the Meiklejohnian understanding of the First Amendment protection of free speech. After carefully reviewing evidence showing that many newspapers besides the *Miami Herald Tribune* had come to enjoy local monopolies,[20] he boldly claims that the First Amendment freedom enjoyed by the press embodies a right to autonomy and, thus, that the imposition of a "fairness standard" (such as that provided in the Florida "right of reply" statute) to ensure exposure of the public to competing points of view is illegitimate. As he puts it:

> However much validity may be found in these arguments [for imposing fairness standards], at each point the implementation of a remedy such as an enforceable right of access necessarily calls for some mechanism, either governmental or consensual. If it is governmental coercion, this at once brings about a confrontation with the express provisions of the First Amendment and the judicial gloss on that amendment developed over the years.

After citing some cases in which editorial autonomy is upheld in other contexts, he concludes,

> The clear implication has been that any such compulsion to publish that which "reason" tells them should not be published is unconstitutional. A responsible press is an undoubtedly desirable goal, but press responsibility is not mandated by the constitution and like many other virtues it cannot be legislated.[21]

Justice Burger's statement is very tough-minded, for it leaves those who have been unfairly treated by the media with no remedy. While it may be true that public figures of national significance may easily find forums in cases where they wish to disseminate their ideas or vindicate themselves when they have been attacked, it is not plausible to hold that this will be possible when the persons or issues involved have only a local prominence or relevance. In these latter cases monopoly media outlets may well be the only vehicle for reaching the specific audience of those who are interested. Yet (as the *Miami Herald Tribune*'s treatment of Tornillo illustrates) a local newspaper may deliberately editorialize in a way that is grossly unfair. How then are individuals to vindicate themselves or pursue their interests in these cases? Surely we do not want to hold, as Burger seems to have, that attempts to ensure that the political process is free from serious distortion are illegitimate.

These are hard questions which Justice Burger does not adequately confront. By virtue of his ruling, neither Congress nor the Florida legislature have authority to ensure that the electoral process is fair. Indeed, unless freedom is abolished as a basic political right in the United States, the problem of an unfair attack by a newspaper with a local monopoly cannot even be solved by amending the constitution! (Because a clause protecting liberty of the press "except when regulations are in the public interest" would be redundant.) We may well ask, then, whether the right to communicate freely includes a discretion to monopolize a forum in the way that the *Miami Herald Tribune* succeeded in doing when it refused to publish Tornillo's reply to its editorials attacking him.

One reason for doubting whether the liberty to speak includes a right to monopolize a forum arises from the very definition of "protected speech" which we arrived at when considering the theoretical justifications for such a liberty provided by liberal theorists. The problem we considered was that of finding a way of distinguishing those speech acts—such as falsely shouting "fire!" in a crowded theater—which it would not be wrong for a government to regulate from those which ought to be protected. A consideration which was relevant in establishing our chosen criteria of demarcation was whether the harm likely to arise from a communication could be remedied by further speech. The reason I gave for holding that we ought not to enjoy a right to mislead others by falsely shouting "fire!" is that, in circumstances of emergency, there is no time for reasoned responses by others. The words carry authority in such circumstances because they are not vulnerable to refutation; thus, it would not be wrong for a government to prevent such authority from being misused. What a government may not do is prevent us from being influenced by our own assessment of a public debate. Thus, so long as speech takes place within the context of a possible dialogue, it would normally be protected. In terms of this criterion, anyone who asserted a right to speak without possibility of contradiction would have a weak claim. Yet this is what the *Miami Herald Tribune* was demanding when it asserted the right to exclude Tornillo's reply.

A second reason for questioning Burger's judgment is that it conflicts with our intuitive sense of moral propriety. The *Miami Herald Tribune*'s failure to grant Tornillo an opportunity to respond was a gross abuse violating standards we would expect from a serious newspaper even if such a duty were not enforceable at law. Moreover, if we look at analogous cases such as the frequently encountered problems which arise because of the presence of hecklers at public meetings, we find that our sense of what would be a proper resolution does not support the notion that the liberty to speak includes a right to monopolize a forum. For example, when someone is heckling a speaker and has come to a meeting specifically to do so (as other members of the audience may have come to cheer), most of us are inclined to hold that he or she ought to be facilitated rather than dealt with in a way which stifles the opinion expressed. The point has been well stated by the California Supreme Court:

> Audience activities, such as heckling, interrupting, harsh questioning, and booing, even though they may be impolite and discourteous, can nevertheless advance the goals of the First Amendment. For many citizens such participation in public meetings, whether supportive or critical of the speaker, may constitute the only manner in which they can express their views to a large number of people; . . . An unfavorable reception . . . represents one important method by which an office holder's constituents can register disapproval of his conduct and seek redress of grievances.[22]

A third reason for questioning Chief Justice Burger's judgment is that he fails to notice that the *Miami Herald Tribune*'s claim to be exercising editorial autonomy is a weak one. The attack against Tornillo did not take place within a news report or even in the context of a feature article but in an editorial. But space allocated to editorials is like that reserved for advertising, for the messages are carried alongside the package of entertainment, informative articles, and commentary which constitute the selling point of the paper. In this way, like advertising messages, they are able to reach an audience which they would not attract in their own right. Editorial space is also somewhat similar to the space often provided in good newspapers for letters from readers. I do not argue that letter columns and editorials ought to be regarded as public forums in the way that advertising forums usually are; only that editors have less moral right to autonomy in managing such forums and that a paper which carries materials in these spaces may incur special obligations.

I conclude that neither *Miami Herald Tribune v. Tornillo* or *Red Lion Broadcasting v. FCC* provide a satisfactory resolution of the tension which we find between the claims of editors to autonomy and the claims which individuals make to justice when media owners discriminate against them unfairly. In the *Red Lion Broadcasting* case, the Court was too inclined to favor "fairness" and ended up ignoring the legitimate claim broadcasters were making to editorial autonomy. On the other hand, the claim of newspaper editors to autonomy was taken too seriously in Tornillo's case. Ironically, the two cases complement one another, for neither resolution would serve as an acceptable standard when applied to the domain of the other. Thus, if the Meiklejohnian functionalism exemplified in *Red Lion Broadcasting v FCC* was taken as establishing principles for the regulation of the print media, most of us would regard the ruling as intolerable. But we would be equally unhappy about applying Chief Justice Burger's Lockean analysis in *Miami Herald Tribune v. Tornillo* when dealing with broadcasting cases.

Some more general conclusions can also be drawn in the light of my review. First, the principle of editorial autonomy must be afforded considerable weight. Thus, we can say that regulations which impose fairness standards specifying what a media outlet must carry will not normally be acceptable. In liberal systems we suppose bias will be corrected by allowing a plurality of outlets rather than by imposing on speakers to ensure that they present all sides of a question and, provided no individual can show that he or she has a right to gain access to a forum (that unless access is afforded, he or she will not be treated with equal concern or respect), editorial claims to determine the content of what is disseminated must be honored. Second, it is clear that the imposition of fairness standards can have a signifiant inhibiting effect because the burden of monitoring coverage to establish bias may be heavy, because the costs in space used or broadcast time are often considerable and because readers, viewers, and listeners can be bored or offended by the messages that a broadcaster or publisher is forced to convey. These problems are compounded by the fact that serious news and commentary is rarely the most popular kind of journalism, so broadcasters and publishers do not lose by being cautious. Third, a speaker, writer, or broadcaster has a right to determine the content of the message he wishes to have disseminated but has no right to control who else will communicate to the same audience. Attempts to stack audiences at public meetings to eliminate hecklers or those who boo and jeer would not be tolerable in a democracy. With regard to the mass media, I have argued that advertising forums should be open and those who establish them regarded as common carriers.

4

Free Speech versus Reputation

In many cases when an individual suffers a personal attack, he will seek to obtain monetary compensation for the harm suffered. The case for obtaining such damages in cases where what is disseminated about a person is true is extremely weak (although in some jurisdictions this can be achieved if the matters published are of no legitimate public interest). In most cases, however, a plaintiff must show that the harm resulted from the dissemination of false claims.

If there is some actual pecuniary loss, the claim to compensation may well be a strong one. Such a case would fall under the general principle that individuals have a moral right to obtain compensation when their interests are significantly harmed by others. Much more controversial is the claim that media companies should pay out money to make amends for any emotional distress which the publishing or broadcasting of defamatory material may have caused. I have suggested that emotional distress of this kind is not usually the kind of harm which should be regarded as "significant." But is this position tenable in the context of libel litigation? It is on this last issue that I wish to concentrate, and I will take it as given that (apart from exceptional cases in which a report is regarded as privileged) media companies should be vulnerable for actual damages (excluding normal psychological suffering) if they disseminate false claims which harm individuals.

THE FUNCTIONALIST CASE FOR DEFAMATION LAW REFORM

Over the last two decades there has been considerable discussion over whether or not the law of libel as this has evolved from the common law is unnecessarily restrictive of speech. The main concern of reformers has been that, by affording individuals a right of action, the law is unnecessarily restrictive; and, in this latter regard, it is often held that the fear of being held liable for damages on the part of media company executives and journalists inhibits public debate. Functionalists who emphasize the importance of freedom of speech within the political process and who have no strong scruples about the alleged rights of individuals when these seem to be in conflict with the public interest have been extraordinarily influential and persuasive in demanding protection for the press. Thus, we find writers such as Schauer arguing that the presumption in the common law that defamatory statements are by definition false (and may consequently be regulated without great loss) is misleading. In his view, regulation of the press even to prevent the dissemination of falsehood may involve significant social costs. Firstly, the practical difficulties and costs which a publisher may forsee (if he or she were required to prove a controversial statement about a person in court) may inhibit that publisher from disseminating the allegation—encouraging a cautious self-censorship. Yet the publisher may have good reasons for supposing the claims to be true. Thus, Schauer tells us, "a rule that punishes falsity may at times punish truth for fear that it will erroneously be found to be false and therefore be penalized," and he concludes that if we recognize the importance of freedom of speech as basic principle comprehending its centrality to the search for knowledge and in public deliberations, we will see the need for institutionalizing some reasonable protection for the press.[1]

This line of argument, which takes its bearings from Alexander Meiklejohn's influential essay, has been exemplified in the treatment of the problem of defamatory speech by the United States Supreme Court. Thus, in exposing weakness in the functionalist approach, a good place to begin is with an examination of the Court's progress in dealing with difficult cases. How well or badly has Meiklejohn's orientation served as a guide for the Court's interpretation of the First Amendment in this area?

The landmark case in the constitutionalization of defamation law in the United States (for, previously it had been assumed that defamatory speech because it was false could not claim protection under the freedom of speech principle embodied in the First Amendment) is *New York Times v. Sullivan.* Here, in a unanimous judgment, the Supreme Court stated the rule that the constitutional guarantee of freedom of speech and the press, reflected in the First Amendment to the Constitution, prohibits a public official from recovering damages against those who have published a defamatory falsehood relating to his official conduct unless the statement was made with "actual malice" (that is, "knowledge that it is false or with reckless disregard of whether it was false or not").[2] Subsequent cases show that the court attaches a very special meaning of its own to this malice requirement: it has held *inter alia* that demonstrable ill will, a careless failure to discover falsehood, and even the repetition of a libel after a denial of the charge had been communicated by the individual concerned are all insufficient grounds for disqualifying respondents from the constitutional protection. It now seems that plaintiffs who wish to defeat a publisher's claim to privilege (in cases involving public officials) will be required to show that respondents either knew what was published was false, or that they believed the defamatory statements were probably false at the time of publication.

We can see from the very restricted interpretation placed on the "malice proviso," established in the *New York Times v. Sullivan* judgment, that the purpose of the Court was to articulate a rule protecting critics of government. It hoped to free the press from any need to resort to self-censorship. The court made the evaluation that the public good requires a fearless, vigorous discussion of both public policy and administration. To achieve this, it required government officals to suffer any libel directed against them without compensation, so long as it was made in good faith.

The main line of argument provided to justify this position involved developing an analogy between the use of the criminal law to censor criticisms of government officials and policy, and the resort to civil litigation to intimidate critics. The court accepted that it had a responsibility to guard against treating seditious libel as a criminal offence; and that open debate about public issues may well include "vehement, caustic, and sometimes unpleasantly sharp attacks" directed at public officials. From these premises it drew the conclusion that because a government may not restrict seditious speech by way of the criminal law, it may not do so indirectly by upholding civil law actions brought by public officials who may have been defamed.

This comparison between the role of the civil and criminal law was not the only consideration which the Court found persuasive in upholding the press's view that defamatory speech was entitled to constitutional protection. Another consideration was taken from Alexander Meiklejohn, who stresses the need which citizens have to be exposed to vigorous public discussion on matters of political significance. Meiklejohn's claim that it is this need to be informed which justifies our protecting speech was endorsed by a unanimous court. In his judgment, Justice Brennan goes so far as to claim that a Meiklejohnian understanding of the significance of liberty was already reflected in the law. In support of this contention, he cites the existence of rules of privilege relating to libel suits which had developed in some state jurisdictions (resulting from controversies arising between members of the public and administrators, or between prominent individuals during debate over matters of great public importance) and the well-established common law rule which affords a qualified protection when government officials are sued for libel by private citizens. Brennan also refers to the important Kansas case *Coleman v. Maclennan* (in which a privilege is extended to speech during election campaigns, unless uttered with knowledge of falsity or a reckless disregard for the truth or falsity of the claims made) as a relevant precedent. The Kansas court reasons that:

> It is of the utmost consequence that the people should discuss the character and qualifications of candidates for their suffrages. The importance to the state and to society of such discussion is so vast, and the advantages derived are so great, that they more than counterbalance the inconvenience of private persons whose conduct may be involved, and occasional injury to the reputation of individuals must yield to the public welfare, although at times such injury may be great.[3]

It is but a short step from this argument to the position adopted in *New York Times v. Sullivan*, for it surely is the case that important discussion of public affairs is not confined to the election period. It is not surprising, then, that Justice Brennan took *Coleman v. Maclennan* as a basis for interpreting the significance of the First Amendment protection afforded to speech, nor that he is persuaded that a very severe restriction of the right to claim against citizen critics (even where these are professional journalists) must be acknowledged. Brennan's argument convinced the other justices to protect journalists and other critics of government even when they are motivated by hatred or by a desire to discredit a particular official. A public official in the United States now has a remedy only in those rare cases when he can show that the libel was made with the knowledge that it was false, or made "with a reckless disregard for the truth."

This reasoning of Justice Brennan in *New York Times v. Sullivan* focuses on audience needs and interests: it is our important democratic concern to be informed which establishes the press's claim to constitutional protection and not their rights as speakers. As a consequence, the court was soon faced with further cases in which the implications of the new reading of the First Amendment were tested. The crucial question was how far the justices were prepared to go in extending the principles established in the case. Citizens clearly need exposure to a wide range of opinions in exercising the ballot, and fearless and vigorous discussion may prove useful even when the criticisms are not directed at public officials. In response to this dilemma, the Court ruled that two standards were necessary: the rule established in *New York Times v. Sullivan*, applying to situations when the public's need to know is clear, and a second standard for those cases when the defamation harms a private individual or when the matters discussed are not of substantial public interest.

The leading cases in which this orientation was articulated are *Curtis Publishing v. Butts, Associated Press v. Walker, Time v. Hill* and *Gertz v. Welsh*.[4] In the first two, which were treated as companion cases, the Court reasons that if the public has a right to criticize those in authority, then this right necessarily includes a protection against libel claims when these are made by important individuals (other than those who hold political or public office). In *Time v. Hill*, a case in which a suit was brought for the violation of privacy (in that the plaintiffs claimed that they had been placed in a false light by a publication), the Court applies the argument to cover matters of public importance even when no officials or important public figures are involved. The plaintiffs in this case were a private family who had been the victims of a sensational crime in which they were held captive in their home. The publicity they complained about related to an article in *Time* magazine discussing the incident and a film that had been made depicting the events. Despite the private nature of the complainants and the nonpolitical subject matter of the offending discussion, the Court held that the plaintiffs must show malice to be awarded damages for misrepresentation.

A problem with the situation after these judgments was that the Supreme Court had traditionally taken the First Amendment to require that the relative importance of a communication be settled in the marketplace of ideas, not by some authoritative ruling. Yet, in supervising the application of the *New York Times v. Sullivan* test, it had now taken up the task of making this kind of value judgment. Moreover, its adjudications were necessarily ad hoc, so no clear guidelines were available to publishers and broadcasters (apart from their knowledge of the prejudices of particular judges). Had the Court resolved to stand clear of this kind of supervision, however, it would have placed in jeopardy any legitimate claims which a maligned individual could make to vindicate himself or herself.

These considerations encouraged members of the Court to seek a way out of the dilemma to which it seemed committed by *New York Times v. Sullivan*. It needed a way of limiting the categories of speech which fell under the Sullivan test which did not depend on an ad hoc evaluative judgment. Justice Harlan led the way with a significant dissenting opinion in *Curtis Publishing v. Butts*. He argues (with Clark, Stewart, and Fortas concurring) that the correct standard for accommodating the conflict of interest (between the public interest in vigorous open discussion of matters of central political importance and the interests of defamed individuals in vindication and compensation) should not protect an incompetent or careless publisher. He reasons that society has little to benefit when a job is done badly and claims that there is no reason for requiring a different standard of care from journalists than from other professionals such as doctors, architects, and engineers. If these latter can be held accountable for the consequences of their negligence so, Harlan claims, should the former.

Harlan's reasoning confronts the Meiklejohnian theory of the significance of the First Amendment at a weak point. He is surely correct to hold that careless speech is of little use and that so long as courageous and conscientious journalists are protected, no great deterioration of the vigor of public debate need be anticipated. Harlan was not able to convince a majority of the court, however, for it was felt by some that the notion of "fault," when applied to the case of journalism, was too indeterminate. These justices feared that any carelessness on the part of a journalist would come to be regarded as "negligence" by juries and that this would undermine the protection afforded to the media by *New York Times v. Sullivan*. A compromise was finally reached in *Gertz v. Welsh*. Here the Court decided to look beyond the Meiklejohnian focus on audience needs as the basis for criteria by which to distinguish cases and to make some evaluation of the "desert" of categories of plaintiff. In this regard, it contrasts plaintiffs who had thrust themselves into the public arena and were capable of fending for themselves (because they had ready access to the media) with those who are vulnerable, perhaps because they had been caught up in matters of public interest against their wills. The basis of this distinction does not depend on a judgment that matters involving the first category of plaintiff are inherently of more legitimate public interest. Rather, the Court argues that governments have a more pressing responsibility to protect the interests of the vulnerable private individual who has suffered a defamation than they have to protect those who have chosen public exposure, risking public attention and inviting comment.

By combining the reasoning in the *Gertz v. Welsh* case with Harlan's claims about the relative insignificance of careless journalism as a category of speech in his *Curtis Publishing v. Butts* dissent, the court reaches the following conclusions: The *New York Times v. Sullivan* test (requiring that malice be shown before compensation can be claimed) applies to cases in which the plaintiffs are public officials or, if they are public figures, when the defamation occurs in the context of a discussion of legitimate public interest. In cases involving private individuals (or public figures when the matters discussed are of a private nature), plaintiffs who wish to claim damages for defamation need to show that the journalist responsible departed from standards of investigation that could reasonably be expected of a competent professional. The court does not attempt to spell out its conception of the circumstances in which a journalist could be regarded as negligent, preferring to leave state governments free to impose any reasonable standard they like, but it does address itself to the substantial matter of the kind of damages which can be awarded once fault had been shown. First, it ends the common law presumption that damages in defamation cases may sometimes be awarded even when there is no proof of actual injury (although it allows that sums may be awarded to compensate personal humiliation, mental anguish, and suffering); second, it rules that punitive damages may not be set.

Before concluding this section, it is necessary to draw attention to some problems with the present state of the law relating to defamation in the United States.

A first point worth noting is that plaintiffs who are "public figures" win all or nothing. If they can meet the *New York Times v. Sullivan* test, they will probably be able to claim punitive damages and sometimes the award will be quite unreasonable (as it was in Carol Burnett's case[5]). On the other hand, if they cannot meet this test, they can claim nothing. It is also relevant in this regard, that editors may well be harassed by discovery actions, for sometimes the only way in which "malice" can be proved is by opening up the editorial process to review in court.[6] Perhaps the most worrying feature of the present law is that the court's concept of the category of "public figure" is not well-drawn. It clearly wishes to define the category without reference to whether or not a person's activities are newsworthy. Yet it is precisely this latter consideration which determines whether or not self-help vindication is possible. Thus, a "public figure" in the United States may well find that he or she has no way of attaining vindication after suffering a defamation. (The case of a Miss Street may serve to illustrate. She had been acquitted many years ago in a widely publicized murder case, yet she recently found herself portrayed in a television documentary about the trial in a way that was most uncomplimentary. She is now an old woman and although she clearly had enjoyed "public figure" status at the time of her trial, no longer enjoys any standing in the public mind. Yet she will be required to show malice if she wishes to win her action for defamation.[7]) On the other hand, some individuals who clearly do have a capacity for self-help vindication may not be regarded as "public figures." (Elmer Gertz himself was one such case. More recently, Mrs. Firestone, a well-known socialite, was not regarded as a "public figure" even though she had held press conferences.[8])

Perhaps the most serious difficulty with the functionalist balancing which the United States Supreme court adopts as its chosen orientation in dealing with defamation cases is the inconclusive nature of the argument: Is the law of defamation really inhibiting? How much protection of the press is desirable in the public interest? Will an absolute privilege against defamation actions lead to irresponsible journalism? – and so on. This problem, that experienced and conscientious observers do differ in their judgments about the social costs involved in protecting people's reputations against unfair attacks, is reflected in the responses to the United States experience in the United Kingdom.

Consider, first, the Faulks Parliamentary Committee's claim that developments in the United States are of little relevance to other parliamentary systems.[9] It argues that, because the Supreme Court in the United States must interpret the First Amendment, it is bound by a constitutional provision which places heavy emphasis on protecting publishers. In this sense, so the committee claims, the United States courts are bound by an historical accident in a way that courts in other democracies are not. Thus, the committee argues, the adjudications of the Supreme Court do not represent an unbiased assessment of the balance of competing interests. And, for this reason, it suggests that the opinions of the justices can only be of marginal relevance to those who live in democracies where there is no similar constitutional protection of press interests.

There are many problems with this understanding of the United States precedent. First, as we have seen, courts in that country have never felt obliged to treat libel as falling under the First Amendment protection. Indeed, for most of its history the Supreme Court has assumed that certain forms of speech (including defamatory and obscene speech) are of no public benefit.[10] Thus, if the United States courts are bound by history, they surely should not include defamatory speech within the ambit of the First Amendment protection.

A second problem with the Faulks Committee's reasoning is that they do not address the arguments brought forward by Justice Brennan, who wrote the opinion in *New York Times v. Sullivan*. His claim that if seditious libel may not be banned by way of the criminal law, the civil law may not be used as a substitute, and the extension of the absolute privilege allowed for during elections in the state of Kansas which he makes, do not relate solely to the task of legal interpretation but have a general application. As we have seen, Justice Brennan attempts to ascertain the minimum protections which it is necessary to recognize for maintaining in operation an effective democratic environment; and, in reaching his conclusions, he is informed by theories about the requirements of a free society and not by debate about the meaning of words in a constitutional provision or about what the framers of the First Amendment actually intended. The unanimous judgment of the Supreme Court of the United States that such an environment cannot prosper when the press are shackled by the threat of expensive libel litigation, strict liability, and the possibility of having to pay substantial damages is an event of great significance for everyone who has a concern for democratic institutions. The court's authority should not have been rejected out of hand.

Finally, it is worth noting that because its institutions have had to adapt to the democratic demands of citizens in a context of civil unrest, racial tension, and conflict over the conduct of a war, as well as a distrust of government officials of a kind not experienced to the same degree in other democracies, the history of the United States over the last few decades has a special relevance in assessing the political impact of defamation law.[11] By dismissing this history as largely irrelevant the Faulks Committee fails to appreciate this.

It is interesting to observe that the negative responses manifested by the British Parliamentary Committee are not shared by an earlier working party set up by the lawyers' pressure group *Justice*. This group, which included members representing the Press Institute as well as lawyers, treat the possibility of self-censorship resulting from fears of libel litigation as a significant impediment to free discussion. In this regard, it agrees with the United States Supreme Court that the central problem is the vulnerability of publishers to awards for excessive damages. (That the danger was a very real one at the time they were writing is reflected in the cases, cited in the report, although there have been changes since then.)[12] The *Justice* party also claim to have heard evidence in which examples of self-censorship on the part of editors was presented,[13] and it is not surprising that it is persuaded that the duty of newspapers to publish controversial material on matters of public interest should be recognized. It urges that a qualified privilege be afforded to publishers so long as they are not negligent and act in good faith. It should be emphasized that (like the protection recognized in *New York Times v. Sullivan* and the subsequent cases in the United States) the underlying concern of the changes suggested by *Justice* is to ensure that citizens are kept informed. It is the citizens' right to know and not a concern to relieve publishers of responsibility for the consequences of their actions which *Justice* sought to protect.[14]

As I have said, the Faulks Committee was reluctant to accept these suggestions. In its view the *Justice* party was unduly influenced by press representatives amongst its members and greatly exaggerated the problems and burdens which newspapers face under the existing law.[15] In particular, the committee finds little evidence of the alleged self-censorship frequently resorted to by editors, although it claims to have "sought earnestly for such evidence." It goes on to quote Lord Goodman as an authority for an opinion which the committee strongly endorses:

> The absorbing question is the one whether the present law prevents editors from printing material which ought to be printed in order to expose villainy and protect the public from villainy. I have heard this contention over many years and remain unrepentantly skeptical of its truth.

Neither Lord Goodman nor the committee provide any support, aside from the latter's wide experience, for this judgment; nor, as far as I am aware, has any satisfactory research been conducted into this issue.[16]

There is conflicting authority, however, for the Australian Law Reform Commission (in its initial discussion paper, *Defamation—Options for Reform*, and in its report, *Unfair Publications*) comes to precisely the opposite conclusion. Indeed, it acknowledges as a fact that newspapers operate under a serious threat so long as there is a possibility that they may suffer heavy damages for libel. Although the commission is clear that the "costs of defamation actions would appear to be significant rather than crippling," it holds, nevertheless, "that the present law unduly inhibits the publication of some information the publication of which is desirable." As for smaller papers and some broadcasters, the commission points out that the position may be even more serious, for "one high verdict might conceivably destroy a small publisher."[17]

Without a clear review of all the evidence and some objective way of assessing the content of communications so that we know when self-censorship is likely to be a significant social cost, there is no rational way to settle the difference of opinion between, on the one side, the United States Supreme Court, The *Justice* Working Group, and the Australian Law Reform Commission, and, on the other, Lord Goodman and the British Parliamentary Committee (Faulks). However, there are some considerations which caution against acting with hasty skepticism regarding the complaints of newspaper publishers and broadcasters. First, we must bear in mind that most publishers are quite prepared to accept liability provided that the damages awarded in defamation cases do not include any compensation for emotional distress (medical expenses for an emotional breakdown would of course count as a legitimate out-of-pocket cost). Second, the most appropriate remedy for any harm done to a person's reputation is certainly not a monetary one but consists of a speedy correction of the falsehood and of an apology. Third (as I shall argue more fully below), it cannot be argued that individuals have a moral right to monetary compensation when they have been defamed, provided there is no negligence and the imputation is made in good faith. Fourth, the claim that publishers should be made to pay for harms when they are not grossly negligent has little moral force. (If society values their role in disseminating news it ought not to hold them responsible for the inevitable harm which will sometimes accompany this.) We must conclude, then, that when we consider the issues at stake in this policy area, balancing the competing interests in the manner favored by functionalists, we find that although the arguments are inconclusive there is no pressing social reason why a qualified protection should not be extended to the press.

At issue is the question whether publishers should be held liable in a general way for the mental suffering which is thought to arise in many cases where reputations have been maligned. Both the *Justice* group and the United States Surpreme Court argue, correctly in my view, that if we allow compensation for this injury we must balance the value of this relief to individuals against the possibility that a fundamental democratic freedom may thereby be restricted. Of course, if Lord Goodman is right and there is no risk of self-censorship even under existing law, the problem of balancing the competing values would be very different. But even so, we may not be justified in asking the press to pay out money by way of compensation for a harm that has some other obvious remedy.

A DEONTOLOGICAL APPROACH TO DEFAMATION

If we are to accommodate adequately the competing interests in the defamation area, we must ask ourselves whether any of these interests are so fundamental that Rawlsian negotiators would be inclined to identify them as a right. I have identified freedom of speech as a residual right in the sense that our enjoyment of it takes priority over any competing claims made in the name of the public interest but must give way when confronted by competing rights. Thus, on a Rawlsian account, Meiklejohnian concerns about the public interest in wide open, vigorous discussion relating to matters of legitimate public interest should have no place. Also, attempts to discriminate categories of claimant so as to afford a different response depending on whether the person who suffers the defamation is a public official, public figure, or undistinguished citizen are misconceived. So also are attempts to identify circumstances when "rights" are suspended (for example, during election campaigns or in parliamentary debate). In terms of a Rawlsian account, if a person can establish a right to some benefit, he or she must have it afforded even when there is a significant cost to the public interest. Thus, for a Rawlsian liberal, unless there are competing rights in defamation cases, speech ought to be unregulated; however, when rights can be identified these must be protected even when this means that citizens enjoy a less extensive liberty.

The most compelling principle involved in considering the issue of defamation seems to be the Lockean notion that innocent persons harmed through the activities of others ought to be able to obtain fair compensation. We could well imagine Rawlsian negotiators discussing such a principle, and they are likely to focus on two issues pertaining to it.

First, there is the issue of fault, for in defamation actions there is often strict liability. Yet, intuitively, it does not seem fair to require publishers and broadcasters, working in good faith, to meet the burden of compensating individuals for harms that could not be avoided except by censoring all derogatory imputations. If society values a free, vigorous press capable of making accusations when these seem warranted, it does not make much sense to force publishers or broadcasters to pay for the inevitable damage which will be associated with this activity. Why should these companies suffer the damage rather than the individual harmed? Or, if the latter is to be compensated, surely the costs should be borne by the community as a whole?

The strongest reason for requiring broadcasters and publishers to shoulder the burden of the emotional injury caused to innocent third parties through uninhibited and robust public discussions is that they are in the best position to anticipate loss. Anyone involved in publishing or broadcasting will know that the occasional defamatory claim will be disseminated and they can take out appropriate insurance, passing on the cost to readers, listeners, or viewers. This reasoning is sound if we assume that the amounts involved will not be large (as would be the case if the amount was limited to exclude any compensation for emotional suffering). It is not convincing if the scale of the damages becomes a serious burden for, in these circumstances, publishers and broadcasters may choose to reduce their risk and the consequent insurance costs by playing safe. Also, insurance companies may discriminate against publishers or stations whose programming or features are a high risk, and they may be forced out of business if no one provides them with insurance at an economically viable price.

The British Faulks Committee (which recently reviewed the case for reforming the law of defamation), in holding that publishers and broadcasters be required to pay compensation, relies on the principle that:

> Persons doing harmful acts without actual legal justification should, in general, have to bear the consequences of the harm caused thereby. The plaintiff is passive, the defendant active. The defendant is wrong in fact even if, in a particular case, he is morally blameless. As between the two parties the loss should be suffered by the active, wrong party—defendant—rather than the plaintiff.[18]

Presumably, this principle is to be found in some other areas of the law (for example, in motor accident cases, where, no matter how morally innocent, the driver of a vehicle may be held responsible for any harm it causes.) But a problem about applying the principle to defamation cases is that it begs the question at issue: What we have to decide is whether the law should be changed so that publishers have some "legal justification" for publishing in good faith. There are often good reasons for this. For example, we can all see that a bookseller is not responsible for any defamatory material which he sells, and because there is a socially significant interest in encouraging the flow of communications, we may see some point in ensuring that his contribution is lawful (and, therefore, protected from the impact of the principle we are considering). But if we recognize the importance of booksellers and the legitimacy of protecting them, what about the role of publishers who give other people space in letter columns, carry political advertising, or use the work of syndicated journalists and other outsiders? What of broadcasters who provide access for concerned groups to voice views on highly contentious matters?[19] Most of us would like to allow that a publisher or broadcaster is often in much the same situation as a bookseller in these kinds of cases, but the principle quoted would not allow us to offer relief to either.

Rawlsian negotiators would have to bear all these considerations in mind when considering the principle in question, and they may be inclined to seek a compromise by relying on a right already acknowledged, namely the right to be afforded a reasonable opportunity to respond when personally attacked. It could be argued that when such a right is enjoyed, the problem of compensating for damage will resolve itself, as there are unlikely to be serious losses suffered. This latter view is unfortunately somewhat wishful and will force our negotiators to address the second major issue relating to the principle of compensation – the issue of whether some kinds of potential harm, specifically, emotional suffering, should be considered insufficiently serious to warrant compensation. This is not a problem which is unique to the defamation area, for Rawlsian negotiators will know that many people take offense at the behavior of others, suffer when they know that others dislike them, and are vulnerable to the ways they are presented because they value privacy. In considering the issue of mental suffering, then, our negotiators will have to take a broad focus comprehending how difficult it will be in a modern industrial society to protect peoples' sensibilities.

Their judgment about the appropriateness of mental damages may also be influenced by an appreciation of how difficult it will be to determine. The following points are worth noting: First, we cannot always tell whether the distress felt about a publication is reasonable, for we know little about how the public image of a person is acquired. The effects of a publication may depend greatly on the reputation of the person making it (thus, a publication which everyone knows will often make unsubstantiated claims is not likely to have great influence, nor will the spokesmen of groups whose opinions are not trusted) as well as on the status and reputation of the person referred to. (A person who is already widely regarded as a scoundrel is not likely to suffer great harm if further evidence is presented supporting that well-established image. On the other hand, a person with a very high record for integrity may also suffer little damage because an unsubstantiated accusation may not be believed.) A further complicating factor which may determine how much influence a defamatory statement is likely to have relates to the context in which it is published. For example, if a publication accuses someone of a repeated offense and is correct about nine of ten instances cited, the mistake of fact is not going to be so serious as it would be if the mistaken case is the only instance relied upon.[20] Presumably a person suffers most emotional distress when friends and acquaintances come to question his reputation. But, often, these are the very people who will know more of the facts and will discount derogatory imputations if these are based on "hearsay" evidence.

Another consideration which will influence the deliberation of Rawlsian negotiators on this issue is the need to be consistent. Most of them will wish to hold that damages should not be paid to compensate for emotional injury in those circumstances when sharp public debate is clearly in order, as in a legislature or during an election. Indeed, the value they are likely to place on frank communication is such that privileges may need to be afforded in other circumstances as well (as when references are provided in good faith or when someone is giving evidence before a tribunal or court). But if they allow these exceptions, Rawlsian negotiators cannot also claim that individuals have a moral right to compensation for emotional suffering when their reputations are falsely called into question in more general public debate. They may claim that such compensation will be a good thing, but they cannot consistently allow that it should take precedence over the right to speak. We do often feel outrage at what we think others have done, and thus we sometimes have an intense desire to force them to account by way of a public accusation. This interest is what freedom of speech protects as a right in a democracy, and no consideration of policy provides a sufficiently strong reason for censoring such speech.

In the light of these considerations, I suggest that, apart from cases where a report would enjoy a common law privilege, there should be strict liability in defamation cases and that reform be directed at removing the vulnerability of publishers and broadcasters to serious financial loss. This can be done most effectively by limiting the damages that can be awarded and by recognizing that the payment of money as compensation for emotional suffering is not a satisfactory remedy. Thus, a plaintiff who can show that he or she has been harmed financially because of the dissemination of defamatory statement for which the defendant is responsible would be awarded damages only for the actual loss shown, and there would be no compensation for any emotional suffering. However, plaintiffs do have a moral right to expect good faith on the part of publishers and broadcasters and, in this regard, the latter should have to pay the legal costs of a plaintiff who is forced to take action in order to obtain an opportunity to reply to a personal attack.

Would the burden of having to provide reply time or space seriously inhibit the press? The answer to this question depends on how the obligation is conceived of as well as on which sections of the media will be held vulnerable. Presumably most media companies wish to avoid litigation and the heavy costs that this often entails; and they would also resent having to keep copious records and would complain if their executives had to spend a lot of time making decisions about what to do in hard cases. Editors and program directors would also wish to minimize the impact which replies or corrections may have on their work. Apologies do not make good copy; nor do rambling excuses for wrong-doing. Broadcasters are most vulnerable when "rights of reply" are imposed, because their viewers and listeners cannot skip over material found boring or distasteful. Book publishers are also in a difficult situation, for it is often unclear how a reply could be afforded unless some other medium is employed.

These considerations should make us cautious about forcing material on editors in ways which would intrude into their traditional area of autonomy, and we should seek to accommodate the conflicting interests involved. I suggest the following guiding principles: First, the burden of providing access need be imposed only in those situations when it is unrealistic to suppose that the individual whose reputation is in question is incapable of a self-help remedy. This will account for by far the majority of cases, for in most instances when someone is attacked in the media, he will usually be a public figure or the context in which the accusation appears will be of such interest to the public that many opportunities for reply will be offered (although not necessarily by the publisher or broadcaster responsible for disseminating the attack). So long as it is clear that a reasonable opportunity for reply has been available (no matter who it has been provided by), there is no reason why any particular publisher or broadcaster should be forced to provide further space or time. Second, editors should enjoy considerable autonomy in deciding how a reply can best be presented and what constitutes an adequate reply. For example, they may refuse to carry a libelous statement or rule that much of the response offered does not address the substance of the original accusation. Third, there is no reason why the opportunity to respond should be carried in the same medium as the original attack. Thus, a broadcaster should normally be allowed to fulfil his or her obligations by purchasing advertising space in a newspaper. Of course, in monopoly situations (such as that in Florida, when the *Miami Herald Tribune* used its editorials to attack a candidate standing for political office) or when the accusation takes place in the context of an on-going discussion, it may be necessary to insist that the reply be carried by the same medium, because no other way of reaching the target audience will be available. Fourth, there is no reason why the media should have to notify those who have been attacked or to seek out a response. Fifth, if the reply that someone makes questions the integrity of the person responsible for the original attack, no further obligation to carry a reply to the reply should arise.

If these principles are endorsed, a broadcaster or publisher who is faced with a complaint from someone about a personal attack will retain much of the initiative. He or she may immediately choose to disseminate a correction, bringing to the notice of the audience the points made by the complainant. This should bring an end to litigation. However, suppose that the plaintiff finds the correction unsatisfactory or complains that relevant points in reply to the accusation have beeen misrepresented. In these circumstances the matter may proceed to a tribunal or court. If the arbitrator finds the correction reasonable, costs should usually be awarded to the defendant. However, suppose that the broadcaster or publisher disagrees that a false and derogatory statement has been made or claims that the plaintiff has already enjoyed adequate opportunity to respond. If this is challenged the matter would again proceed to arbitration to resolve the factual dispute. Whoever the verdict goes against would be vulnerable for costs; and if it is the publisher or broadcaster, he or she would also have to facilitate the dissemination of a correction and pay any actual damages.

This kind of burden on the media will not be greatly resented. A good journalist will generally try to ensure that persons who are attacked have an opportunity to reply, and this practice is recommended by the codes of behavior endorsed by most associations representing the profession. It is far more likely that the principles will be criticized by those who fear that the press will be irresponsible if they are too free from accountability, and that they will make accusations without taking sufficient care to safeguard the interests of those they attack by checking the facts carefully. Here, I can only emphasize that the very point of the principles I have recommended is to ensure an improvement in public discussion by making sure that people who are attacked are afforded a proper chance to reply. It is worth noting in this latter regard, however, that those sections of the media who are frequently careless because they adopt a policy of seeking to disseminate accusations even when these are not supported by evidence, will invariably be burdened by the many replies which will be imposed upon them. This is because more respectable outlets will not usually be bothered to comment on stories which appear in the "gutter press," so the only means for achieving a reply will be by imposing on those who are responsible for the original accusations. Thus, programs and papers which embark on a policy of sensationalism will find that they are heavily burdened with replies. Hopefully, this will encourage them to improve their journalistic practices.

Nor will there have to be great changes in existing practice if a tribunal with authority to enforce such a right of reply were to be established. In most areas of the media where abuse seems likely, there is already some mechanism by which newspaper publishers and broadcasters can be held accountable. For example, in the United Kingdom, newspaper publishers are answerable to the Press Council, to whom complaints can be brought. (However, anyone who takes a complaint to the Council is required to waive all right to legal redress.[21]) Although it enjoys no legal authority, this body can often succeed in securing a right of reply in cases where such an opportunity seems appropriate. As for the BBC and IBA, these bodies operate under a statutory obligation to supervise programming in the "public interest," and each has established mechanisms by which complaints from the public can be reviewed by a responsible committee. Thus, most people who complain after being personally attacked in the broadcast medium would be able to obtain a reasonable opportunity for vindication.

These provisions in the United Kingdom fall short of the principles I have articulated, in that an attacked person should not have to rely on the willingness of a broadcaster or publisher in seeking social justice. However, one has to allow that the self-regulation system appears to work quite well in the broadcast area. The Press Council has been less success-ful.[22] The British Annan Committee (*On the Future of Broadcasting*, 1977) recommend that one body be set up as a complaints commission to which any misrepresentation or unjust or unfair treatment in broadcast pro-grams can be brought. They envisage such a a body as having the power to enforce the broadcasting of an appropriate apology as well as its find-ings when any injustice has occurred.[23] This suggestion has significant merit. Ideally, such a body should also regulate the print media; it should also (as Annan recommends) be able to consider complaints about inva-sion of privacy.

In the United States the Federal Communications Commission (FCC) acts as a tribunal of review. The rules relating to personal attacks evolved as an interpretation of the "public interest" standards imposed by the *Communications Act* on stations to whom a license to broadcast had been awarded. A station's obligation to afford opportunities to reply are clearly specified. The rules require that licensees who broadcast what amounts to a personal attack upon an individual (or group) notify that person (or group) not later than one week after the attack and make an offer to carry a response. The obligation does not arise if the target of the attack is for-eign or if he is campaigning for election (provided, in this latter case, the attack is not made in an editorial opposing or endorsing one of the candi-dates); nor does it arise if the attack is made during a newscast, news in-terview, or on-the-spot coverage of a news event.[24] If an attack is made in a newspaper, however, there is no legal remedy, and the person attacked would have to rely on the good will of the particular publisher involved.

These provisions (in the United States) seem to have no proper ration-ale. Why should a person suffer an injustice just because the attack against them takes place during a news interview or report? Why should newspapers be immune from legitimate fairness obligations? As for the rule requiring a broadcaster to notify the subject of an attack, this seems an unnecessary burden for we can surely suppose that an individual will learn if an attack against him has been made. The most relevant question in determining if a broadcaster or publisher should be vulnerable is whether the person or group attacked has a capacity to answer any of the charges made against them. Public figures and those caught up in a news-worthy events will enjoy such a capacity for self-help and, as a general rule, so will groups.

5

Free Speech versus Privacy (Part One)

I have argued that freedom of speech falls into a residual category and that when an individual is able to establish some competing interest as a moral right, the latter claim must take precedence. Thus, in dealing with the competing claims of privacy and the liberty to speak, a first question we must address is whether it is plausible to hold that there is a moral right to a level of privacy which must consequently be afforded to all individuals who claim it. This is the task I address in this chapter.

Our privacy interests are far-ranging and include solitude, intimacy, and anonymity; they also encompass our desire to have control over how we are presented to others.[1]

There are many circumstances in which facts about us which we find embarrassing are legitimately publicized (as in court proceedings), so it makes little sense to suppose that there is a general moral right to privacy. However, we clearly do enjoy some limited entitlement to control when and how we are presented to others (for example, we enjoy a right to be free from intrusions so that we are not caught unaware). My difficulty is to determine whether any specific claims to autonomy of this kind can be asserted as a matter of moral right. I wish to delineate the circumstances, if there are any, when a person may legitimately demand that a specific claim to privacy ought to be afforded a priority over competing social interests.

In answering this question, what we have to ask ourselves is whether individuals who have no knowledge of their own specific circumstances and who are asked to make a judgment binding on future generations would be inclined to recognize some privacy interests. This way of posing the problem would not be useful if we were considering the matter of subjective feelings, for we would have no knowledge about how deeply anyone is likely to feel about being vulnerable to scrutiny by others. But moral rights do not depend on how deeply we feel about our various interests but on whether these can be shown to be fundamental in a more general sense. In this regard, I distinguish three specific claims to privacy protection which I believe would have general application and argue that the notion that the interests identified should be protected as a matter of moral right would carry force. First, I distinguish a utilitarian justification for recognizing a right to privacy where this is understood as a basic minimum seclusion of our most intimate experiences (birth, the moment of death, ablutions, sexual acts). I argue that the utilitarian argument establishes the right in these cases because there is no competing public interest which can carry weight. Second, I distinguish a sense in which we assert the claim that there is a right to privacy, where what is referred to is the violation of a legitimate presumption of privacy. What I have in mind here is the impropriety of allowing someone to think they are private when, in fact, they are being snooped upon. Finally, I argue that we can claim an entitlement to some privacy on the grounds that certain protections are a necessary prerequisite for the effective exercise of political liberties.

OUR PRIVACY INTERESTS

We may usefully begin by looking at the legal discussion of privacy, for certain core elements among our privacy interests have been distinguished as delineating some sort of legal profile. Thus, the legal scholar William Prosser, after noticing that a privacy tort has evolved in the United States (partly because courts had developed the common law but also through legislation) distinguishes four different interests which, if violated, are recognized as giving rise to a basis for civil action.[2] He lists: intrusions upon seclusion as solitude or into private affairs, public disclosure of embarrassing facts about an individual, publicity which places an individual in a false light, and the appropriation of an individual's name or likeness. These four interests have subsequently provided a basis for most discussions of privacy in the United States.

For my part, I am persuaded that Prosser's distinctions help immensely to clarify the various issues which arise when we reflect on the value of privacy. If we set aside a person's commercial interests in their name and likeness, we are left with the notion that our privacy interest has to do with our concern to control when and how we are presented to others. Even our worry about publicity which presents us in a false light reflects this, for we distinguish violations of privacy from defamation by the fact that it makes sense to complain about misleading publicity even when it is flattering. Our interest in controlling how we are presented to others is, of course, also reflected by the great trouble people often take to create a space which is free from arbitrary intrusions into which they may retreat if they wish to be away from the public gaze.

Privacy, in this sense, seems to be associated closely with the ideal of personal autonomy. If we allow ourselves to be exposed, it is no violation of our privacy if others observe us — even if what we do is something quite personal. What is important to us is that we have control over how and when we are presented to others. Thus, there may be times when we choose voluntarily to make disclosures of our personal selves, and this is not a loss of privacy but intimacy. Of course, some individuals may display a low appreciation of their own privacy by behaving in over-familiar ways with relative strangers, and in these cases we are usually critical of them. Besides controlling their intimacy, individuals are also concerned to control what happens to their own bodies.[3] We can see, then, that privacy usually involves the control by individual actors over matters of deep concern to them, and it is best characterized as an aspect of the exercise of human autonomy.

Of course, as J. S. Mill points out so eloquently in *On Liberty*, a good deal of privacy may be justified as a means to other ends in that it may have an enabling purpose, allowing us to develop potentialities which it would be difficult to nurture if there were no privacy (for example, our capacity for friendship through the sharing of intimacies would not be possible if nothing were private in the first place[4]). But someone who valued privacy only because it was instrumental to the realization of some other value is not sensitive to its intrinsic worth, for the value of privacy and our entitlement to enjoy it do not always depend on whether we make a good use of it or on whether some social interest is served thereby.

It would seem that our privacy interests, insofar as these can be listed at all precisely, have to do partly with our legitimate attempts to create a space which is free from arbitrary intrusions, and partly with our wish to control how we are presented to others.

Historically there have been differences in the degree to which these interests have been valued, for what people demand often reflects what they have come to expect. Clearly we enjoy far more privacy in modern societies if this is measured in terms of the availability of a closed off space into which individuals may take themselves apart from others and in terms of anonymity. As the British Parliamentary Committee (Younger) puts the point:

> . . . the modern middle class family of two parents and their children, relatively soundproofed in their semi-detached house, relatively unseen behind their private hedge and rose trellis, travelling with determined reserve on public transport or insulated in the family car, shopping in the super-market and entertained by television, are probably more private in the sense of being unnoticed in all their everyday doings than any sizable section of the population in any other time or place.[5]

As the committee sees it, the increase in the amount of privacy available to people today is due to a number of historical changes. First, the modern citizen is far more mobile than has been the case even in the recent past. We are more likely to move our areas of residence so that it is often true that very little may be known about us in our neighborhoods. Also, when we travel within or between cities our anonymity protects us from the embarrassment of having our activities monitored, for if nobody around us has an idea of who we are, we become merely a face in a crowd and our activities are rarely remarked upon. Second, kinship networks have been narrowing so that in the United States today the standard group is normally the parents and their dependent children—even grand-parents have left the family home. As for friends, it is usual to have a number of different contacts and intimates who may not be known to one another. This is possible in modern societies because people can keep dif-ferent aspects of their lives, such as sporting activities, work, and family life, quite separate.

I do not deny that our enjoyment of anonymity and solitude, when we choose to enjoy it, is threatened by certain aspects of modernity, or that people such as public figures or those caught up in events of public inter-est may suffer a deprivation and need protection. Nor do I necessarily want to embrace the argument that because freedom from intrusion is greater today than it has been in the past, we should be grateful with what we have and not seek for more. But it is important to keep in mind that human beings have been able to live very fulfilled and worthwhile lives with far less privacy than is enjoyed by many people today. Also, we should comprehend that the case for regarding an increase in seclusion and anonymity as a good in itself may be controversial: we cannot claim that people are better off today than they were in the past, or that they are happier, merely because they enjoy more potential to isolate themselves from others. Indeed, it may be that privacy in the sense of enjoying a pro-tected zone and relative anonymity goes together with a certain level of anxiety and may involve loneliness and even what sociologists describe as anomie. Certainly, we would have to allow that the aged are not happier today living anonymously in flats than they may have been in the past in the midst of family life.

Nevertheless, it must be said that a certain level of privacy to protect in-timacy seems to be essential to human dignity in the modern context (it may not have been in other societies) and that it is barbaric to violate this unless there is some very pressing concern.[6]

I turn now to consider whether it makes much sense to claim that we have a moral right to some more narrowly defined privacy interest.

A functionalist approach is to seek a way of delineating a category of in-formation "private facts." The characteristics of this category must be that the information in question is of a kind that is unlikely to serve any useful social purpose. Thus, on utilitarian grounds, we may justify affording individuals a right to control the dissemination of this kind of information about themselves.

The problem with this strategy is that it is virtually impossible to plausibly distinguish such a category of "worthless information," so that when any authority is asked to frame or administer laws which make reference to so-called private facts, a good deal of inconclusive balancing must inevitably take place. That this will be the case, can be seen from the wide range of matters which in some circumstances would clearly be of legitimate public interest (for example, information relevant to a person's professional activities or to the assessment of his or her character when this is a factor in a matter of public concern.[7]) Thus, it is clear that matters which we normally take to be private (for example, those relating to the health, private behavior, home life, personal family relationships of individuals) would have to be regarded as of legitimate public concern in some circumstances. And, if we were to seek to protect privacy, the problem of distinguishing legitimate from illegitimate reports would be complex.

One problem is that some public figures affect our lives not merely by what they do but also because of the role model they set. This seems to be especially so of those whose public image is a virtual fiction. Considering the impact that Marilyn Monroe had as a film star who helped to change our perception of women, it matters a great deal that the public be properly informed that her private self was nothing like the public image – that she was very difficult to live with and desperately unhappy.[8]

More importantly, if moral prejudice is to change we need role models who confront us with alternative conceptions. A lesbian sports star or a ballerina who has numerous love affairs each in their own way helps to break down prejudice. We may all feel that Princess Margaret has been made very unhappy by the publicity which has focused upon her private affairs, but it should, nevertheless, be understood that ordinary folk need to know that the rich (and even the royal) also run into difficulties in coping with their emotions.

A better approach is to ask ourselves whether any of our privacy interests is so fundamental that Rawlsian negotiators would be inclined to recognize that they must be protected as a right. Here, there would be no question of balancing, for what is meant by a "privacy right," in the strong Rawlsian sense, is that elements of our privacy interests are of a kind which make us reluctant to see them balanced against other competing interests which governments may be concerned to pursue (for example, crime prevention or efficient welfare support for single parent families). Furthermore, in asserting that there is such a right to privacy (in this strong sense) we undertake to substantiate this claim by somehow including it, as entailed by or compatible with, our basic conception of the democratic commitment that people be treated with equal concern and respect.

As I mentioned earlier, I do not think there is a general right to privacy (including all the elements listed by Prosser) in this strong sense, for it seems true that governments and the public (through the press) often have a legitimate interest in intruding into the private realm (for example, if a serious crime has been committed). Generally, also, the private realm needs to be penetrated at times simply because there is a public interest in learning how people live and because we are interested in what motivates people in life. Of course, these kinds of intrusions should mostly take place after permission is granted and when warning is given that some investigation is to be made (researchers, biographers, or the makers of film documentaries are not usually granted, nor do they usually expect, a special dispensation to violate privacy at their discretion). On the other hand, a society which allowed for no intrusion into the private realm would impoverish its capacity for self-reflection—and perhaps even compassion.

One way in which we learn about the private realm is through public proceedings dealing with crises (as in custody cases before the family courts, or when there are disputes over a private estate). Although, I would not argue that it would always be wrong in these cases to insist on secrecy to protect privacy, I would suggest that this kind of protection is often bad policy. I certainly do not think that adequate arguments have been put to show that individuals ought always to have their interest in preventing public disclosures at these times respected—that is, that they have "a right" to privacy in the strong sense I have noted.

In my view, then, the philosopher Judith Jarvis Thomson is entirely correct when she states boldly that "none of us has a right over any fact to the effect that the fact shall not be known by others . . . there is no such thing as violating a man's right to privacy by simply knowing something about him."[9] Of course, people do often claim such a right and many of the current disputes about privacy relate to the strong interest which individuals have in controlling facts about themselves (such as their bank statements or medical files). However, it should be remembered in discussing this kind of claim, that information is often relevant to policy and that if individuals are afforded a right to keep secrets, a cost will inevitably be paid by somebody. For example, when a bank or finance company is assessing an applicant for a loan, they may need to know something about that person's financial arrangements and character to make a reasonable judgment, and they will force disclosure of information that they may need in assessing the person's worthiness for credit. If we do not allow for this, people may be granted loans which they cannot afford; or, what is more likely, banks and finance companies will only loan money to the rich. In general I would argue that the more information we have about each other, the better, and that the richer and more powerful the person, the more imperative it is to force disclosure of his or her affairs (all tax returns, and not just those of a willing prime minister or president, should be available for public scrutiny if this is likely to serve the public interest).

But having granted these limitations on whatever privacy right we do have, I wish now to argue that there are at least three different considerations which establish a moral right (in the strong sense I have delineated) to certain significant elements of our privacy interest.

PRIVACY AS A RIGHT NOT TO BE DECEIVED

Consider first how moral rights are usually established through authorization of one kind or another. I make a promise to meet you in the city at a specific time, and in doing so I establish an expectation on your part that I will be there. We can say that you have a right to expect that I will meet my commitment—you are free to organize your own arrangements on this understanding, and may legitimately complain if I disregard my commitment to you. The moral force behind your complaint, if we are to suppose that I do not meet you when I said I would, arises because of the respect we share for each other as moral agents. We strive to relate responsibly as persons who undertake to meet our commitments so as to allow others to rely upon us.[10] Of course, there may be good reasons why I cannot do what I have committed myself to do, and in this kind of case I may have a relevant excuse. Not every consideration of convenience and comfort will serve, however, for whenever an undertaking is made, there is a presumption of special concern which will, of course, vary depending on the circumstances. (In the case of my promise to meet you in the city, we would normally balance the inconvenience which I put you to against the difficulties and costs I would have had to endure to meet my commitment, qualified in subtle ways by our common understanding of the circumstances in which the original undertaking was made. For example, it would make a difference if you reluctantly cancelled some other arrangements saying that you knew I was unreliable; and your case would be strengthened if you only agreed to rely on me because I had promised to make great sacrifices to meet the commitment if this was necessary. In these last mentioned circumstances I could hardly use the kinds of excuses for not meeting you which would normally be acceptable.)

If we consider the case of privacy, we can see that there is some analogy with promising: individuals often do have a presumption of seclusion which they justifiably assume others will respect, and may, therefore, claim this area as "a right." Consider the typical married couple in the presumed privacy of their bedroom. Their situation here is very different from what the case would be were they to find themselves alone in a public place such as a holiday resort. In these latter circumstances, provided they look about carefully, they may presume that they are private, but they have no right to assume this. And if some innocent party of bush-walkers comes upon them, our couple's privacy has not been invaded, for they had no right to suppose that this would not happen. If these bushwalkers had intruded into their bedroom, on the other hand, they would most certainly have violated the couple's privacy. In these cases the expectations are the way they are because of legal rules (the couple may legitimately assume that the bedroom is private because an intruder would have to break the law, but may make no such presumption at the resort), but our expectations about how others will behave—that is, whether they will intrude into our private realm—sometimes depends more on convention than on law. For example, the police may have had a legal right to place a listening device in Martin Luther King's hotel bed-room but he, nevertheless, had a moral expectation that his privacy would not be violated in this way. I would argue that we can generally claim a moral right to privacy provided we can show that by the standards of behavior accepted in our community we could reasonably assume that nobody would intrude. Thus, if the couple had taken a room at a motel on their way home from the resort, they would assume that they would not be spied upon by the management, and they would be justified in doing so. And if some electronic device was used to monitor their conversation (perhaps to check whether they were planning to leave without paying their bill[11]) they could legitimately complain that their right to privacy was violated. This would be so even if there was no law against anyone using such a device. And, as I have said in my reference to Martin Luther King's case, it would be so even if it was not the management who was intruding but the police.

Even though this is a narrower sense of "a right to privacy" than most people would like, it has some significant implications, for once it is es-tablished that people have a moral right of the kind delineated, we must expect and demand that the law be used to protect it. Also, the right we are talking about lies at the core of the modern privacy dilemma, for most of our worries about the violation of privacy do not relate to the fact that there are not sufficient zones into which we may retreat, but to the fact that they are vulnerable to electronic intrusions. We worry that we may not know when we are in the public realm, and so will be caught una-wares. We certainly have a right to expect that this should not happen.

But how much weight does this assertion carry? When we were dis-cussing the hypothetical situation in which it was supposed that I had broken an undertaking to meet you in the city, I said that the moral force of your complaint would depend, first, on how serious an inconvenience I had put on you (for even a clear undertaking to meet someone is not the sort of commitment which we would never be prepared to renege upon);

and, second, on how much assurance I had given you. The situation is somewhat similar when privacy is violated, for we have to take the competing interest into account.

Let me take first the issue of the harm which individuals may stand to suffer when assurances about privacy are violated. Clearly, we do sometimes have a serious interest in our privacy, for its violation may undermine our sense of personal dignity. We would, therefore, require that very serious competing considerations be provided before we would concede that a policy which put people at this risk was justified. On the other hand, the value of privacy to an individual may not be substantial and it certainly varies depending on the circumstances. Is it a violation of privacy to publish the letters and papers of a person who is already dead? Clearly in this latter kind of case the person whose privacy is violated does not suffer. Whatever harm is caused is suffered by those nearest to him or her who have empathy if these publications involve a loss of dignity, or those who are hurt or embarrassed by what is written about them by the deceased person. Does a person have any moral right to claim that information about his or her financial affairs is private? What of other information such as medical records or the information held in personnel files? The legal answers in these kinds of cases are easier to provide than the moral ones.

As a quick response, I would say that even though individuals have a moral right in circumstances when they can presume (by convention or law) privacy, this does not entitle them to control information about themselves. If we are asked to state our finances we are not caught unawares. All we can say is that those who keep a private file in their acknowledged private space have a right to expect that its contents will not be disclosed, but only while they are alive. The presumption here does not carry a great deal of weight, however, for we would accept many reasons as sufficient to justify an intrusion, especially if the substance of the material concerned related to matters of legitimate public interest. Information available elsewhere would, of course, normally be public unless confidentiality is clearly guaranteed.[12]

Turning, then, to the question of when individuals may presume that their privacy will be guaranteed, we find that most cases are straightforward, for some express assurance of confidentiality will normally have been given. This is usually the case when information about a person is collected from that person or when third parties are asked to provide references. Although I believe that too much confidentiality is generally guaranteed in most modern communities—often hypocritically, for not much care is taken to preserve it—this opinion is beside the point for the purposes of the present discussion. Here, I merely claim that where assurances have been given, so that a person acts on the understanding that what he or she says or does will be private, the person involved has a right to expect that the commitment will be honored. Thus, although it may be good policy for legislators to enact laws which make it an offense for most agencies to hold private files (and, as I have said I think they should), we ought, nevertheless, to respect the rights of those who have dealt with agencies on a prior understanding of confidentiality.

As for less formal types of assurance, these generally relate to those circumstances where individuals indicate their presumption of privacy by withdrawing behind closed doors. If privacy is not complete in such circumstances, as it may not be in airport toilets or the change rooms in large department stores, then very clear warnings ought to be given.

Generally, then, the scope of our moral right to privacy, where what we are referring to is our right not to be deceived into supposing that we are out of the public gaze and free to relax where this is not the case, is very narrow. However, when it is established, such a right is usually a significant one for it counts heavily against the practice of surreptitious surveillance. Nor would such a right fall into abeyance if for some very pressing reasons of law enforcement embarrassing private material is collected. Clearly those who take possession of material which is of an intimate and highly personal nature, such as recordings of people making love or of their intimate conversations, have a great responsibility to keep this material confidential, and it should not be shown to anyone unless this disclosure is relevant to the purpose for which the private information was collected (perhaps to demonstrate a conspiracy to commit a serious crime). It should certainly be kept completely confidential if the surveillance merely showed the innocence of the parties involved. Thus, when J. Edgar Hoover used his recordings of Martin Luther King's intimate moments to try to discredit him and to precipitate a crisis in his marriage, this represented a significant abuse of whatever power to intrude had been given to the FBI director by the United States Congress.[13] Also, those who took a delight in playing these tapes to friends for malicious and prurient reasons (like President Johnson), demonstrated their own moral depravity.[14]

PRIVACY AS A RIGHT TO POLITICAL LIBERTY AND MINIMAL DIGNITY

I turn now to distinguish the second sense in which I think we can claim "a right" to privacy. I wish to argue that we can substantiate a claimed right to privacy by showing that it is an element of some more basic right. Thus, if it can be shown that privacy is a necessary prerequisite for political liberty, we would have effectively established our moral claim to have this interest protected. When we establish a privacy right in this sense, we are talking about that minimum freedom from surveillance and intrusion which is necessary if citizens are to perform their democratic responsibilities adequately. Thus, a government which kept so close a watch on citizens that it intimidated them, making them unable to experiment with ways of living or to explore controversial ideas, would violate their right to privacy. The political importance of privacy is demonstrated very clearly by the confrontation in the United States between the organization known as NAACP, which served to represent Blacks who were being prosecuted in civil rights cases, and some of the white-dominated state governments.[15] A few segregationists thought that the NAACP could be intimidated if its list of members were made public, for those who supported the organization financially would then have had to risk suffering whatever social pressures might be brought to bear upon them. As is well known, similar pressures were brought to bear during the McCarthy hearings on members and ex-members of communist and socialist organizations. By forcing people to declare their political affiliations, their right to association is often undermined by the resulting social pressures, particularly those affecting their job security. We can see, then, how our privacy interest can serve to supplement our claim to political liberty.

Privacy is not merely necessary as a feature of our right to associate. Another politically significant reason for valuing solitude and intimacy is that it is conducive to our developing an effective capacity to perform as self-governing citizens, for it is only because we are able to retreat from public surveillance into a private sphere to think and to gather ourselves emotionally and spiritually that we are able to reach a maturity of judgment. Thus, those of us who share the humanist belief that what distinguishes persons is the development of a capacity to make responsible choices, so that we are able to regulate our lives in the light of our own comprehension of what it is important for us to do, must concede that privacy is a central value. Without some protection against public exposure, we would not easily develop a capacity for individual judgment and action.

This is an attitude which, as Sir Zelman Cowen rightly points out, needs to be sharply distinguished from the totalitarian impulse which despises the private realm.[16] If one holds that the moral realization of the individual depends on his or her conformity with a given value structure, then one may be tempted to dismiss claims to privacy as exhibiting a bad tendency. In modern times the notion that what is important is total control over the individuals who make up a society has become widely accepted. Many government leaders believe that progress will only be achieved through the mobilization of significant resources of coercion and surveillance. They wish to manipulate sources of information so that no dissenting doubts emerge loosening the degree to which individual citizens identify their interests and duties as conforming, even emotionally, with what is required by the social planners. In earlier times, of course, conformity was achieved without conscious effort, for people literally belonged to a community and they had little ability to shape their fundamental values.

Given that we regard privacy as a fundamental liberal value of the kind that Cowen says it is, how much of it do individuals require if they are to participate effectively as citizens? Also, is our interest in privacy ever in conflict with liberty (widely conceived to include the right to assemble and to associate, the right to free speech, and a claim to equal privileges of citizenship)?

There is no clear-cut way in which these questions can be answered. However, I would say that where freedom and privacy are in conflict, it is the former rather than the latter which should normally be afforded priority. The reason for this is that we can most usefully comprehend the democratic commitment as requiring us to set a higher value upon facilitating an individual's ability to participate as an equal in the democratic process than on most other competing values.[17] We do this because as democrats we regard it as imperative to ensure that it is possible for citizens to exercise their sovereignty. Of course, the rights of liberty may not be as important to individuals as their other personal interests (for example, their interest in a good job, or a happy family life, or in their health and education). Nevertheless, we place a higher priority upon the protection of their right to democratic participation, for it is only in this way that we avoid tyranny and respect their dignity. (On the other hand, privacy protection, when this extends to afford individuals a right to enjoy a substantial power to control how they are presented to others, can inhibit political participation.)

For the most part, as I have indicated, it is possible to include many of a person's privacy interests within the basic liberties which must be protected if they are to serve as effective citizens. However, this is not always so, and some claims to privacy, particularly our concern not to have facts about ourselves made public, may come into conflict with liberty. In these cases, we must balance a concern for the sensitivity of an individual who resents being exposed (perhaps a candidate for office who dislikes having his or her financial affairs looked into, or who is shy about a health problem) against some significant democratic right (most usually, the right to evaluate the character of social and political leaders). Luckily, privacy is rarely seriously threatened by democratic processes, and we can usually find ways of accommodating our interests without harming the core institutions (a free press, the inviolate home, autonomous associations, and independent courts) which provide the framework for democratic politics.

Finally, I turn to the last of the lines of argument which may succeed in establishing a claim to privacy protection as a matter of right.

Intuitively, most of us feel that a certain level of freedom from intrusion is essential to human dignity and that it is barbaric to violate this unless there is some pressing concern. In the first place, most of us would be inclined to the view that people have a right to be free from violations of their person and personality. Thus, we would say categorically that people ought to be protected against sexual assault and torture, even if this involves great public cost. We would be inclined, also, to support the view that they should not be violated by special techniques of intrusion which can expose intimate thoughts (such as by truth drugs and lie detectors—even aptitude tests are controversial). Most of us would also agree that people should not have their moods and dispositions manipulated against their will by drugs and that, along with the right to the sanctity of their person, individuals are also entitled to a minimum protection of their intimate moments.

The claim that we have a right to the protection of our person and intimacies cannot always be established by utilitarian argument, for in some circumstances there may be very great social costs involved if the use of intrusive methods is foregone. Also the degree to which we are humiliated varies considerably. For example, it may be much fairer to use aptitude and intelligence tests in selection procedures than other indicators, and it may also be more efficient. Indeed, even if we take the extreme case of torture, the violation may serve a good purpose (for example, when the lives of innocent persons are at risk). Not surprisingly, then, when we turn to review cases where a person's intimate moments are violated, we often find that some good purposes may be served. For example, Hoover was able to persuade Robert Kennedy to authorize the surreptitious surveillance of Martin Luther King, Jr., and these men are not alone in making judgments of this kind. Many people argue today that the problem of organized crime, especially as it relates to the illicit importation of harmful drugs, can only be effectively controlled if the police are given authority to violate people's privacy. Terrorism is another threat to society which some people believe warrants this kind of response.[18]

The moral right to some miminum standards are established by the utilitarian argument, however, for some violations cannot have very much utility, if any. The case of sexual assault is an example, as there do not seem to be any conceivable circumstances where any good purposes could be served by this kind of violation. As for privacy violations, there is often very little public benefit from them, and this is especially so where the motive is clearly a prurient one—no obvious social interest is served apart from the satisfaction of a perverted delight in spying on others. In these cases, it seems that the utilitarian arguments so clearly support the protection of privacy that we can speak about a moral right to privacy.

I must add one qualification. Some of our most private moments (I have in mind moments of great emotion) inevitably occur in public and can involve matters of great social importance. One case, reported by the British Parliamentary Committee, involved the reunion of a foster child with its natural parents.[19] This was a moment of great trauma, for the child had to be removed from its foster parents, who, understandably, were emotionally upset. It was argued in this case that the national press manipulated the situation for their own commercial purposes, disregarding the feelings of the parents involved. Against this point of view, we must place the social interest which is served when the public is faced with evidence demonstrating the impact on the lives of individuals of a given public policy. Without graphic public exposure it would not have been possible for the human dimension of the foster parent program to be illustrated. This case serves to highlight the general problem that our private moments are sometimes caught up in matters of genuine public interest. Disasters catch us unawares, we may be distraught and in pain, we may be frightened or simply exhausted after an ordeal, and at these times we may not welcome publicity; yet an important public interest may be served by this.

We must allow, then, that whatever protections are afforded to private individuals to secure their most intimate moments against intrusions, they ought not to be worded so that they prevent the press from reporting what takes place in public. The most we can justify using utilitarian arguments is a right which protects people at the inner core of their private selves, at times when they enjoy intimacy in private, or at moments of birth and death.

6

Free Speech versus Privacy (Part Two)

Thus far I have shown that privacy is an important individual interest – so significant that we can sometimes successfully establish that an individual's interest in his or her privacy ought to be afforded a priority over other social values when there is a conflict. The problem is, of course, to establish when this kind of priority should be given, as it is clear that there is no general moral right to privacy. I have suggested that such a right is established only when one or more of the three lines of argument delineated in the last chapter is put forward in a convincing way.

I turn now to test the orientation articulated above by briefly reviewing some hard cases when freedom of speech is in conflict with privacy. We find that there are two kinds of problems which need to be reviewed separately: there are first those which arise because an individual objects to the manner in which a news story is investigated, complaining of harassment or embarrassing questions (perhaps because a reporter insists on phoning at all hours of the night, trespasses into private property, or investigates matters which are of a confidential nature). However, second, the same complainant may have no objections to the way that a reporter investigated a story and may, in fact, have enjoyed the interview and the interest taken in his or her affairs. The complainant's objection may be to having certain facts or photographs made public.

In the light of the values articulated in my analysis of a Rawlsian approach to these problems, we can conclude that the press should generally be free to disseminate information as they choose; however, they may not deliberately catch people unawares in a manner which violates privacy or any other right (although deception as a strategy for news gathering may sometimes be in order when such rights are not jeopardized, for example, suppose a journalist pretends to be a client so that he can expose quackery or a violation of professional ethics); nor may they gather materials in a manner which involves intrusion, for example, using surreptitious forms of surveillance to penetrate private places or by trespassing. How well or badly does this way of resolving dilemmas serve in practice?

INTRUSIONS AND THE PRESS

It should be pointed out that the greatest threat to our interest in enjoying a private realm does not come because of the activities of the press so much as from investigators working for government agencies. Apart from the activities of the police in combating crime and terrorism, many other agencies resort to intrusion. Of course, not all of these investigators would trespass or use electronic gadgets to intrude. But there are often good reasons why these methods may be thought justified in some circumstances. In the social welfare field, for example, strong utilitarian reasons are found to protect children who may be abused by their parents or to ensure that people are not claiming benefits to which they are not entitled. An agency which wishes to use methods of electronic surveillance or to intrude in some other way into the private realm must usually obtain some warrant authorizing such actions, and for this they need to state clearly the specific purpose for which the information is to be collected.

If we consider the current practice of journalists, we find that the evidence does not give cause for serious worry. The case of an Australian politician who complained that an interview he had given had been televised using a hidden camera without his knowledge is a typical example of the kind of case brought before Press Councils.[1] (But the problem here is really breach of confidence rather than intrusion.) By far the majority of complainants object to surreptitious photography, whether by stealth (the photographer behind the bush or the camera hidden) or by use of telescopic lenses. In most of these cases the person caught unaware is in a public place and is not embarrassed because of a violation of privacy but because they resent publicity which is not sought out. (For example, three British football stars resented a photograph taken of them playing a game in the prison yard after they had been convicted of accepting bribes.)

The Younger Committee's research provides examples of how useful recorders and sophisticated cameras can be to journalists.[2] It lists the following cases: (a) A film documentary on the prevalence of industrial espionage and its dangers included scenes in which private detectives plant a "bugging" device in an office telephone and steal documents. This material was obtained by reporters who had arranged a decoy assignment for these detectives, who were unaware that they were being filmed or recorded. (b) Two television reporters had posed as arms dealers and their subsequent meeting in Geneva with an agent trying to buy arms for Biafra during the Nigerian Civil War was recorded and filmed using a telescopic lens and a hidden microphone. (c) Reporters recorded telephone conversations relating to matters of public interest such as drug trafficking and the breaking of economic sanctions against Rhodesia. (d) Reporters took a ride in a taxi from London Airport pretending to be foreigners, and the journey was recorded and filmed to show how customers were cheated. With regard to newspaper journalism the committee asked the Press Council to provide details of their adjudications since 1953. Only three cases of surreptitious surveillance gave rise to a complaint, and none of these involved telephone tapping or the recording of conversations.

Journalists who violate privacy are more likely to accomplish their goal through deception or breach of confidence, and they very rarely use sophisticated surveillance equipment apart from cameras and recorders. A California case, *Dietemann v. Time, Inc.*, may serve to illustrate. The plaintiff in this case, Dietemann, was a herbalist who practiced from his home, charging people for medications which involved nothing more than clay, minerals, and herbs. Two reporters posed as a married couple seeking treatment and advice because the "wife" had detected a lump in her breast. Photographs and recordings were taken of their consultation with Dietemann about this problem and his diagnosis that the ailment was due to rancid butter eaten eleven years, nine months, and seven days previously was noted. The magazine *Life* subsequently published an article on medical quackery discussing Dietemann's practice which was illustrated with photograhs taken in the latter's consulting room. When Dietemann sued the company for invasion of privacy, the California court awarded heavy damages against *Life* on the grounds that the photographs had been obtained in an intrusive way. The photographs themselves were not embarrassing; rather, it was the manner in which they were acquired (that is, the use of a hidden camera) which constituted the alleged invasion of privacy.[3]

This ruling is in conflict with the standards I have articulated earlier. How are reporters to gather evidence of a practice such as quackery if they are not allowed to pretend to be members of the public? Had they arrived with cameras, recording devices and a press card all clearly visible, Dietemann would not have exposed himself. Nor did the reporters intrude into his privacy, catching him unawares. At each stage he was dealing with what he took to be clients as someone offering a service. The reporters had no interest in surveying his behavior when he was in private, rather they duped him into supposing that they were innocent members of the public. Not surprisingly, then, other courts have not tended to support this ruling. Thus, in a similar Kentucky case, *McCall v. Courier Journal*, a young woman surreptitiously recorded a conversation with her attorney, John T. McCall, using a small recorder lent to her by reporters on the *Louisville Courier Journal*. During the conversation McCall violated the code of professional ethics he was bound to uphold as an attorney by guaranteeing that he would get her "off the hook" of her indictment on a drug charge offense if she could come up with $10,000. He said he would return $9,000 if he failed to have her set free. The transcript of the conversation was published by the newspaper and McCall sued in the hope that, like Dietemann, he would be awarded damages for violation of privacy. Unfortunately, for him, the court chose to distinguish the cases, making much of the fact that the young woman involved (unlike the reporters in the Dietemann case) was a genuine client and had been invited into McCall's office at his request.[4] (This basis for distinction is rather inadequate, and one suspects that it is more of a rationalization for reaching a different evaluation of the competing claims. Deception by journalists acting as surrogates for the public has long been an accepted practice.)

We are left with the following dilemmas:

(a) Ought newsmen to be authorized to use telephone tapping devices, hidden cameras, microphones, telescopic lenses, and other sophisticated surveillance equipment in some special circumstances?

(b) If reporters break the law by intruding, should they be vulnerable to criminal and civil prosecution like everyone else?

(c) Should editors ever be allowed to use materials gathered in ways which involve a violation of privacy? (Often film or other information that is passed on to a journalist could not have been collected without a violation of privacy. For example, the break-in by Nixon's plumbers into the office of a psychiatrist to obtain a copy of Daniel Ellsberg's file was part of a campaign to discredit him, and embarrassing information collected by way of this intrusion would certainly have been passed along to journalists).

(d) Does it make a difference whether reporters are responsible for collecting the material or whether it is passed on by others who are guilty of the illicit intrusion in the first instance?

With regard to my first two questions, I have already acknowledged that surreptitious surveillance of others violates a fundamental right and should not be tolerated. The practice involves catching persons unawares, often exposing intimate moments and, if widespread, it would leave us all vulnerable. However, telescopic lenses for cameras and sophisticated microphones are readily available so it would be absurd to require that journalists obtain a license to make use of them. Nevertheless, they surely should be vulnerable at civil law if they use these devices to catch people unawares. The question we must ask is whether individuals being presented to the public on the media are behaving in a way that they would normally reserve for times when they believe themselves to be private. (Thus, the publication of a photograph taken of a woman bathing topless when she has obviously taken care to choose a spot that is remote should be regarded as a violation of privacy if it was taken with a telescopic lens; whereas the publication of a similar shot of a woman in a crowded section of the beach should not.)

Questions (c) and (d) raise issues which are far more difficult to answer, but we may make progress if we begin by noting the interests which the protection of privacy is supposed to serve. As we have seen, although our privacy right is a very narrow one, it includes the enjoyment of a private zone into which a person may relax without worrying about his public image. It would be contradictory to hold a person vulnerable for violating this privacy by way of an intrusion (for example, hiding in a private garden to photograph someone relaxing) but not to hold him or her accountable if the harm caused by this intrusion is compounded by further publicity. After all, our enjoyment of privacy is often a matter of degree and can be violated to a greater or lesser extent. Thus, a public figure may not resent a passing stranger who mistakenly enters his property. He might become very concerned, however, if it turns out that the stranger subsequently sold photographs taken at this time. Even when an intrusion is justified on the grounds of national security and has been properly authorized, the violation of privacy can be compounded by further publicity (for example, the authorizaton that J. Edgar Hoover enjoyed to bug the bedroom of Martin Luther King, Jr., could not have extended to the playing of the tapes for prurient reasons).

If our interest in not being presented to others without having a chance to compose ourselves is what the right to privacy protects, it should not serve to safeguard a person's interest in keeping his activities secret. A good deal goes on in houses and other places where people feel free from the scrutiny of others which the public has a significant interest in learning about and which individuals have no strong claim to keep secret (for example, criminal conspiracies and practices such as child abuse, cruelty to animals, or quackery). Journalists who obtain information concerning practices of this kind ought to be able to expose them so long as privacy is not compromised by the publicity. I do not imply here that a journalist who intrudes to collect information should not be prosecuted or vulnerable to a civil action for doing this, but merely that material that may have been collected by way of an intrusion is often not relevant to the legitimate enjoyment of privacy.

This brings me to my final question: does it make a difference whether the intrusion necessary to collect private facts or photographs about an individual is conducted by someone other than an agent of the publisher or broadcaster who disseminated it? Surely not. If material is gathered which is of public interest but which harms an individual's legitimate privacy rights, a publisher or broadcaster should have to ensure that further publicity does not compound the harm. Thus, when embarrassing material candidly exposing persons caught unawares in a private place is disseminated, the media company concerned should be regarded as implicated in the violation of privacy involved and vulnerable for any damages a court might award in amelioration.

I turn now to consider the less technical means by which investigators can be intrusive. I have in mind here the use of deception and the resort to harassment.

The most notorious case of persistent and harassing journalism is that of the photographer Ron Gallela who made a good living (or so it would seem from his devotion to duty) from taking pictures of Jacqueline Kennedy Onassis and her children. After an incident in which Galella's efforts caused the horse on which John Kennedy, Jr. was riding to bolt, Mrs. Onassis sought an injunction to restrict the photographer. The court enjoined the latter from coming within twenty feet of her and within thirty feet of her children, from blocking their movement in any way, from doing anything which might put them in danger or might harass, alarm or frighten them, and from entering the children's play area at school.[5] This unusual case has a sequel, for Gallela was subsequently charged with contempt and only escaped a prison sentence by promising not to photograph Mrs. Onassis or any of her family again. As far as I know, this is the only case where a journalist has been restrained by an injunction to prevent his or her harassing a particular individual. Many complaints are made about the behavior of journalists, however, and some celebrities have been known to resort to self-help measures in dealing with reporters they have regarded as rude or intrusive (as Frank Sinatra did when he visited Australia). Reports from Press Councils (in both Australia and the United Kingdom) as well as from the New South Wales Privacy Committee show that reporters do at times pursue their enquiries beyond the point that people consider reasonable. The press seems to harass public figures and even minor celebrities. A Melbourne case reported to the Australian Press Council is typical:

> A television journalist separated from her husband. A Melbourne newspaper thereupon investigated her personal life to determine whether there was "another man." This involved camera surveillance of the woman, interviews with a male suspect in which he was questioned as to his relationship with the woman and asked to confirm a previously typed statement, extended camera surveillance of his home and the photographing of some 30–40 guests entering a private party attended by the couple. He declined comment insisting that the matter was private. Nonetheless the newspaper carried stories on two separate occasions about the relationship.[6]

Even if a strong case could be made for offering some protection against the over-eager press reporter, it is very difficult to see how the use of harassment in the gathering of information by investigators can be curtailed without passing laws which would threaten free expression in a very serious way. As the Younger Committee put it:

> We are unable to devise any general rule which could help a newspaperman to decide at how late an hour he would be justified in disturbing a private citizen, or for that matter a public figure, or how far he should pursue him to a holiday retreat in order to get information or comment on a piece of news, or how far the importance or urgency of the news should effect his decision.[7]

It is equally difficult to establish when and to what extent deception may be a justifiable means of ferreting out important facts. The British Broadcasting Corporation (BBC), for example, could not have exposed their story about the breaking of sanctions imposed against Rhodesia or their revelations about the selling of arms to Biafra had they not been prepared to provide false credentials.[8]

Both the Younger Committee and the earlier Committee of *Justice*, which reported in the United Kingdom, suggest that the best solution against the irresponsible or over aggressive investigator is some form of self-regulation, and they recommend that journalists accept a code of ethics monitored by their own profession.[9] What the Younger Committee hoped to see is a situation in which editors and others in senior positions hold themselves responsible for the conduct of their staff. It argues that any attempt to use the law to discipline the press would constitute a serious threat to liberty.

Of those who complain about the behavior of journalists it is often the representatives of certain institutions who most strongly object to harassment by the press. The argument put is that some organizations, such as schools and hospitals, do not function effectively if there are frequent intrusions by outsiders who have little or no comprehension of how these institutions function or of their particular needs. What these spokesmen would like is for certain institutions to be regarded as closed communities into which the press should be admitted only if they receive permission. They seek laws specifically directed at making it difficult and hazardous for reporters to gain access through deception and trespass or to harass staff officers.

One reason why reporters so often offend the executive heads of large public or private institutions is that their role as newsgatherers often puts them in an antagonistic relationship. Editors expect reporters to gather newsworthy information concerning corruption, incompetence, or mismanagement, and it is to perform this function as well as to gather illustrative materials that they seek access to the files, personnel, and clients of major institutions. Not surprisingly, administrators and managers are not eager to accommodate, and they have ways of establishing a significant degree of control over information held by or about their own institutions. For example, they can appoint trained public relations officers to liaise with interested outsiders, conduct official tours, and censor all information put out. They can also discipline staff members who make embarrassing disclosures or offer opinions when they are not authorized to do so. Nevertheless, it is often difficult for a large organization to keep secrets, and persistent journalists may be able to penetrate by hanging about looking for leaks. There are usually employees who have a grudge or who feel that they have an obligation to make disclosures about newsworthy incidents. Furthermore, it is clear that reporters do often behave ruthlessly when they are out to get a story and may resort to bribery and even stealing. (The worst case of aggressive journalism I have heard of involved placing a bugging device in a hospital ward so that the conversation between an injured football star and his fiancee could be recorded. Another more typical case involved stealing information relating to the grades for course work achieved by members of college sports teams to use in a report about how sport was affecting academic achievement.)

So long as there are independent journalists, there will be an antagonistic relationship between the managers of most large socially significant organizations and the press. This is all to the good, even if the zeal of reporters to get stories does sometimes result in abuse. On balance, then, given the significant role which the press plays in exposing corruption and incompetence, it would not be wise to enact special legislation to protect the privacy of major institutions. Indeed, many aspects of life which presently escape public scrutiny should be more exposed to review, and a strong case can be made for framing laws to assure access to and protection for the investigating journalists rather than to establish greater secrecy.

It is worth noting that these issues have been raised in the context of a demand by journalists that they be afforded a right to keep their sources of information secret, as well as a special license giving them access to institutions not normally open to the public. I have already discussed the issue of the so-called "newsman's privilege" to keep confidence with an informant and will not say more about the problem here (see page 28 ff.). With regard to the matter of affording the press a special right of access, the issue has been joined most forcefully with regard to the debate about reporting events which have taken place within prisons. As usual in the United States, the Supreme Court has had a word to say about the constitutional status of this claim. The cases I have in mind involved disputes with authorities about whether reporters had a right (based on an appeal to the First Amendment) to interview specific prisoners whom they regarded as useful spokesmen, and whether they had a right to inspect and take pictures in the Santa Rita County jail in California in which an inmate had committed suicide (*Pell v. Procumier* and *Saxbe v. Washington Post*).[10]

The Supreme Court was not sympathetic to these demands. In an opinion for a narrow majority (four to three), Justice Burger claimed that the First Amendment guarantee of freedom to the press did not include any right to expect that others will be compelled to supply all the information that reporters may seek.

Burger's point is convincing. I would argue, however, that the cases in question should have been handled differently, in that the status of the prison rule preventing prisoners from obtaining reasonable access to journalists who wish to interview them could have been questioned. Unless we hold that citizens lose all their communication rights when they are committed to a prison, we must surely hold that those who are detained have a right to meet with journalists who choose to listen to them. Thus, although the prison rule which regulates access to prisoners cannot violate any First Amendment right of the press (in that they enjoy no special right of access), it surely violates the right of prisoners.

THE PROBLEM OF UNWANTED PUBLICITY

Thus far I have focused on the privacy interest individuals have in protecting a sphere which is free from intrusion. It has long been recognized that restraints must be placed on investigators, and most of us take it for granted that the law may legitimately prevent unauthorized invasions of our person and property. If we focus our attention on some of the other core elements of privacy we find that there is another serious conflict between the public interest in uninhibited discussion and the privacy interests of individuals. The kind of conflict I have in mind occurs when there is no intrusion of a private zone, nor even the passing of confidential information (which is a form of intrusion by way of deception); rather, what is objected to is the publication or broadcasting of information (or photographs) which cause embarrassment or harm by making public intimate facts or by placing the person in a false light.

I wish to consider, then, the set of problems which arise because of the power of the media to harm individuals simply by making certain facts about them public. Many of those who are worried about the threat to privacy which modern media present are concerned with this problem. Samuel D. Warren and Louis Brandeis, for example, in their famous *Harvard Law Review* article, were inspired by the former's sense of outrage at the reporting of a private party.[11] Although Warren's concerns about the Boston gossip columnists may seem somewhat over-sensitive to modern readers, the notion that there should be some protection against the publication of private facts remains alive. The Younger Committee summarizes the basic complaint:

> In publishing news and comment, they [the press] are said to have made known, mainly to satisfy idle curiosity facts which would otherwise be gener-

ally unknown about private misfortunes, calamities and other incidents, so aggravating the distress or embarrassment; or to have published with critical innuendo, stories about unusual but lawful private activities and behavior which are judged to be objectionable to current conventional opinion; and in all these situations to have identified directly or indirectly the individuals concerned. These practices, it is claimed in the critical evidence presented to us, can do grave damage to private individuals, out of all proportion to any general benefit derived from the dissemination of the news.[12]

It may be useful to distinguish different ways in which unsought publicity can cause harm to an individual. We may begin by looking at some of the complaints put before the British Committee. By far the biggest group of complainants objected to the publication of names or other means of identification (such as photographs and addresses) of people involved in the news. One difficulty about this relates to the social implications which may follow when the veil of anonymity is lifted. For example, publicity in a local paper reporting someone convicted of a minor offense such as drunkenness or petty theft in a supermarket may lead to ridicule, ostracism, or even loss of employment. In one case put to the committee, a report about a women's practice of witchcraft resulted in the invasion of and damage to her property by local hooligans. In another, a former schoolmaster complained that he had lost his position in a school because of publicity given to his conviction for a minor sexual offense. Often publicity is resented because it is embarrassing. For example, people complained that there was no need to identify donors of heart and other organ transplant cases. Another group of cases involved publicity which disrupted or made more difficult the performance of sensitive activities. For example, the West Sussex Council argued that the reunion of a foster child with its natural parents "is something which has to be done gently and quietly and privately" and complained that the behavior of the press entirely disregarded the feelings of the persons concerned through unnecessary publicity.

The response to these kinds of complaint in most democracies has not been substantial. In most democracies legislation has been enacted to curtail the activities of court reporters. The reasons why the reporting of trials has often seemed to be in need of regulating often go beyond the issue of privacy protection, however, involving other rights (such as the claims of an individual to a fair trial) as well as wider considerations of the public interest. For example, we serve the public interest if we encourage people to report crimes. To ensure this, however, we may need to protect the anonymity of witnesses so that they feel safe, and we may also need to protect their privacy. At the present moment these kinds of protections are usually secured by convention more than by legal right. However, we find that a person's interest in a fair trial is secured by placing restraints on the reporting of cases at the committal stage. In Australia anonymity is also offered to those involved in proceedings in the family and juvenile courts.[13]

In the United States where privacy has been afforded more protection than in other democracies, there is now a cause for action in cases when a plaintiff has been placed in a false light. Typical cases arise when editors decide to embellish stories in various ways. For example, an editor who used a photograph from his file (of a young girl who lay crying in the street after being hit by a car) to illustrate a story about how children cause accidents by darting into the street from between parked cars was held answerable. (However, "false light" cases are complicated by the fact that editors must be shown to have acted negligently before an action against them will succeed. Also, the plaintiff who is a "public figure" must show that the editor knew or had good reasons to suspect that the offending material would place him or her in a false light. Malice or negligence on the part of an editor is, however, easier to show in this kind of case than in most actions for defamation.) A privacy action in the United States may also succeed when a publication exceeds "tolerable levels of decency." However, it would seem to be the case that the protection afforded would reach only to communications that touch an inner core of intimacy. As Emerson puts the point in his summary statement of the law in this area:

> Descriptions or photographs of a woman in childbirth, of sexual intercourse, of similar personal and intimate details of one's life would receive . . . protection. Beyond this point, however, disclosure of embarrassing facts or fictionalizations would not be embraced by the legal system of privacy.[14]

We can see, then, that even in the United States it is no longer significant in practice to distinguish "what is in the public interest" from "what has public interest," and there is very little censorship to protect a person against unsought publicity of this kind.

I conclude from this review of the way that privacy dilemmas have actually been resolved that the Rawlsian liberal framework I outlined does offer solutions which are generally compatible with informed opinion. Given the fact that news reporters do not often use surreptitious and other intrusive surveillance methods, it is realistic to hold that individuals should enjoy a right not to be caught unawares. Also, my suggestion that individuals should not be afforded any fundamental right to control how they are presented to others (except when a publication touches their most intimate moments) is reflected in the protections afforded to the press in both the United States and the United Kingdom.

7

Free Speech versus The Public Interest in Regulating Offensive Speech

In pursuing the public interest, governments often regulate speakers so as to ensure that they do not cause a nuisance. The most usual context in which this occurs is when a speaker interferes with the legitimate activities of third persons. (Can we object if a library imposes a rule of silence in its Reading Room?) Speech can be a nuisance in a general way (for example, pamphlets which a speaker has distributed may come to cause a serious litter problem; advertising billboards may be displeasing aesthetically or constitute a traffic hazard; speakers may use resources needed for other purposes). However, it may be that the content of the speech itself causes the nuisance because it is offensive or provocative.

In my theoretical analysis, I indicated that when a government pursues some legitimate objective (preventing litter, preserving the peace, or ensuring that travellers can make use of the streets) in such a way that it has an indirect effect on someone's communication interests, an accommodation could be found if the regulations (a) fall short of a complete banning of speech, (b) do not discriminate on the basis of message content, (c) are reasonable (in the sense that there is no obvious less intrusive remedy available), and (d) are carefully framed so that their impact on the liberty to speak is kept to a minimum. What a government needs to be prevented from achieving is indirect censorship (that is, from so framing regulations that it imposes its own view about what should or should not be said).

The categories of expression which give rise to the most common forms of nuisance are those which impinge on parties who may not have consented to the exposure, or which involve forums or facilities which may be scarce between competing speakers or may be needed for other purposes. Advertisers often indulge in forms of speech of the former kind. And those who demonstrate in public places create both forms of nuisance, in that they confront the public with their message and use forums which may be needed for other purposes. Broadcasters also create a significant nuisance not only because government licensing has established the broadcasting spectrum as a scarce resource but because the switch mechanism on receivers does not ensure that only those who have chosen to listen or view a program are exposed to it.

In most cases when governments regulate speakers to minimize some indirect consequence of a form of communication, the issues are fairly straightforward. Although hard cases do arise, our difficulty in resolving them is usually one of judgment, for we may disagree about whether some consequence is serious enough to warrant regulation, about the kinds of regulation which are best suited to the goals of a policy, or about whether a proposed set of regulations will have an inhibiting effect. Philosophical analysis cannot contribute much to the resolution of conflicts of this kind.

Two categories of nuisance problem have given rise to considerable conceptual and theoretical difficulties, and the issues need to be looked at carefully. The first set of problems I have in mind occurs when the nuisance is not the physical aspect of a communication (noise, litter, the disruption of a facility) but arises because the message is provocative, insulting, indecent, or shocking. Many laws regulating speakers are directed at preventing them from indulging in communications which can have these kinds of effects. For example, the common law crime against the dissemination of blasphemous matter is best interpreted (whatever the original rationale) as protecting religious sensibilities, and laws proscribing the dissemination of indecent or obscene matter can also be interpreted as protecting sensibilities. A second set of problems occurs when the consequences of a communication is that it may indirectly bring about harm to others by influencing the attitudes of third persons. For example, the law in the United Kingdom relating to the communication of matter likely to stir up hatred against any racial group is an example of an attempt to regulate this form of nuisance.[1]

The reason why the problems mentioned in the last paragraph raise controversial theoretical issues is because liberal principles countenance restraining speakers only when their influence is achieved through the deliberate propagation of information known to be false or misleading, if they use subliminal methods or in situations when a reasoned public dialogue is not possible. It seems illiberal to censor speech if the purpose is to prevent a speaker from influencing someone else by means of emotional appeal, reasoned argument or by conveying genuine beliefs about matters of fact.[2] Also, liberals do not normally count the harm of offense as a serious interest which can justify imposing restraints on the behavior of others. As for provocation and incitement, a liberal must allow for this if his commitment to freedom is to be meaningful, for a speaker may incite someone merely by holding opinions which the latter detests or finds threatening. In any event, the liberal way of responding to social disruption is to deal with those who resort to physical means of settling disputes rather than to inhibit speakers even when the former have been provoked by the latter.

Nevertheless, censorship of this kind is often imposed and the arguments for and against such programs need to be carefully reviewed. I shall do this by considering the case which has been made out for censoring offensive speech.

LIBERAL THEORY AND THE OFFENSE PROBLEM

A liberal approach to the problem of offensive speech was worked out by J. S. Mill in *On Liberty*, and his way of resolving the competing claims is still relied upon by most liberals. His judgment is reflected in the following passage:

> . . . there are many acts which, being directly injurious only to the agents themselves, ought not to be legally interdicted, but which, if done publicly, are a violation of good manners, and coming thus within the category of offense against others, may rightfully be prohibited. Of this kind are offenses against decency; on which it is unnecessary to dwell, the rather as they are only connected indirectly with our subject, the objection to publicity being equally strong in the case of many actions not in themselves condemnable, nor supposed to be so.[3]

What Mill has in mind in this passage seems clear enough: he is surely referring to practices such as the wearing of clothes or the requirement that people refrain from public defecation and love-making, which are insisted upon more or less universally, without discriminating between actors on any moral basis. Thus, it makes no difference whether one's sexual relations are socially approved and sanctified by marriage or whether they are homosexual, or involve adultery or prostitution, the requirement that they be restrained within the private realm remains the same.

Mill's way of resolving the issue of offense by way of his public/private distinction accommodates the conflicting interests in a way that most of us find (intuitively) acceptable. On the one hand we have a fundamental political right and, on the other, is the fact that some person in exercising that right causes a nuisance to others by offending their sensibilities. May a government confine such activity to the private realm? Surely, says Mill, for the point of the activity is not lost and the social purpose (in protecting the sensibilities of others) is a serious one.

Unfortunately, although the solution to the problem seems to be a promising one at first sight, it seems unavailable to those who (like Mill) restrict themselves to purely utilitarian arguments, for what the latter fail to make clear is why the harm of offense can only be regarded as serious when the behavior giving rise to it takes place in public. Suppose people were to object to an act taking place at all, even in private. The offense caused by a form of behavior (say, the eating of pork in a Muslim community) may be no less when it takes place in private. Also, some kinds of offensive behavior or expression (for example, the wearing of one's hair in a particular style) which cannot be confined in the private realm may nevertheless cause significant offense. Thus, if a young man was to grow his hair long he could offend a great many people and in some communities a strong utilitarian argument could be put for insisting that he have it cut to a less offensive length. Mill wishes to hold that so long as the point of the activity (the wearing of long hair) would be lost if it were not public, regulations to protect the sensibilities of others would not be justifiable. But it is not easy to see how this conclusion can be reached using purely utilitarian arguments.

Mill's dilemma here, and the ambiguity of his position which it gives rise to, has been the subject of sustained criticism. For example, Lord Devlin (In his Maccabaean lecture[4]) tells us that if offensive behavior is classified as self-regarding (as causing no serious harm to others), Mill's notion that the only legitimate justification a government can have for regulating the behavior of an individual is to prevent harm to others commits us to an extreme libertarian position which not many people would endorse. In the light of this principle (given that "offense" is not to count as a serious harm), it would not be legitimate for governments to forbid acts such as incest, bestiality, and sodomy which many people find it difficult to tolerate even when these take place in private; nor could it prevent a private performance of such acts in front of a willing audience. On the other hand, Devlin tells us that if offensive behavior is regarded as "harmful" (and it is hard to see why it should not be), Mill's liberal position would be broken-backed, for it would allow the conclusion that those with the most deeply felt prejudices would simply require the rest of us to conform to their standards. We would offend them if we practiced our nonconformity in private, and we would outrage them if we performed what they regard as our wicked acts in front of them.

Mill does not provide much response to this challenge, but his position has been championed by H. L. A. Hart in a famous exchange with Devlin and by Joel Feinberg in an influential paper.[5] Let me consider the former's analysis first.

Hart's way of defending Mill involves shifting the debate away from the issue of whether offensive behavior is really harmful, by interpreting the "harm principle" as proscribing moral paternalism (the imposition by a government of a particular public conception of the good). In this regard, he claims that Mill's public/private distinction can be read as reflecting the claim that it is possible to distinguish the regulation of indecency as a form of social nuisance from attempts by governments to impose standards of behavior on others. Thus, in response to Devlin, Hart argues that various provisions in the criminal law regulating offensive behavior (which Devlin had claimed that most of us would be reluctant to jettison, as would be required by the application of Mill's principle so long as "offense" was not to count as a harm) can be explained on grounds which have nothing to do with the morality of the acts concerned. His strategy is to counter Devlin's claim that the law is shot through with regulations which enforce moral standards which most of us nevertheless approve of, by claiming that the legitimation of a government's imposition of standards of decency raises problems quite distinct from those which arise when a government attempts to impose a public morality by way of the criminal law.

Hart takes as his case for study the law relating to bigamy and asks whether those who wish to retain the law against bigamy, on the grounds that it protects a deeply felt religious feeling from offense by a public act desecrating the ceremony, would be inconsistent if they also denied that the law may be used to punish immorality as such.

Bigamy, as Hart ably shows, is an excellent example for illustrating the distinction between the immorality of a practice and its aspect as a public nuisance. This is because many countries which punish bigamy allow open cohabitation between parties who have been previously married to other spouses and are not free to go through a marriage ceremony. As Hart points out, this fact can be most plausibly explained by saying that "the law interferes in order to protect religious sensibilities from outrage by a public act." He argues that the bigamist is punished "neither as irreligious nor as immoral but as a nuisance." Hart does not, of course, defend the law against bigamy; he merely illustrates the kinds of argument he would find relevant. In this regard, he suggests that we may calculate the utility of various policy options, taking into account the moral prejudices and deeply felt beliefs of people as one factor which may be brought into the balance. It is for this reason that he allows that:

> opponents of the law (against bigamy) may plausibly urge, in an age of waning faith, that the religious sentiments likely to be offended by the public celebration of the bigamous marriage are no longer very widespread or very deep and it is enough that such marriages are held legally invalid.[6]

Hart imposes one significant qualification which must be noted: he tells us that the process of neutral calculation can legitimately take place only within certain definite limits, for otherwise factual claims about prejudice and feelings of disgust would be decisive in any argument. He is very clear that recognition of individual liberty as a value involves, as a minimum, acceptance of the principle that the individual may do what he wants, even when others are distressed when they learn what it is that he does—unless, of course, there are other good grounds for forbidding it.[7]

This is why the distinction between public and private realms is so important: the distress we feel when exposed to what we regard as indecent behavior, no matter how well-founded, is no justification for interference which violates personal liberty, although it may sometimes justify driving the offensive behavior off the streets. Hart's point is that this kind of distress may never provide a pretext for preventing others from enjoying a particular activity, but this does not happen when we insist that it be conducted in private.

How successful is this response to Devlin? From a utilitarian point of view, we can concede that regulations which require that certain kinds of behavior be relegated to the private realm do not impose heavy burdens on those who wish to practice them. No one would normally want to claim that the point of engaging in a sexual act with someone would be seriously frustrated by a law which makes public copulation an offense. Similarly, the enjoyment people derive from the viewing of pornographic materials is not seriously frustrated by laws which impose a ban on public displays of such materials (although the interests of those who are commercially involved in distributing them would be). Thus, in balancing the interests of a speaker who wishes to communicate pornographic materials, the interest of an audience eager to receive such material, and the interests of a significant third group who have a strong desire not to be exposed to material of this kind, we must allow (ignoring for the purposes of this example the commercial interests of the distributor) that relegation to the private sphere may be a useful response.

This solution may not represent an even-handed balancing of the competing interests, however, for those who find the materials offensive may be by far the majority, and their feelings of outrage may not be assuaged by having their own sensibilities protected. They may strongly desire to have the material banned so that no one may view it. Why should the feelings of those who are so moved by the very thought that certain communications are sinful, disgusting, or degrading be ignored in the balancing process? If we reflect on this issue, we see that neither Hart nor Mill provide an adequate response to Devlin's *reductio ad absurdum* argument that the public/private distinction is broken-backed because the harm of offense (the general nuisance which governments seek to protect the public against) may result from activities which take place in private.

It is not Hart or Mill's conception of liberty which is under challenge. Devlin's point is the logical one that the harm people experience when they are exposed to public displays depicting or exhibiting behavior which they find offensive is no different from the harm they experience from the mere knowledge that such behavior is taking place in private. What he challenges, then, is Mill's utilitarian argument. His claim is that if utilitarian reasons can be found for regulating public displays, then these same reasons should be decisive in justifying the censoring of private conduct that is offensive to the sensibilities of a clear majority.

Let us now turn to review Joel Feinberg's attempt to save Mill from Devlin's criticisms.[8] In his "Harmless Immoralities and Offensive Nuisances," Feinberg argues that it is possible to consistently hold (1) that a government may sometimes treat offense as a sufficiently serious harm to warrant the regulation of the activity causing the offense; and (2) that a government may never legitimately enforce a morality as such. He concedes, however, that the two principles (which combine Devlin's approach, exemplified in (1), with Hart's proscription of moral paternalism) appear to contradict one another, for very often what causes us to take offense are forms of behavior we regard as immoral (for example, some people are offended by the knowledge that a medical clinic is used by those seeking abortions, others when they learn that their favorite bar is a meeting place for homosexuals). Thus, Feinberg accepts that the onus is on him to show how his principles can be reconciled.

The problems he confronts in achieving this goal are complex, for what we need is an account of his offense principle (1) that allows us to apply it in a way which does not entail the enforcement of public standards or the protection of popular prejudices about the way others should behave. Thus, we need a set of criteria for distinguishing when someone's taking offense constitutes a sufficiently serious harm to warrant a government's interference to protect his or her sensibilities and some way of determining whether the harm in question is undeserved (the result of irrational prejudice, for example). Moreover, the criteria have to be morally neutral if they are to be compatible with Feinberg's second liberal principle proscribing moral paternalism. Further, whether or not a case of offense is serious must not be allowed to determine whether it is also deserving.

In response to these dilemmas, Feinberg offers two morally neutral filtering principles. The first of these is the standard of universality, that the reaction of taking offense must be one that can "reasonably be expected from almost any person chosen at random, taking the nation as a whole"; and the second is the standard of reasonable avoidability, that "no one has a right to protection from the state against offensive experiences if he can easily and effectively avoid these experiences with no unreasonable effort or inconvenience." Taken together, these principles show us that Feinberg's position is very similar to that of Hart in that he thinks it important to comprehend the regulation of offense as a form of public nuisance. It is clear, however, that Feinberg intends to face more squarely the problem of showing why some forms of offense may count as harmful for the purposes of a utilitarian calculation whereas others may not.

Unfortunately, Feinberg's principles also illustrate how intractable this problem is, for it is clear that various forms of offense which he clearly would like to ignore—as undeserving—would have to be counted as harms unless further considerations are brought into play. An example he provides of an interracial couple holding hands in a community where many would take offense illustrates this: while Feinberg's claim that his standard of universality filters this case is plausible if we suppose that the community is Jackson, Mississippi, because a very large number of Americans would not take offense in the way that the whites of Jackson are likely to, it would not be if we were assessing the propriety of a South African Airway's rule which required interracial couples to sit at the rear of its planes (supposing that it had adopted such a rule). So long as the airway officials responsible for such a rule can plausibly argue that almost any member of the community of likely passengers would take offense if asked to sit next to the couple, they would surely establish their claim that the offense is a serious nuisance. In any event, they would have shown that their regulation falls within Feinberg's standard. Yet it is clear that Feinberg would be unhappy about this result, and he certainly anticipates problems of this kind, for he adds a qualification to allow for exceptional cases when offense is caused through racial and other prejudices. Thus, he tells us that we may allow for exceptions to his universal standard so long as we can show (a) that the persons taking offense are being subjected to the "flaunting of abusive, mocking, insulting behavior of a sort bound to upset, alarm, anger, or irritate those it insults"; provided that (b) the offense is not the result of an abnormal susceptibility. Under these provisions, we could accuse the South African Airway's management of insulting behavior. However, even allowing that the offense taken by the interracial couple when confronted by a rule which requires them to be segregated at the back of the plane may now be taken into account, it is not clear that we would be able to show why the South Africans would not still insist on their segregation rule. What Feinberg fails to demonstrate is that when we balance the hurt to the interracial couple's feelings against the harm suffered by the racists (who would take offense at having to share facilities), the balance favors protecting the couple. Yet a balancing of this kind will be involved in all such cases, and it is not clear why the balance should favor the victims rather than those who are prejudiced.

Even allowing that Feinberg's principles and his ad hoc adjustments enable us to deal with most cases in a way that seems reasonably congruent with our basic intuitions, there are still some hard cases which would be impossible for anyone using his framework to accommodate. For example, most Australians do not take offense when Aboriginal sacred sites are violated by tourists, mining companies, or anthropologists, yet many would want to see the sensibilities of these traditional people protected. Feinberg cannot argue in accommodating this case (supposing that he would also like to see Aboriginal people protected) that they are targeted deliberately for special insult or derision, for the people who violate their sensibilities may not even be aware of the harm they are causing. Yet, once the problem is pointed out, almost everyone recognizes that the harm in question is serious. If Feinberg is to allow for protection even though this case does not fall under his universal standard or any of the other ad hoc exceptions he has allowed for, he must surely face the consequence that not all behavior which causes a serious harm of this kind can be effectively proscribed or ought to be. But how is he to distinguish this case from others which seem analogous yet intuitively less deserving (for example, conscientious advocates of animal rights who are deeply offended at the sight of slaughterhouses). The problem which Feinberg faces, here, in seeking neutral principles which will enable us to determine why some offense is to be regarded as a legitimate ground for regulatory actions, whereas other cases are deemed idiosyncratic or not serious, are intractible so long as we are debarred from making moral judgments (for example, that racist responses are unacceptable and should be discouraged rather than protected).[9]

A better way of responding to the nuisance when speech causes offense is to allow that Devlin is correct to hold that the problem is a serious one for anyone defending Mill's harm principle—supposing that they wish to defend a utilitarian position which is also liberal. What we need is a fresh approach.

If we embrace a deontological ethical framework of the kind I advocate, the awkward balancing (of prejudice versus liberty) which Feinberg, Hart, and Mill all find themselves confronted with can be avoided. All we need, in challenging moral paternalism, are arguments which can justify the liberties in question as a right (for example, the right to view or hear what one chooses, to engage with other consenting adults in sexual acts that others may disapprove of, and so on). Mill's arguments in *On Liberty* address this task but are inconclusive. Other arguments are readily available, however; for example, my own commitment to the principle that each person's choices as to the nature of the good life be afforded equal respect itself constitutes a rejection of moral paternalism. From this perspective, the private/public distinction is introduced not to justify our claim to the liberties in question (to view or hear what we choose or to engage with other consenting adults in sexual acts which others may disapprove of) but to accommodate attempts by governments to minimize the nuisance that may result from the exercise of these liberties.

There will, of course, be cases when no compromise is possible and when this is so, the public must simply endure the offense. For example, some people may find the advocacy of homosexuality offensive but, in terms of the principles I have articulated, this is not a harm from which they can be protected in a democracy. All that a government may do in this kind of case is ensure that the manner in which a communication is disseminated is of a kind that meets standards of taste. Thus, the slogan "Gay is Beautiful" on a public poster will need to be given the same protection as, say, "Make Love Not War" or "Jesus Saves" even though it is clear that it will cause more offense. The governing consideration must be that the censorship of an expression or a form of behavior should not be such as to make it impossible for a speaker to make a point or enjoy a liberty. Also, any restraint must be applied in neutral manner. Thus, if the "Gay is Beautiful" poster is censored on the grounds that it depicts nude models in a suggestive way, all other posters will necessarily have to meet this same standard of decency.

Usually in cases involving indecent behavior the most readily available compromise (between the public interest in avoiding offense and the claims of an individual to the enjoyment of a fundamental liberty) is a requirement that the offensive form of behavior be restricted to the private realm. Luckily this remedy is easily applied to the case of offensive speech, as many communications are clearly private in that the reader or viewer must take the initiative to gain exposure to it. Video cassettes, books, records, and magazines readily fit into this category and, even though they may be publicly available in shops and libraries, they should be regarded as essentially private. Regulations directed at eliminating possible offense should not, then, be directed at this material.

As for communications which address the public at large, the problem of finding a compromise is usually more difficult, but some regulations may be justified so long as our right to free expression is not violated: First, communications conveyed in an offensive manner but which can be restricted to the private realm without compromising the point of the expression may be so restricted. Thus, a bookseller would have no grounds for complaint if he were required not to confront the public with offensive material to drum up business, and similar constraints could legitimately be imposed on those who advertise violent or obscene films and other potentially offensive materials. Second, in cases where the offensive material cannot be restricted without unacceptable costs, a government can nevertheless insist that a warning be given (as is typically required of film distributors). Thus, in regulating broadcasting in the public interest, it would be reasonable for an authority to insist that stations announce in general terms what their policy is regarding potentially offensive material. It may even be necessary, as a way of protecting the public, to impose standards on those stations which broadcast to a very large general audience.[10] When this limited form of censorship is imposed to prevent people from being confronted by offensive materials, some stations would still remain at liberty to broadcast what they like so long as warning is given and a specific category of viewer (excluding children) is targeted. Finally, some forms of communication are so intrusive that a government would be justified in regulating them. For example, it would be reasonable for a government to insist that advertising should not be offensive. Outright censorship of this kind would, however, only be legitimate when it does not prevent a speaker from making his or her point; it ought not to represent such a severe restraint that it makes the expression of an opinion impossible.

These principles reflect Justice Black's recommendations which I articulated at the beginning of the chapter: that the regulation of speech may be legitimate so long as it does not involve discrimination on the basis of message content, is not an unnecessary burden, or does not have the effect of frustrating a speaker completely. I now turn to test this framework by considering some further problem cases, when the accommodation of interests cannot be easily secured by delineating a private realm.

DEALING WITH OFFENSIVE SPEECH IN THE CONTEXT OF DEMONSTRATIONS

The problem with offensive speech is that it certainly causes harm. Thus functionalists and utilitarians have difficulty accommodating such speech under a free speech principle, and they usually allow for a considerable flexibility, allowing pure balancing to take place so that the nuisance to those who are offended can be adequately dealt with. The dilemmas which arise because of the nuisance caused through political demonstrations provide a suitable test for the case for banning some assemblies and marches because they are likely to cause significant offense. This case is often a strong one. Yet, as liberals, most of us wish to hold that such censorship is illegitimate. I shall argue that the absolutist approach advocated by deontological liberals offers the best framework for accommodating this intuition and the competing interests in this area.

People seem to have a need to express their commitments, and they like to share with others in doing so. This makes an assembly or a march a special and important event. Such occasions can be useful to those who wish to reaffirm conventional opinion and, of course, they are of vital concern to radicals and minority groups who would otherwise not be able to communicate effectively either to their followers or to the wider public. Also, demonstrating seems to have a cathartic effect on participants, providing psychological relief to those who feel that something must be done about a problem and evoking feelings of solidarity and mutual support.

Mass demonstrations also serve as a warning device giving governments time to react by anticipating a possible crisis.

Although public assemblies are recognized as having a useful democratic role, they place a significant burden on society. In the first place, wherever large crowds assemble a public nuisance is created. This is because there is usually disruption of traffic flow, an increase in rubbish and litter, and often a need for considerable police resources to maintain order and to prevent crime. More importantly, what can distinguish political assemblies from other crowds (such as those attending sporting, religious, or musical functions) is that they are sometimes deliberately disruptive; they may also be provocative, providing an occasion for conflict when rival groups come into contact. Moreover, the communicative and psychological functions of an assembly are closely associated with the threat it provides to law and order, for there is often little dynamic to public protest if the expression of feelings is so restrained that the consequent emotional responses are not potentially disruptive. Indeed, some of the advantages listed as flowing from public assembly would not be likely were it not also the case that this kind of enterprise often brings social conflicts to the surface, often in dramatic ways. (I have in mind here advantages such as those which flow from the interest taken by journalists, the cathartic release of tensions, and the realization on the part of those in authority that something has to be done about an issue.) An effective legal right of assembly, then, will require a great deal of tolerance and will often strain social consensus, especially when the groups who are active are unpopular.

There is, of course, no doubt that citizens have a democratic right to assemble and to demonstrate. So long as we concede a right to speak we must acknowledge that physically to present oneself standing for some point of view is an essential collorary right. Any government which forbade assemblies or marches would clearly violate the democratic commitment. The problem we face, then, in reviewing public policy relating to the use of assembly rights, is to find a satisfactory accommodation between our social commitment to afford a right to assemble and to march and the legitimate efforts governments often make to minimize the various nuisances which inevitably occur whenever large crowds gather or intensely felt emotions are publicly expressed.

Those who are against affording citizens a right to demonstrate on the grounds that this will at the same time create an atmosphere in which civil disobedience, disruption, and disorder will follow, correctly perceive the connections here. What they do not see is that we have an obligation in a democracy to face these risks. Also, in the long run, there are likely to be less violence and more possibilities for compromise and response through a policy of tolerance than would be the case if public expression is severely restricted. It is also significant that many of the nuisances which society must face when citizens demonstrate arise simply because large numbers of people gather together. All crowds are potentially disruptive, to some extent at least, and they inevitably litter. Further, there is always danger that a crowd will turn to violence when emotions are heightened, as is the case at sporting events, religious and political gatherings, and some concerts. If we are willing to allow religious, musical, and sporting assemblies, we should surely be prepared to tolerate crowds who gather for political reasons. In any event, the regulation of a crowd by an authority is a general problem, and the principles we articulate to allow for this will have a wide application.

Clearly the streets and other public places in which crowds are inclined to assemble are forums of a peculiar kind, for they have a use besides that of providing a space for demonstrations. It is, therefore, often possible for authorities to argue, plausibly, that regulation of the use of this public facility must be resorted to if competing claimants are to be fairly accommodated. Administrative controls provide authorities with fair warning of the likelihood that a crowd will be assembled, thus facilitating their capacity to have the necessary personnel for supervision. They also enable those in authority to impose reasonable restrictions as to the time and place of prospective assemblies. The necessity for this kind of regulation often arises because of the fact that where two or more groups of people wish to assemble at the same time and the same place, some arrangements must necessarily be made so that they do not come into conflict.

The problem is to find a way of preventing administrative controls, which taken in themselves may not be objectionable, from being used as a form of censorship. That this is a real possibility has been demonstrated time and again for, in practice, when authorities wish to intimidate or otherwise harass demonstrators, they have been able to rely on a wide range of considerations to provide a justification. All of the following have been important: protecting the public from offense, allocating a scarce resource between different claimants who wish to use the same facility, preventing crime, protecting some legitimate proceeding, and maintaining order.

In most assembly cases what is meant by offensive behavior is the use of foul language which it is reasonable to suppose will produce strong emotional reactions in others. The standard here is often vague. This is because the context in which words are used is clearly relevant in establishing the nature of the speech act (an expletive uttered in exasperation has a very different meaning and is usually regarded as less offensive than when the same word is used to insult others). It is also significant that in most instances where demonstrators cause offense, the persons abused are members of the police force or other public officials.

In terms of our general analysis of the offense problem, it would seem that the legitimacy of a government's regulation of a speaker will depend on whether his speech does shock an unwilling audience, discounted by an assessment of how easy it may be to avoid (switching the radio off, walking away from a demonstration). In terms of this criterion, it would be conceded that offensive speech, insofar as it takes place in a demonstration, would not usually represent a serious injury to anyone. Most people in these modern times have heard foul language and are not greatly shocked by exposure even though they may disapprove. The problem is compounded, however, when the offensive speech is used as a form of abuse. A leading case in the United States, *Chaplinsky v. New Hampshire,* illustrates the point.[11] Here the defendant, after he had already been taken into custody, on confronting the city marshal said to him: "you are a God damned racketeer . . . a damned Fascist and the whole government of Rochester are Fascists or agents of Fascists." The Supreme Court in this case concluded that Chaplinsky could be convicted under a statute which made it an offense to address others in a way which is "offensive, derisive or annoying." What bothered the Court in this case was not so much that Chaplinsky's words were offensive but that they constituted an insult directed at a specific person. (This aspect of *Chaplinsky v. New Hampshire* has remained good law in the United States, and it is clear that "those personally abusive epithets which, when addressed to the ordinary citizen, are, as a matter of common knowledge, inherently likely to provoke violent reaction" are regarded by United States courts as a category of unprotected speech.)[12]

Abusive insults are legitimately proscribed in a democracy when they are addressed to private individuals in public. The reasons why this is so are twofold: First, as the legal scholar Thomas Emerson has correctly noted, abuse often crosses the line that can be reasonably drawn between speech and action because it can constitute a kind of challenge. As such, it forms no part of any useful dialogue, for it carries an illocutionary force which distinguishes it from a simple statement of fact or evaluation. Thus, we cannot translate "I feel abused, angry and hurt by what you have done" by "You fascist pig," even if the same emotions are conveyed. A second reason why it may be legitimate for a government to proscribe personal insults is that our dignity is directly called into question if we are singled out for personal abuse especially in public. It is, however, more questionable whether those who direct insults at public officials acting in their capacity as authorities responsible for dealing with the public should be vulnerable to criminal prosecution. Here we can presume that officials will not usually take the abuse personally and it is clearly the case that those who heap insults upon them have a pressing need to indulge in this form of expression. Indeed, unless some protection is allowed for this kind of speech, many sections of society, particularly poorer groups who feel most intensely about administrative actions and who may be less refined in manner than those who have more privileges, will be very vulnerable to harassment when they assemble to demonstrate, for they will inevitably direct abuse at police and others who may be the focus of their anger.

The United States Supreme Court has, for the most part, recognized this and has been wary of upholding convictions when demonstrators have not directly threatened or insulted private persons. Thus, citizens in the United States enjoy constitutional protection in most circumstances when they employ foul language in a public place.[13] This contrasts with the practice in the United Kingdom, where demonstraters are vulnerable under many statutes which proscribe offensive speech.[14]

A problem occurs, of course, when speech which is not directed at any specific individual nevertheless has an effect on an audience that is provocative. Ought the speaker to be held to account for the effect of his or her words in circumstances when such an effect could have been predicted as a very likely outcome, given the kind of things said?

This question introduces the complexity of a hostile and potentially violent audience into our discussion, and I shall deal with the issues this raises shortly. At this stage, my focus is with the preliminary prophylactic maneuver often resorted to by concerned governments of banning forms of speech which may be provocative because offensive to sections of a community. Of course, in terms of my analysis of the significance of liberty, a government may never censor speech simply because other citizens do not appreciate the ideas which are communicated. Every citizen has a fundamental right to speak even if what he intends or is likely to say will arouse the hostility of others. However, it may be a less significant violation of liberty if a government resorts to a more specific ban by focusing on offensive insults and even libels directed at particular groups. The British Race Relations Act of 1976 provides a model of such a statute. Section 6 (1) provides that

> A person shall be guilty of an offense under this Section if, with intent to show up hatred against any section of the public of Great Britain distinguished by colour, race, ethnic or national origins: (a) he publishes or distributes written matter which is threatening, abusive or insulting; or (b) he uses in any public place or at any public meeting words which are threatening, abusive or insulting, being matter or words likely to stir up hatred against that section on grounds of colour, race, or ethnic or national origins.

Clearly, this kind of statute is directed at the kind of speech that is thoroughly disapproved of by most people. However, there are reasons for distinguishing group insults and abuse from those directed at individual persons who are singled out. First, the amount of speech that will be vulnerable under such a statute will be substantial. Also, unlike personal insults, which may be distinguished as making a very small contribution, if any, to political discussion, attitudes and emotions directed at specific groups are significant and important and the expression of these affects are consequently a matter to take some notice of. Further, it is much more difficult to distinguish abuse from opinion when the communication is directed at a group, for in such cases an insult is usually paraded in the form of a derogatory assertion and is rarely delivered by way of a string of simple expletives. If I provocatively assert "A woman's place is either in the home or on her back," I am insulting half the human race by implying that they are fit only for nurturing and are useful as sex objects. But were this opinion put forward in a carefully reasoned and serious way, it would have to be protected in the light of any liberal conception of liberty. Yet it is the conservative Catholic view of women which does far more damage to them as a group than the heated words of a few poorly educated male chauvinists whose intensity of expression lacks caution. Moreover, the latter's strongly held emotions are often the product of the very ideas disseminated by the more careful ideologue, and it is quite unfair to punish him and not the former. Finally, it is worth noting that groups who are singled out for abuse often retaliate with insults, so a law proscribing offensive sexist or racist speech can have the effect that the position of the very groups which such a law would presumably protect becomes more precarious. It is ironic that one of the first people convicted under the British Race Relations Act was a Black leader abusing the white community.[15]

Speech may provoke not only through insult or because foul language is used. Sometimes the ideas expressed themselves are offensive to those to whom they are addressed. Moreover, speakers may know that this is so and yet persist in that expression. That this can give rise to serious problems is illustrated very dramatically by the dilemma faced by authorities in the United Kingdom with regard to the activities of the National Socialists (a racist organization modelled on the Nazi movement). Many local authorities have refused to provide facilities such as halls to this organization, and some have refused to issue permits to allow them to march. One reason for this is, of course, that most people detest what the National Socialists stand for. However, a more pressing consideration has been that they have provoked extremely hostile reactions amongst the Black communities in the United Kingdom, as well as from some of the more militant left-wing organizations such as the International Socialists, the International Marxist Group, the Communist Party of England (Marxist-Leninist) and others, leading to violent confrontations.[16]

The issue raised by this case is known as the problem of the "hostile audience," and it occurs wherever a group's activities are so disliked by some sections of a community that they are no longer prepared to be tolerant of its right to expression. Similar problems occur, however, when militant but minority sections of a crowd resort to violence. In these cases, the rights of a majority who wish to protest peacefully are placed in jeopardy by those intent on violence. The central issue, then, is whether the right of one group of citizens to demonstrate peacefully should be suspended when, through no fault of theirs, the demonstration becomes associated with violent disorder.

One answer to this question has been provided by the United States Supreme Court in their judgment in the case *Milk Wagon Drivers Local 753 v. Meadowmoor Dairies*.[17] The problem here involved a dispute between a trade union, representing the milk wagon drivers who delivered milk on a door-to-door basis to customers, and certain dairies who were distributing milk through local shops using independent contractors to make the delivery. The union decided to organize pickets outside the stores which were involved, and this activity, although itself peaceful, was associated with serious acts of violence on the part of unknown agents directed against the dairies, the transport contractors, and the stores. The Supreme Court agreed, by a six to three majority, to uphold an injunction prohibiting further picketing to prevent a possible breach of the peace (not on the part of those who were picketing, but by others). It reasoned in this case that the picketing, although itself peaceful, was so "enmeshed with contemporaneously violent conduct" that it could be legitimately proscribed.

This answer effectively denies peaceful citizens the right to demonstrate if others express their intensely felt feelings more aggressively. On the face of it, this would seem a silly result for, as I have noted, demonstrating is a form of action which may have a cathartic effect. Also, the outrage felt by angry citizens is likely to be exacerbated by denying them a right to demonstrate peacefully, thus causing many of them to join the already violent minority. Another reason why a policy of banning marches may not help to achieve the objective of establishing order is that it may itself become a focus for confrontation as groups of citizens defy the order, forcing the police to respond by making mass arrests or by forcefully dispersing the demonstrators. A strong utilitarian case can be made, then, for not denying angry and outraged citizens a right to assemble peacefully. Of course, in the circumstances of the Meadowmoor Dairies case, a contrary judgment was made by those who sought the injunction to prevent the trade union from picketing. But, when asked to uphold the injunction, the Supreme Court should have had some thought for the precedent it set at that time. Luckily, since then, it has shifted away from its judgment in the Meadowmoor Dairies case, and it is more likely now to uphold the claimed right of citizens to demonstrate peacefully, even when some fraction of those who support a common cause have turned to violence.[18]

The importance of distinguishing peaceful from violent demonstrators is highlighted by the well-documented events in the United Kingdom during disorders which occurred in Red Lion Square, London, in 1974.[19]

In the circumstances there, the police had the very difficult task of keeping two hostile groups apart. Past experience had shown that there was likely to be violence if they came into contact; yet, despite this, both were granted permission to demonstrate in the square. The police saw their duty to maintain order as requiring them to ensure that the hostile assemblies kept to different corners of the square so that there could be no provocative physical contact between them. Accordingly, they ordered one group of demonstrators to turn right as they entered into the square from a side street (Old North Street), and the column of marchers peacefully obeyed the request. Or, most of them did. Justice Scarman in his Report into the incident describes what happened:

> Perhaps as many as 500 marchers had followed the directions . . . turning right into the square. A gap opened up between the rear of those 500 and those following the banner of the IMG [International Marxist Group]. I have no doubt that this gap was deliberately created by the IMG slowing its pace a little. The gap having appeared, the IMG banner (mounted on three poles carried by demonstrators spread across the width of the roadway) was removed to the side, leaving a front line of determined-looking men with their arms linked. Disregarding the direction taken by the march ahead of them they led a charge round the corner into the police cordon. Thus began what Mr. Hawser (leading counsel for the Inquiry) in his final speech accurately described as a "deliberate and sustained attack" on the police cordon. It was unexpected, unprovoked, and viciously violent. It was the beginning of the afternoon's violence in the course of which one young man sustained a fatal injury, and an unknown number of demonstrators and 46 policemen were injured.[20]

The police proceeded to clear the short side street (Old North Street) of marchers but they allowed those who had entered the Red Lion Square to remain peacefully assembled in the corner designated to them. Those who brought up the rear of the march were able to join this group by entering the square from another road. The police wisely decided to tolerate all those who remained peaceful and calm. The reason for this may well have been that they had their hands full coping with the others, but, if so, this merely illustrates the point that had they moved to disperse the peaceful crowd they may well have provoked more of the demonstrators to resort to violence.

In the Red Lion Square disorders, as in the Meadowmoor Dairies case, the law-abiding demonstrators and those who used violent means were in sympathy on the issues. In other cases this has not been so, for the threat to the peace has come from hostile audiences. Nevertheless, the principle at issue is the same for, in these kinds of cases, we must judge whether peaceful citizens exercising their right to demonstrate may have that right restrained because some authority has judged that others will be provoked into breaking the peace. It makes no difference here, except perhaps to our emotional response, whether the violence is committed by those who support the case of the demonstrators or by those who are opposed.

It is interesting to observe that although there seems no principled reason for this, the United States Supreme Court is more sympathetic to demonstrators where their right is placed in jeopardy by those who are hostile, and in most of its decisions subsequent to *Milk Wagon Drivers Local 753 v. Meadowmoors Dairies,* that judgment is qualified. The response of the Court to these problems produces no clear doctrine as to the way in which central issues are to be resolved, however, and there are disagreements about how to deal with particular cases.[21] The majority view allows for police or government interference to preserve the peace when the judgment of the officials concerned seems to be well-founded (as was claimed in the Meadowmoor Dairies case), but it reserves a right for the court to overrule an authority when the evidence brought forward to show that a particular demonstration is a danger is insubstantial. This ambivalence is reflected in somewhat contradictory findings. In *Feiner v. New York* the Court upheld a conviction for disorderly conduct after a police officer had arrested Irving Feiner because he had mounted a soapbox to address a mixed audience in a way which was extremely provocative to the whites in his audience and had refused all requests by a police officer that he desist. The officer who arrested Feiner also believed that a breakdown of order was imminent. In *Edwards v. South Carolina,* however, the Court ruled that action taken by the police to disperse a crowd of students constituted an infringement of their constitutionally protected right to freedom of speech, free assembly, and freedom to petition for redress of grievances.[22] It, consequently, reversed their conviction for the common law offense of breach of the peace with which they were charged after failing to disperse when instructed to do so. In practice, even when "hostile audience" situations have been difficult to manage, the Court has been more inclined to support demonstators than to uphold police who order them to disperse. It clearly believes that peaceful demonstrators must be protected even when the cost is high. For example, in one case, an orderly but small group marching against segregation in public schools was confronted by a large hostile audience, jeering, turning sprinklers upon them, and even pelting them with eggs and rocks. The police dealt with the situation by ordering the demonstrators to disperse and by arresting them for disorderly conduct when they refused. This action, however, was not upheld by the Court. (This case, *Gregory v. Chicago,* can be distinguished from the Feiner case because the demonstrators did not act provocatively. It is the cause they stood for rather than the manner in which they presented it which provoked hostility in the audience. Also, the police had sufficient numbers present to take alternative action, directing their attention towards the hostile audience rather than the demonstrators.[23])

Some may criticize the Court for assuming an authority to review the judgments of legislative and administrative authorities. This questioning would not be constructive, for, if there was no review of the use made by local authorities or the police of their discretion to act anticipating a possible breach of the peace, there would be very little of substance left to the citizens right to assemble freely.[24]

As I have shown, this view has tended to prevail in the United States, for the Supreme Court is prepared to review the use of whatever discretion is exercised by administrative authorities in regulating the behavior of demonstrators. Nor does the Court limit itself to restraining police powers. It is also prepared to review administrative restraints enacted to impose time and place limitations on the right to assemble or to march. While recognizing a legitimate state interest in protecting the public against serious nuisances which might occur because of a demonstration, the Court has taken upon itself the task of ensuring that no prior restraints on the right to assemble are imposed. In this regard, it has sought to ensure that statutes are not discriminatory or unnecessarily restrictive in their impact. This practice reflects a correct understanding of the fundamental issues, as any judgments about when the regulation of a demonstration is expedient or desirable should not be left solely to the police or to those who are politically involved.

If we turn to review the situation in Britain, we find that there is virtually no protection afforded to the rights of assembly against a legislative authority intent on preserving the peace, or even when it is pursuing some less significant public interest such as traffic control or the avoidance of litter. There is no common law right to demonstrate, nor is there any constitutional protection. Thus, citizens cannot assume that their claim to assemble or to march will be accommodated. They enjoy only the residual right to do that which is not proscribed. Thus, the popular belief that there is a right of meeting in such well-known centers as Speaker's Corner in Hyde Park or in Trafalgar Square is erroneous. Meetings are held there under terms set out by the relevant local authority or park management and the availability of these venues can be withdrawn.[25] Legislative authorities may, then, deny assembly rights without very good reason. Luckily, some tolerance has been shown towards demonstrators in practice. However, this is a matter of discretion, and there have been notable instances when the right to demonstrate has been virtually suspended.[26]

Police in the United Kingdom also have a great deal more authority to order demonstrators to disperse, to arrest them, or otherwise to harass them than have police in the United States. First, they may make use of the many statutes which make it an offense to use provocative, indecent, inciting, or offensive speech.[27] These provide a readily available pretext for arresting particular members of a crowd regarded as agitators. They also provide a plausible charge with which the police may threaten almost anyone in a vocal demonstration. Indeed, a citizen is vulnerable even after arrest if he or she protests too vigorously at the police station. Second, in many jurisdictions there are administrative controls which ensure that, unless permission is given, a march or assembly will be deemed unauthorized. In these circumstances, the police will decide whether or not to break it up, and anyone who refuses to disperse after being so ordered is guilty of an offense. Third, the law of criminal obstruction is very wide-ranging. This is particularly relevant when police are dealing with those who are protesting or marching on a highway. Demonstrators may not cause an unreasonable obstruction and they may be ordered to move along or off a highway if this is thought desirable to facilitate free passage for other users.[28]

Further, in the United Kingdom, the police may arrest demonstrators if they perceive a threat to the peace. The common law relating to unlawful assembly makes it an offense for one or more persons to be gathered together with the intent to commit a crime or to carry out any purpose, which may be lawful or unlawful, in such a manner as to give firm and courageous persons in the neighborhood reasonable grounds to apprehend a breach of the peace. Of course, as we have noted, even if a gathering is peaceful, a breakdown of order may nevertheless be threatened by a hostile audience. In these circumstances, the police will not usually succeed if they charge demonstrators with unlawful assembly. However, they may resort to some other expedient if they wish to apprehend a demonstrator who is provoking a hostile audience. The simplest technique is to order the demonstrators to disperse or to gather or march elsewhere. So long as a police instruction is made in the exercise of duty and is reasonable, it is binding. Moreover, what the courts count as "reasonable," here, leaves a good deal of discretion to police officers. A leading case is *Duncan v. Jones*, in which the judgment of a police inspector who refused to allow Mrs. Katherine Jones to address a small group of people near the entrance of an unemployed training center, ordering her to hold her meeting 175 yards away, was upheld. There was no obvious obstruction to the highway and the only consideration which influenced the officer was the fact that when Mrs. Jones had addressed an assembly at the same center in the previous year, there had been a disturbance. In most circumstances, then, citizens who are demonstrating are very vulnerable to harassment and can be convicted for unlawful assembly, for obstruction, or (if they fail to comply with requests made by a police officer) for willfully preventing the police from carrying out their duties.

These arrangements are unacceptable. It should not be possible for an important political right to be eroded by authorities wherever they find it expedient. The general principles here which should be applied in a democracy are: (1) Speech should be protected even at great cost to the community. Indeed, short of a state of emergency, there ought to be a near absolute protection of speech. As for assemblies, we need to keep in mind that peaceful demonstrations are, for the most part, a form of speech and should not be regarded as a physical challenge to the authority of the state. They only become so when they are disruptive, disorderly, or violent. (2) Because any regulation of an assembly may constitute a form of censorship, the exercise of any discretion by government authorities to limit demonstrations should be subject to review. This applies especially to the discretion exercised by police, who (by virtue of their role and the difficulties which they undoubtedly experience in handling demonstrators) are inclined to hasty judgment. (3) There must be some way of affording demonstrators the right to accuse administrators and of obtaining a remedy if the latter abuse their authority.[29]

In applying these principles it is essential to keep in mind that only actions which attempt to bypass democratic processes may be subjected to control, and that so long as citizens are attempting to communicate, their actions ought to be protected. Of course, it is not always easy, especially where feelings are intense, to make a sound judgment about which actions fall into this category. Indeed, even after reflection, it is not always easy to be clear. Nevertheless, if we agree about the guiding principles, we may find that there is less disagreement about how the problem cases should be dealt with.

8

Free Speech versus the Public Interest in Regulating Broadcasting

What I wish to evaluate in this chapter is the propriety of regulating broadcasters, treating them as a special category of speaker less entitled to freedom of speech than others. In terms of my analysis of our right to speak, as a residual right, a government may not impose on speakers to secure policy goals such as achieving a desirable balance in the public discussion of matters of controversy, the development of art and science, democratic accountability, and the maintenance of a community's capacity to create programs with local content. Thus, the widespread acknowledgment that broadcast speech is a category which ought to be regulated when this serves these social purposes is embarrassing to my thesis. This is why I need to explore the precise nature of this contrary intuition (so I will be concerned to make explicit the main lines of argument that have been put forward to justify regulating broadcasters). And it is also why I shall provide a statement of the considerations which someone committed to my conception of freedom of speech may nevertheless take into account, either when trying to accommodate the plausible claim that broadcasters ought sometimes to be regulated or in trying to account for the strength of this intuition.

A problem that must be confronted before we proceed concerns the notion of spectrum scarcity, which is so often cited as the reason why the regulation of broadcasting is a necessity. While this claim may have been plausible at the time when radio and, later, television emerged as major media, it is no longer supportable, as technological advances allow communities to make far better use of the spectrum than they actually do (all that is required to allow for more broadcasters is the introduction of more sophisticated receivers). And the reasons why this technology is not exploited are political and economic.[1] There certainly would be more broadcasters if the licensing requirements in place in most systems were lifted.

That the claim that there is scarcity in the broadcasting spectrum is a fiction has been widely known and accepted for some time, so there is a puzzle as to why so many serious and conscientious observers still acknowledge the need for regulating broadcast services. Indeed, we may well speculate that scarcity is not the real concern of regulators, but that what they are really troubled by is the power of communicators who for one reason or another have managed to gather a mass audience. Clearly once a huge number of people can be addressed regularly, those who gain access to such an audience—sometimes virtually every member of a community—enjoy a tremendous capacity to shape sensibilities and influence opinions. So, the demand that these communicators be held accountable is understandable. Also, the public has an obvious interest in ensuring official access to such audiences to convey vital messages (for example, Fire Ban Notices in Australia) and to encourage democratic ideals by requiring that the public be kept informed of current events through adequate news services and public affairs commentary.

A full explanation of why broadcasters enjoy something of a monopoly in most systems today and exhibit a capacity to attract such large audiences would require the skills of a talented historian, and I will not attempt to provide an account here.[2] However, I think it would be accepted by anyone who looks at the evidence that one significant factor giving rise to the scarcity of the programs broadcast in commercial systems, and partly accounting for why stations mostly aim at attracting and holding such large audiences, is that the revenue from advertising is limited and there is no obvious alternative source of funding, for it is virtually impossible to collect payments from viewers or listeners. The problem here is that a capacity to charge viewers a fee for service requires the installation of scramblers or other devices which can ensure that only those who pay the fee receive the service, but consumers have shown that they are very reluctant to invest in any new equipment of this kind before they are convinced that it offers clear advantages over what they already enjoy.[3] It follows that if a broadcaster is to continue putting a program to air, he must be confident that advertisers will be willing to pay to have their messages brought before the audience it is likely to attract. Thus, he will aim at gathering the kind of mass audience which advertisers find it profitable to communicate with.

Although commercial stations funded through advertising have enjoyed something of an immunity from competition so that, at this stage, we can only guess at how much of their income most consumers would be willing to pay for a better service, they have been faced by the constraint that the incentives at work encouraging marketing companies to use broadcasters to carry their messages also dictate the marginal rate they are willing to pay per viewer or listener delivered (for it is not in their interest to pay more than they can anticipate recouping through any increase in commercial activity advertising is likely to bring about). Thus, if it were possible for one broadcasting company to hold a massive audience while carrying all the advertising, there is little doubt that most communities would eventually be served by only one television station—just as many are now served by only one newspaper. As it is, most stations carry far more advertising than the average person wishes to put up with and, if it were not for regulations, would probably carry more.[4] Also, only those stations which can succeed in delivering large audiences can hope to attract advertisers; moreover, once they are established with something of a monopoly (as they usually are in television), they have little incentive to improve the quality of the programs they put to air. Thus, what we are faced with, in effect, is a market process which seems to give rise to scarcity and encourage mediocrity!

A further preliminary point worth noting is that new technologies are rapidly undermining the dominant position which broadcasters have enjoyed during most of this century, and they also allow for alternative sources of funding to that provided by advertisers. The most important change is that a majority of people in the advanced systems will soon be satisfying nearly all their consumption needs with communications received via cable systems (which in many cases will be linked with telephones and or satellites as well as supplemented by home recording devices). This is not to say that broadcast services will disappear or that advertising revenue will lose its position as the major source of funding. However, it is clear that once cables are established, it will be possible to charge viewers and listeners for the programs they receive and to cater more easily to minority tastes.

What is controversial is whether the prevailing pattern, in which a few producers cater to a vast, only partially differentiated audience, will disappear in the immediate future. (If it does, the perceived need for regulating the media may also.) What we can say at this stage is that because it is now easier for programers to reach selected audiences, some may choose to indulge the interests of consumers who have minority tastes (such as for the game of chess, for a poetry reading, or for a program which offers a sophisticated treatment of historically significant events), for it may soon be just as profitable to aim at reaching a market of this kind as at an undifferentiated market. Of course, the audience for a special program (say, a good chess analysis and interview with players) will often be widely scattered throughout a very large population (for example, all English speakers throughout the world), yet the new technologies make it feasible to deliver programs to this audience.

Present experience indicates, however, that we would be wise to be cautious in our speculation about likely changes in the world's communications system, for it must be allowed that newer technologies have only been introduced when they are able to serve as more efficient conveyors of the kinds of program which are currently put to air by the major broadcasting networks. Thus, for the immediate future, the characteristics giving rise to the call for the imposition of public interest standards will remain a reality.[5] It will be instructive, then, to review the case for regulating broadcasters as this is put forward at the present time.

PUBLIC BROADCASTING

The imposition of obligations upon broadcasters needs to be sharply differentiated from other ways in which governments interfere with the communications system, for they often sponsor speakers of various kinds to promote community goals, assisting those judged to be important or otherwise deserving or those who would not be able to disseminate their ideas without government aid. For example, public education is a massive expenditure on forms of communication, especially at the university level. But education is only the largest of the many investments liberal governments are likely to make in communications. Most governments spend considerable funds on cultural funding to promote the arts or to ensure that there is a wide appreciation of history, and they also help selected scientists by funding research. What distinguishes these kinds of involvement from the broadcasting case, where governments impose standards, is that the autonomy of the communicators affected is not usually directly compromised (unless intrusive conditions are laid down as a prerequisite for government aid). It is one thing to ensure a plurality of outlets by sustaining communicators who would not be able to operate if they had to depend on market forces and quite another to impose standards on speakers.

I do not wish to imply that governmental involvement of a promotional kind in the communications system is not controversial. Far from it. The allocation of money for education, cultural promotions, and research is often highly contentious. Why should "quality" leisure activities such as attending ballet or completing an arts degree at a good university be subsidized by the state? Apart from aid to schools, which often helps children who would otherwise be deprived, the beneficiaries of public funding in communications are almost always those who aspire to knowledge or who have a creative talent developed to the point where they can contribute to the arts or to science (of course, the public also benefit in the long term through the activities of these elites). Not surprisingly, there are many who regard these subsidies as grants to the upper-middle class paid out of general taxes.[6] Nevertheless, most people think that this kind of governmental assistance to communicators is important and legitimate.

Liberals agree that governments who act affirmatively to promote communications have an obligation to respect the autonomy of important institutions. Thus, funding for universities is usually made in a very indirect way so that a single university or even a particular department cannot be isolated by a government who dislikes its work. Similarly, it is normally regarded as a breach of liberal convention if a government seeks to intrude party political bias in allocating funds to various categories of communicator. Thus, government departments do not usually administer the selection processes in terms of which funds are given to specific groups or persons, and it is usual for independent agencies to be set up for this purpose. Of course, there is still considerable bias (for example, politicians inevitably attempt to appoint persons who share their own values to significant funding agencies), but when this is exposed those responsible often suffer public disapproval.

In most democratic systems governments are deeply involved in supporting broadcasters. Again, efforts are made to avoid party political bias, and conventions upholding the autonomy of those agencies responsible for the administration of the national resources allocated for this purpose are widely respected. The British Broadcasting Corporaton (BBC) provides the best known example of such an autonomous body, and similar statutory authorities in other systems are often modelled upon it. The British system works well primarily because the BBC has such high prestige and because conventions requiring ministers to respect the autonomy of the corporation are deeply entrenched. The BBC also enjoys more independence from the British parliament than most other statutory corporations, in that part of its funds are allocated through a listener and viewer licensing system. (This independence has been seriously eroded by inflation, however, for the corporation must get parliamentary approval if it wishes to raise the fee.[7])

Whether they enjoy a government subsidy or not, broadcasters usually operate under a very wide range of public interest standards of a kind that would not normally be imposed on those working in film, theater, or even education. For example, they may be required to carry a percentage of material produced within the community they serve (local manufacture rules[8]). This kind of standard provides a subsidy to artists (which could be accomplished by direct grants in aid), but it also deliberately shapes sensibilities in ways that are thought desirable. Broadcasters may also be required to carry different kinds of programs (for example, catering to those with minority tastes for material of a religious or educational nature), and they usually have a duty to provide news services as well as commentary on public affairs.[9] For the most part, the latter obligation is coupled with a duty to be impartial and, often, a broadcaster may not editorialize.[10] Also, specific obligations to provide access to others may be imposed (as in the requirement that broadcasters carry the message of a prime minister or president or that they offer time for reply to contenders for public office or to those who are personally attacked). Children's programing is another sensitive area which is often the focus of regulation. In this regard, stations may be obliged to carry certain kinds of material at particular times and they may be forbidden to broadcast programs which are classified as suitable for adult viewers only or instructed not to air them until quite late at night.[11] Finally, broadcasters operate under a special duty not to offend their listeners and viewers with materials that many of the latter would regard as indecent.

One serious issue regarding the imposition of these "public interest" standards is that it seems to constitute a form of direct censorship. Is it possible to find reasons showing why "public interest" standards do not constitute an undesirable interference with the autonomy of broadcasters? Why is it necessary to impose regulations on broadcasters and not on publishers? Rather than obliging all broadcasters to carry children's television programs, even though they find this unprofitable, a government could set up a special children's television station. Surely this latter expedient is better policy in a democracy than the imposition of standards which force all broadcasters to carry material they would not voluntarily choose to disseminate?

I have already looked at the scarcity argument, which is often used to justify regulating broadcasters. One problem I noted is that the argument is inconclusive in that even if we concede that there is a spectrum scarcity and that licensing is necessary, it does not follow that licensees should be vetted by a governmental authority to ensure that they are "responsible." But why should we concede claims about spectrum scarcity? The main impediment to the establishment of further stations seems to be that licensing authorities worry about the affect a new competitor is likely to have on the viability of the broadcasters already established. In fact, governments could license more stations than they do and leave the matter of viability for the market to determine. Even leaving this consideration aside, it is no longer plausible to maintain that radio stations are scarce, for there are often more radio broadcasters in big cities than mass circulation newspapers. Furthermore, as I have previously noted, the advent of cablecasting and the use of satellites will soon make it even more anomalous to distinguish the broadcast medium as a special category.

Once scarcity is established through government action (because of the establishment of a restrictive licensing system or if it is decided that commercial broadcasting will not be allowed), a strong case for imposing standards can be made out. A government which is implicated in establishing a monopoly within the communications system surely has a duty to ensure that sinister interest groups (which may include the government itself) do not come to take advantage of it. The case for establishing independent authorities to regulate monopoly broadcasting stations carries special force in those systems where all sectors of the broadcast service are nationalized.

The case of the BBC provides a suitable example of a politically imposed monopoly for, prior to 1954, all broadcasting in the United Kingdom was undertaken by the corporation, and the governors appointed were responsible for monitoring the service it provided in the public interest. Of course, since the advent of commercial broadcasting in 1954,[12] the monopoly of the BBC has been eroded. Nevertheless, entry into the broadcasting system in Britain is not free, and the corporation continues to enjoy significant political protection. For this reason the corporation's governors have assured parliament that they will monitor all its programs to ensure that there is no abuse of the public trust. Once appointed by the Queen in Counsel (that is, on advice from the responsible minister), however, governors of the corporation enjoy considerable autonomy from their political patrons. It is they, rather than the responsible minister or parliament, who are expected to serve as a watch-dog body to ensure that "proper" programing standards (mostly left to them to determine) are respected. Furthermore, they have the power to appoint the director general and senior management of the corporation. In practice, it is the latter who run the broadcasting services, but policy guidelines are worked out in conjunction with the governors, who must give their approval and take full responsibility.[13] What we have, in effect, is an oligarchy of senior executives who see to it that the programs aired by the corporation are comprehensive in coverage, decent, and are not biased in an unacceptable way (that is, against one of the major political parties or a powerful pressure group). These arrangements successfully reflect two ideals: first, that broadcasters should be free from politically motivated interference from the government of the day and, second, that they should be "responsible." In practice, the system provides a relatively uncontroversial service because a convention of political neutrality (also well-entrenched within the British civil service) has been successfully incorporated as a norm within the corporation. In addition, the governors enjoy genuine independence from their political patrons, to whom they are only very indirectly accountable, and the persons they have appointed as managers have tended to be cautious about what they allow to be broadcast without being prudish or illiberal. Nevertheless, it is a censorship system, albeit a benevolent one, and power is vested in very few hands.

Insofar as the justification for censorship is based on the circumstances of monopoly or near monopoly (set up deliberately in the case of the BBC by way of the Royal Charter), the regulations which seem most appropriate are those directed at avoiding bias, especially as this relates to the presentation of candidates standing for political office and the credentials of rival political parties. But this should not be confused with the notion that public funding for communications should be allocated only to program-makers who agree to be neutral in presenting controversial points of view. If we insist on this, we would also have to hold that it would be wrong for a government to fund other committed communicators with public money (unless we can find reasons for supposing that broadcasting is a special category of speech deserving much greater regulation than other forms of communication). Thus, our principle will require the withdrawal of government funding for universities, for film production, and for the arts. Another implication of a programing policy requiring strict neutrality which most people would not accept is that it would preclude our making use of the cheapness of radio to help those minority groups who would not normally be able to communicate effectively by providing a means for them to propagate their point of view.

In practice the BBC has adopted a flexible policy with regard to its commitment to neutrality, and program-makers and commentators are afforded a considerable degree of freedom. Although they are required to ensure that all significant points of view on any controversial topic that has been the focus of attention in a program are eventually aired, there is no insistence that every program broadcast be neutral. Rather, when a committed one-sided statement is given an exclusive coverage, it is expected that the planners of the program series involved will make it clear that the opinion is not necessarily shared by the BBC and indicate that other points of view may be relevant in reaching an informed conclusion about the matters discussed. Wherever possible, they are also expected to announce when a reply to the program or further analysis of the controversial issues will be provided. This policy is not enforced in a rigid manner, however, and the internal censorship system mostly works on the basis of trust between management and program producers, rather than by way of a daily review of content or supervision of the creative process. Influence is exerted mainly through the various codes of policy distributed to producers. Although some specific policy objectives relating to the coverage of general elections and the treatment of political parties and leaders have been laid down,[14] most are loosely worded, allowing a good deal of discretion. Moreover, program-makers are expected to refer problems up the hierarchy for advice on their own initiative and do not have to suffer having someone more senior looking over their shoulder as they perform their duties.

As I have said, the imposition of standards of this kind embodies a commitment to the notion that producers on the state-funded broadcast service have a trusteeship obligation to be impartial. Nevertheless, the fact that the governors and management of the BBC have been reluctant to interfere at the level of program production indicates that they are mindful of the fact that good professional journalists may not be able to be completely neutral in the way that they present controversies.

COMMERCIAL BROADCASTING

If we leave aside the special case of public-funded broadcasting and turn our attention to commercial stations, we find that the best reason which has been provided for imposing standards is that we cannot trust market incentives to result in a system in which the public is served with quality programs and a well-balanced choice. So long as the majority of broadcasters are competing to obtain revenue, they will seek out audiences to attract advertisers. This means that they will mostly create programs with a wide appeal. Occasionally, they may seek to satisfy a specific group interest, hoping to attract an advertising sponsor who might be interested in communicating with them (for example, a station may focus on male sports such as football because breweries are often willing to sponsor such programs). In general, however, programs of educational or cultural value very rarely survive the scrutiny of marketing executives, who usually determine what is broadcast. As for news services, these are designed to be as entertaining as possible, even when this means they are less informative.

As I have said, one community response to the cultural wasteland of commercial television is to impose standards in the public interest. This is understandable, but is the response legitimate (that is, does it violate any moral right that broadcasters may claim) and is it wise?

Let us take the latter issue first. A problem in any process for holding broadcasters accountable is that it is very difficult for a review body to make judgments about the quality or significance of a particular program. All that can be done without too much controversy is to list the categories of speech which are thought to be desirable and to insist that stations make an effort to provide programs of this kind (for example, broadcasters may be required to devote a percentage of their time to children's television, to religious programing, or to providing news services and public affairs commentary). But unless regulative agencies do make qualitative judgments, the very point of imposing these kinds of standards may come to be undermined. For example, we may intend to improve the programing for children by requiring that stations carry material made specially to cater for their needs. However, the quality of any program actually presented will depend very much on the resources that production companies are willing to commit to the task and on the care that is taken by film-makers. Commercially orientated stations may be less eager to promote materials which make the best possible use of television and radio to help children develop through entertainment than they are in capturing an audience for those who wish to sell potato chips or other "junk" foods. Similar considerations apply to other standards imposed.

Put simply, then, the problem is that station managers will often seek to meet their obligations in a manner that has the minimum standards in mind. This should not surprise us, for if a category of program is profitable, it would be provided by commercial stations and "public interest" obligations would be otoise. On the other hand, if the material that broadcasters are required to present is not profitable, managers will meet the obligation in a way which does as little damage as possible to the interests of the shareholders to whom they are ultimately accountable.

It could be said, nevertheless, that it is costly for the state to have to provide an alternative to commercial broadcasting and that it is much easier to impose standards to counterbalance the deleterious influence which commercial incentives seem to have on the quality and nature of programs which profit-motivated stations are inclined to offer. This argument cannot stand close scrutiny, however, for the performance of publicly funded broadcasters in Britain shows that the cost of a successful alternative is not beyond the reach of reasonably affluent communities. Even if the costs were higher than they are, people may be willing to pay for a wider choice and better quality than commercial stations willingly offer. In any case, it is the public who pay for advertising in the long run (indirectly when they purchase the goods promoted), so it is not true to hold that commercial broadcasting is a consumer-pays system. Many of those who use a commodity and have to pay for its promotion (reflected in the higher prices charged for it) do not benefit directly as viewers of or listeners to the programs with which its manufacturer is associated as a sponsor. The revenue received through carrying advertising is, then, analogous to that collected by way of the imposition of an indirect tax on consumption. It differs from most other forms of taxation only because it is not usually imposed by governments. Nevertheless, governments can and do collect part of this revenue to use for public purposes simply by taxing the media companies involved.

These points suggest that it is wise for communities to promote a strong alternative to commercial broadcasting. They do not show that there is no good purpose served by allowing for autonomous commercial communication companies who seek profits by carrying advertising, or that the imposition of some "public interest" standards on such broadcasters would not serve a good purpose, given that broadcasters enjoy an artificial scarcity in the product they provide and that this has been established partly through the licensing system itself.

Turning to the question of whether it is legitimate for a government to impose "public interest" standards, the answer depends very much on the kinds of restraints imposed, for some are clearly more intrusive than others. Perhaps the best known of the standards imposed are those which proscribe the broadcasting of offensive materials. The basic principles which apply here have already been discussed in chapter 7. I have also evaluated standards which are designed to promote fairness in advertising or which force broadcasters to provide access to politicians for promotional purposes during election campaigns (see chapter 3, where I argue that standards of this kind may not be illegitimate so long as they do not concern the content of a station's own programing). Other standards which can be imposed without intruding directly into the editorial process may also be legitimate (for example, the requirement that a percentage of the programs be made locally, that programs be provided that are suitable for children, or that a news service be provided). Where a standard goes beyond listing the kinds of service which broadcasters must agree to supply so that its imposition involves evaluating the quality and the content of specific programing, a more serious legitimation problem arises.

Almost everyone concedes this. Indeed, it is interesting that when duties are imposed on commercial broadcasters, a significant amount of discretion is usually left to editors and producers. In most systems, the broadcaster is seen as someone in whom the trust of the community is placed. It is his or her willingness to accept this trusteeship role that is mostly relied upon to ensure that public interest standards are honored. I am not saying that a broadcaster who abuses this trust cannot be held to account in some circumstances. Review bodies such as the FCC in the United States usually have power to fine a station, add conditions to its license, and suspend or even refuse to renew its license. These powers are exercised reluctantly, however, and regulation mostly proceeds more by moral persuasion and threat of action, by the extraction of a promise of good performance in response to complaints, than by close supervision of editorial judgment.[15]

One reason for this, as I have said, is the widespread acknowledgment that there is something improper about governmental censorship over communications, even if it is well-intentioned. But other problems relating to the imposition of standards have also discouraged close supervision and are worth noting.

Consider the problem of subjectivity. As is well known, what one person thinks is a reasonably balanced report, another will regard as biased. All programing involves selecting between materials, and the items chosen for presentation will not usually exhaust every relevant point of view which could have been presented on any topic; nor is it easy to say how many or which of them a broadcaster needs to present in order to be regarded as "objective" or "neutral." We surely do not want to hold that broadcasters must canvass all possible interpretations on any matter they have chosen to discuss. But once we retreat from an absolutist position, allowing that some discrimination regarding the significance of the opinions in question or their desirability have to be made, we are forced to set out criteria, and it is precisely because it is impossible to do this in an objective way that review bodies have tended to defer a good deal to the judgments made by broadcasters themselves.

The British Annan Committee makes an attempt to provide criteria but insists, nevertheless, that these can only serve as a rough guide to help journalists exercise their trusteeship role rather than as standards against which editorial judgments should be measured. Also the committee is clear that "impartiality" is a matter to be aimed at through overall program balance rather than by imposing upon the autonomy of particular journalists who may be forcefully articulating specific value commitments. They suggest that "due impartiality" can be best interpreted as a programing policy involving three elements:

> The first is that it should allow the widest possible range of views and opinions to be expressed . . . [The second] is that the broadcasters must take account, not just of the whole range of views on an issue, but also of the weight of opinion which holds these views. Their duty to let the public hear various voices does not oblige them to give too much weight or coverage to opinions which are not widely held . . . [The third is that] in their exercise of due impartiality, broadcasters have to recognize that the range of views and the weight of opinion are constantly changing.[16]

These generalizations serve more to draw attention to the problem of subjectivity than to solve it. Who is to decide the weight of opinion behind a point of view? In any case, the number of people who hold an opinion is no indication of whether it is worthy of serious consideration. Sometimes one person's judgment carries great authority and should be afforded deference even when he or she is a minority of one (for example, Bertrand Russell). On the other hand, some widely held opinions are just plain silly and should not be deferred to.

Besides the problem of subjectivity, the Annan Committee also illustrates the difficulty editors face when presenting points of view which they find unacceptable. In this regard, they sympathize with the BBC, who said that they could not be impartial about people dedicated to using violent methods to break up the unity of the state. The BBC told the committee that in its judgment the views of the IRA (Irish Republican Army) and other illegal organizations should be broadcast only "when it is of value to the people that they should be heard and not when it is in the IRA's interest to be heard." And the Annan Committee comments:

> Broadcasters cannot be impartial about activities of illicit organizations. Nevertheless, these organizations are a political force in Northern Ireland and it would be unrealistic for the broadcasters not to take account of them. This does not mean, however, that the proponents of illicit organizations should be allowed to appear regularly on the screen . . . still less to appear in order to argue their case.[17]

Clearly, decisions relating to the airing of unacceptable opinions when these are politically significant will give rise to many hard questions. Nor is it possible to lay down criteria in advance as to how journalists ought to proceed. It certainly is not desirable to allow the government (or any other administrative authority such as the army) to establish committees to censor reports as they see fit. Thus, the Annan Committee is forced to conclude in reviewing the British media's treatment of the conflicts in Northern Ireland, "We think that the decision [whether to allow the Irish Republicans to put their case] must remain with the broadcasting organizations, and should not rest on the fiat of the British Government."[18]

From the point of view of the journalist responsible for presenting material, an obligation of "due impartiality" will be bitterly resented. A problem is that the presentation of different competing views may well interrupt the flow of a program. For example, someone making a documentary for television may find that an obligation to present alternative perspectives forces the filming of conversations and, as all film-makers know, "talking heads" are difficult to present in an interesting way. Also, most broadcasters are required to present material within definite time limits, often no longer than a few minutes, and they often have trouble enough organizing a program's material into the required format without having to take on the additional burden of ensuring that all points of view relating to the topics dealt with are heard. Sometimes a program will focus on material of special interest that has come into the hands of a journalist (for example, film depicting a meeting with IRA members or other revolutionaries), and it may be difficult to present this as well as other material which may be needed to provide balance. Good journalists are also aware that an audience has a limited concentration span and can take in only a few points (preferably reflecting one perspective). Cramming too much information into a documentary or play can have a counterproductive, cluttered effect. Finally, it is not always easy to say which points of view are relevant to a topic, and a journalist may well feel strongly about his or her decision to exclude some spokesman or point of view. It is also worth mentioning, in this regard, that journalists are usually opinionated people (if they were not they would not be able to interest us), and impositions which disallow them from disclosing their own points of view violate their right to speak.

A United States case (*NBC v. FCC*, 1974) involving a program exposing pension fund frauds illustrates many of these points. [19] Here an NBC documentary "Pensions, The Broken Promise" portrayed a number of older workers who were left after retirement without pension benefits because of failures in the pension plans. All persons interviewed suggested that serious defects existed in many private plans, and the presentation left no doubt that the narrator found the situation deplorable. Not surprisingly, a complaint was filed alleging that the program was biased and thus violated the FCC's requirement that broadcast stations ensure that all significant opinions about matters of controversy are presented. NBC responded that their program did not address the overall performance of pension funds but raised particular problems about the management of some of the funds. It claimed that all significant opinions relating to the specific cases of abuse dealt with in the program had been explored and that there was no need to get into a wider discussion about the performance of the majority of pension schemes offered to the public. That this judgment was controversial is reflected in the subsequent history of litigation. The FCC found that there was significant bias, ordering that NBC offer the insurer spokesman an opportunity to reply. But the courts reviewing this judgment were not happy with this way of resolving the conflict. The Appeals Court of the District of Columbia held that because it was arguable whether the performance of pension plans other than those selected for discussion in the program was relevant to the issues raised in the documentary, the judgment of the NBC program-makers was not a clear abuse of their trusteeship obligation and it ordered the FCC to defer to the former's editorial judgment.

The court of appeal was wise to support editorial autonomy in this case. In many circumstances when bias is alleged by powerful interest groups, there is a serious danger that they hope to use their public relations resources to confuse the analysis of an issue. Such groups will often raise extraneous issues simply to defuse adverse publicity, and program-makers justifiably try to avoid this by carefully selecting materials. If they exercise their discretion too cautiously their programs will lose impact.

In practice (apart from special obligations set out in the Federal Election Campaign Act of 1971 which arise only during election campaigns), most commercial stations in the United States are free of close supervision. They are not obliged to devote equal time to all sides in a dispute, nor does the FCC indulge in close supervision on a program-by-program basis. Indeed, stations may broadcast committed programs so long as they present all significant points of view at some time in their coverage. Their most important "public interest" obligation is that they provide a right of reply to persons or groups who are specifically attacked in a program. (However, as we have seen, even this obligation falls away in many situations.) A further duty, which the FCC used to impose but which it now leaves to the discretion of station managers, is that they devote a reasonable amount of time to the analysis and discussion of controversial issues, especially when these have relevance to the communities they serve. This avoids any bias that might result from stations choosing to neglect certain topics which may be embarrassing to clients or political leaders they support.

It is worth noting that even though the "trusteeship" obligations imposed on commercial stations in the United States often amount to nothing more onerous than that managers make an undertaking to self-regulate, broadcasters have found themselves imposed upon in cases when they manifestly abuse the trust placed in them. However, there has to be clear evidence and the matters in question have to be of significant public importance before the discretion normally afforded to a broadcaster would be imposed upon. Nevertheless, controversial cases do arise, especially with small radio stations controlled by committed groups, and the FCC has actually taken away the right of some stations to broadcast. In one case, a Southern radio station, WLBT in Jackson, Mississippi, routinely refused to air the viewpoints of a substantial local Black community and it subsequently lost its license.[20] In 1970 a Pennsylvania radio station owned by a fundamentalist preacher was also denied renewal for refusing to present points of view with which it disagreed. These are exceptional cases, however, and a station would have to show significant and persistent abuse, usually amounting to a refusal to comply with standards, before its license would be revoked. Also, the tendency of the FCC to reserve judgment about the value of a broadcaster's performance until license renewal comes up and to restrict evaluation to overall performance, rather than judging on a program by program basis, tends to support the autonomy of stations.[21]

Despite the looseness of the supervision (relating to the issue of whether stations are providing an "impartial" service), systems of review aimed at preventing bias ought to be scrapped. In the first place, the standard which tribunals are willing to enforce is so minimal that deregulation is unlikely to make much difference to the overall system. Yet small broadcasters are vulnerable, because the cost of contesting an action can be severe. (A typical answer to a complaint can cost between $500 and $1,000 in the United States, and even if a station contests a charge of bias and wins the hearing it may be out of pocket thousands of dollars.[21]) Second, the very point of issuing licenses to committed groups or individuals such as the fundamentalist preacher MacIntire (who owned a station which lost its license in Brandywine, Pennsylvania) is to ensure that strongly held minority and extremist opinions have some access to the airwaves. Besides the need which groups and individuals of this kind have to voice their opinions and make public their anxieties, it is important for us all to be exposed to some communications which are not impartial. So long as the overall system is reasonably well-balanced, there seems no reason why committed groups should be made to carry views which they strongly disapprove of. Certainly the case for affording radio broadcasters full autonomy must be regarded as a strong one.

9

Freedom of Speech versus Democratic Authority

In this chapter I wish to address a completely fresh set of considerations: whether the deontological approach I have been recommending is (a) compatible with a firm commitment to the democratic ideal of government by an accountable congress or parliament, and (b) can serve as the basis for an adequate theory of adjudication when appeal is made to a constitutionally protected right to freedom of speech (or any other listed freedoms or advantages usually afforded to individuals by way of an entrenched "bill of rights"). To understand the difficulties here, it is necessary to contrast the functionalist and deontological approaches in the context of an ongoing debate within liberal philosophy concerning the competing claims of legal and democratic sources of authority. This will be the task addressed in the first section, below, where I shall argue that when courts are set up (through the entrenchment of rights) with special authority to frustrate democratically elected governments, a serious problem of legitimation arises, for we may well ask why a small group of elderly, unaccountable judges should be able to frustrate a popular majority.

Most of us who are in favor of freedom of speech would like to see the entitlement established as a matter of legal right so that individuals who enjoy the liberty can effectively establish their claims. But if we are in favor of such constitutional entrenchment, we face the legitimation problem: How can the practice of judicial review be reconciled with a commitment to democratic accountability? I shall argue (1) that functionalist approaches provide an inadequate basis from which to develop a theory of adjudication or a justification for judicial authority, and that (2) the deontological approach I recommend allows us to develop a more satisfactory conception of the relationship between legal and democratic authority.

LEGAL VERSUS DEMOCRATIC AUTHORITY

A central problem which classical liberal theorists focus upon is that of re-stricting or otherwise controlling the power of the state, preventing it from becoming an instrument of tyranny and ensuring good govern-ment. Two techniques for accomplishing this have been widely en-dorsed: The first is to establish legal authority. Here, what is important is to develop some source of law other than the declarations of a political sovereign, thus establishing a measure of autonomy for the judiciary. This objective is usually accomplished by reference to "natural law" or to "custom" and by developing conceptions of the rule of law. The second is to rely on democratic authority, requiring governments to compete in fair periodic elections if they wish to remain in office. Here the political sover-eign is established only in a temporary capacity. Moreover, the govern-ment must answer to a parliament which will contain political rivals and critics.

We can distinguish three modern liberal traditions characterized by conflicting models of the relationship of priority allocated to legal and democratic authorities. The first (which I have earlier called Lockean) in-cludes those who are distrustful of politically imposed solutions to social problems and skeptical about whether representative parliaments can prevent the abuse of power. Thus, when through necessity or humanita-rian concern, the state intervenes to provide services or relief (such as helping the destitute, providing pensions for the aged, or securing public goods such as energy supplies, transport, sewerage facilities, hospitals, and schools), writers of this disposition argue that the scope of such legiti-mate activities ought to be kept to a minimum.[1] They defend a strong conception of rights and take them very seriously, hoping for judicial so-lutions to what they see as an inevitable abuse of power by democratic states. The second includes those who view the classical fears as largely inappropriate, place great faith in the efficacy of democratic decision pro-cedures and consequently hope to subordinate "law" to politics. These liberals argue that a state instrumentality capable of acting positively in the general interest is a vital necessity in modern circumstances and that because courts are not representative, the authority of the judiciary should be narrowly defined. The third tradition, which I shall defend as the most coherent, is also interventionist. Liberals in this group are more suspicious of democratic claims to authority than those in the second, and they consequently wish to legitimize some judicial review. However, their concern is to reconcile egalitarian goals with the protection of lib-erty; thus, far from inhibiting welfare initiatives promoted by govern-ments in the way that classical liberals recommend, they wish to accommodate them while also protecting individualistic values such as privacy, dignity, and liberty.[2]

I will be concerned to explore only two of these traditions, the second and third identified. Thus, I will not have much to say about Lockean liberals such as F. A. Hayek who, although they may concede that democratically controlled states are likely to produce better government than those which are authoritarian, nevertheless distrust all political instrumentalities, preferring to rely, whenever possible, on market mechanisms.[3]

My reason for not discussing this tradition is partly that the space available makes some selection desirable, but, also, the fact that the massive expansion of state interventions in social life during this century has closed off the option favored by minimalists. We are stuck with the modern state, and if we are to control its many interventions, we have to rely on some form of democratic accountability or some conception of law which is not grounded on the claim that most of the attempts by states to provide services, manage the economy, or redistribute in the name of justice are illegitimate. Thus my focus is on those currents in contemporary liberalism, the functionalist and Rawlsian approaches, which attempt to come to terms with the modern welfare state rather than wish it away.

The deferential tradition of judicial restraint, in which legal authority is regarded as essentially subordinate, has been exemplified by the positivist tradition of British jurisprudence and is manifest in the doctrine of parliamentary supremacy. This latter notion informs a widely shared understanding of the Westminister democratic system. Few authorities on the British Constitution have done more to promote these ideas than Sir Ivor Jennings. What we are provided with by him is a democratic conception of British culture in which liberties such as freedom of speech are guaranteed by the character of the people engaged in governing and being governed. Jennings concedes that there is a close connection between the legal protection of rights and the proper functioning of a representative system. Indeed, he tells us that if we view the system of parliamentary government historically, we can see this relationship quite clearly, as the development is sequential. First there is a recognition of liberties and then the emergence of democratic representation. However, Jennings argues that once the modern period characterized by parliamentary government is established, there are very good reasons why the old methods of protecting liberties, through judicial authority, should be regarded as largely outmoded. As he sees it, "[T]he 'principles' of constitutional lawyers are always a dangerous foundation for the formation of policy" whereas

> parliament can be relied upon to preserve liberties . . . because [in Britain] political power rests in the last analysis on free elections, carried out in a state

where criticism of the government is not only permissible but a positive merit, and where parties based on competing policies or interests are not only allowed but encouraged.[4]

When confronted with the view that these last mentioned political liberties (freedom of speech, freedom of assembly, and of association) are so fundamental that they should be placed beyond the reach of parliamentary majorities, Jennings makes the following observations: first, rights which are thought appropriate at one time may eventually become a burden, placing an inconvenient limitation upon legislative power by one generation on another; and, second, rights are never absolute, so that in delineating their scope a considerable amount of balancing of the competing interests will have to take place. Faced with a choice between democratically elected parliaments or courts as the appropriate authorities charged with preserving liberties and specifying how they are to be interpreted, Jennings prefers the former. In his view, although the British parliament "passes many laws which many people do not want . . . it never passes any laws which any substantial section of the population violently dislikes."[5]

Jenning's views are widely accepted by British lawyers and have been given jurisprudential support by the persuasive account of positivism defended by H. L. A. Hart and his disciples at the University of Oxford. A significant consequence of the legal positivism which Hart has helped to popularize and justify is the limited scope allowed for legal authority. In the light of his analysis, judges who are mindful of their responsibility to ensure lawful government would never seek to secure an independent claim to legislate. The reasons for this are, first, such an assumption of authority involves a conflict of interest for, if the source of law is always a declaration made in conformity with recognized procedures and if courts are established with a capacity to make such declarations, they would not only be responsible for stating what is to be law but for judging whether their declarations are valid. Secondly, courts have no standing as an appropriate policy-making body for, so long as it is accepted that law is promulgated rather than discovered, no strong reasons can be provided for accepting a rule which stipulates that courts should be a recognized declarer of the law. We cannot claim that judges are elected or that they have special expertise, or even that the procedural processes adopted by most courts are appropriate for policy-making.

The concern that English positivists exhibit about the nonrepresentative nature of the judiciary and the inappropriateness of a judge's claim to make policy is well-founded. Unfortunately, the solution advocated by Jennings (that is, that we eschew the American system of judicial review, relying entirely on democratically elected officials to make wise choices) is not. Although democratic systems offer hope that government policies will have wide support, and we can say that unless governments must seek electoral endorsement we have no reason for thinking that powerful groups will not dominate politically, we cannot assume that competitive, representative processes will ensure that a government's policy will necessarily reflect a majority opinion or even that it will always constitute a fair compromise between the competing interests of groups. Thus, the trust Jennings places in democratic processes is misplaced and must be viewed with some skepticism in the light of experience.

A number of serious problems giving rise to a legitimation crisis are worth identifying as being of special significance at the present time in assessing the standing of claims to democratic authority in the United Kingdom and the United States:

First, parliaments have for the most part abdicated, either delegating the responsibility for making policies to other institutions (such as the Federal Reserve Board, the Federal Trade Commission, the Federal Communications Commission, to mention only the best known agencies in the United States) or have elected to defer to the executive branch.[6] The fact that parliament would have to delegate is anticipated and endorsed by classical theorists, and the phenomenon comes as no surprise. Indeed, J. S. Mill includes a chapter in his essay *On Representative Government* in which he argues that the British parliament is not well suited to the tasks of planning or governing and should not assume such duties. What Mill hopes for from the representative process is a watch-dog institution which will carefully monitor the activities of governing agencies, holding them to public account and capable of dismissing officials who fail in their duties.[7] Unfortunately, even Mill's minimal hopes have not been realized, and modern parliaments have been content, in most circumstances, to become toothless tigers whose normal role is to rubber-stamp decisions made elsewhere in the system. Thus in the United States there is the problem referred to as the imperial presidency and, in the United Kingdom, it is clear that the cabinet has taken most of the initiative from parliament, which is tightly controlled, in both houses, through party discipline.[8]

Of course, if we could rely on administrative agencies to make good law and provide just, efficient government, it could be held that parliaments may be relied upon to delegate wisely. Unfortunately, there is no ground for optimism and some evidence that, as the chains of democratic accountability are attenuated, organized special interest lobbies become increasingly effective, reaffirming the status quo.[9]

Second, if we look at the actual outputs produced by these democratic systems using as evaluative criteria the degree to which certain ideal goals have been realized (such as the achievement of enough social justice to allow us to feel that the system is responsive to the needs of the very poor, the achievement of greater equality of income, and the provision of general services such as public transport, education, and health care), their performance is not reassuring. Not only can a significant proportion of very poor people suffering from malnutrition and other associated diseases still be identified, but very little progress has been made in redistributing wealth or in providing adequate welfare services. Moreover, if we compare their performance (that is, of Britain and the United States) to communist authoritarian countries (looking at the degree to which each approaches equality or the level of welfare made available to the poor), we find that it is not markedly different (indeed, welfare would be less generous in the two democratic systems if we include expenditures on education as a welfare payment).[10]

Third, when we turn to the electoral processes themselves, there is further cause for cynicism. There is the fact of low turn-out. For example, Charles Lindblom reports (in 1977) that only 47 percent of United States citizens claim to vote in local elections regularly and only 72 percent in presidential elections. Less than 30 percent say they have ever tried to influence how others vote or have worked for a party or candidate or have contacted an official about a problem.[11] Moreover, if we take as our ideal the goal of political equality set by Lindblom (and Robert Dahl), which requires that "[c]ontrol over governmental decisions is shared so that the preferences of no one citizen are weighted more heavily than the preferences of any other citizen," we have to allow that the two democracies fall far short of it. A difficulty here is that political equality cannot be comprehended in purely formal terms, for there are many ways of influencing policy outcomes. Besides the political liberties which may be enjoyed equally (but rarely are), effective influence requires resources which clearly cannot be enjoyed equally, such as access to decision-makers, wealth, community standing, time and expertise. Perhaps the most important political resource of all is the ability to find others who are willing to coordinate their activities with one's own. This is why groups who are already active in other areas of life and who control significant resources of wealth and skill and enjoy an administrative capacity of their own (that is, those mostly pursuing economic objectives, such as trade unions, manufacturers, and farmers) have a great advantage in competitive political processes.[12] What people are beginning to become aware of today is the very significant influence of large corporations, which make-up the commercial, mining, agricultural, industrial, and finance lobbies. Also worrying is the growing presence of the military as a force to be reckoned with in the political life of the United States.

Finally, neither the United States Congress nor the British Parliament can be regarded as reliable protectors of liberties. Year after year, Congress renews the vast budgets of the Federal Bureau of Investigation and the Central Intelligence Agency without carefully reviewing the work done by these organizations or taking adequate cognizance of the growing evidence that they systematically violate standards of civility embodied in even the most minimal conception of the rule of law.[13] In the United Kingdom there is evidence that prisoners have been tortured in northern Ireland and even that freedom of speech is not fully honored, as the suppression of the thalidomide scandal and the coverage of the Falklands war show. There is also evidence of jury vetting on the part of government prosecutors seeking convictions in cases involving Irish suspects and evidence that privacy is routinely intruded upon through telephone tapping.[14]

My list of the defects of the two selected parliamentary systems is highly impressionistic and merely records what I take to be major areas of concern in the systems I know best. Other people would come up with a different list—more than likely a far more comprehensive one.[15] However, for my present purpose, the observations made are adequate, for it must surely be conceded that the standing of democratic authorities is, in practice, often very low. Indeed, all we can claim for parliamentary government is that well-functioning representative systems ae unlikely to make very bad laws, that they will be somewhat responsive to most groups who have a capacity to organize a political lobby, and that they will serve as not very conscientious guardians of liberties (allowing them to flourish or decline, according to what parliaments find the most expedient). This is perhaps the most we can hope for from any system of government. But it is hardly sufficient to establish the absolute priority of democratic over legal forms of authority.

The legitimation problem, now widely perceived, concerning the claims to supremacy of democratically elected parliaments, has encouraged many contemporary liberals to look more favorably on legal claims to authority. Thus, we find that moves are being made to have bills of rights entrenched in many democratic systems. Moreover, those countries who have joined the European Economic Community have agreed to allow rights cases to be taken to the European Court of Human Rights on appeal. Although this court does not as yet enjoy any power to enforce its findings, the move to allow cases of this kind to be evaluated by an independent tribunal is itself a recognition that parliamentary controls may need supplementation.

One problem with this very widespread shift towards the recognition of rights and the autonomy of courts of review is that conventional wisdom among jurists is still positivistic. Although it is widely conceded now that a constitutional court may sometimes legitimately frustrate even democratic governments (provided a bill of rights has been entrenched and someone complains of a violation), the prevailing wisdom is towards a narrowly defined judicial discretion. The central idea is that judges should not seek to impose their own values in giving judgments but must faithfully defer to the wishes of properly constituted and popularly elected political authorities. The reason why this deference is thought appropriate is that it is in accordance with the democratic requirement that those who make policy hold themselves accountable to the people whose lives are affected by their decisions.

Those who adopt this point of view exhibit an embarrassment about the fact that when a constitution sets out certain rights which are declared to be fundamental, courts, in interpreting those rights, are sometimes forced to frustrate parliaments. Also a constitutionally protected list of rights confronts courts with the tasks which Jennings alludes to as inappropriate for judicial resolution—that is, delineating the scope of the rights, balancing other competing interests, and declaring when they have become a burden binding one generation to the inappropriate judgments of another. Thus, it seems to many that the positivist jurisprudence which democratic Englishmen feel most comfortable with has no easy application once a bill of rights is recognized; also that in upholding a constitution against the wishes of a government supported by a majority, courts must inevitably act undemocratically.

In his recent book *Democracy and Distrust*, John Hart Ely argues that a response to these problems has been made by most of those who both support the system of judicial review established by the list of rights embodied in the United States Constitution and recognize the need for courts to defer to those who have a claim to democratic authority.[16] The apparent paradox involved is resolved, according to Ely, by the claim that the Constitution itself embodies democratic authority—as opposed to legal authority. Those who claim this as an interpretation of the United States Constitution argue that the written clauses of the document protecting rights offer a device whereby the American people have protected themselves against the possibility that a majority, representing a temporary coalition of political forces responding to a prevailing tide of emotionalism, should become tyrannical. Thus, in ratifying the Constitution and by designating certain fundamental liberties, the people forestall this possibility of majority tyranny, agreeing that "it is saner and safer to set [fundamental liberties] down in advance of particular controversies than to develop them as [they] go along in the context of a particular political problem and its accompanying passion and paranoia."[17]

In terms of this account, then, when an American judge appeals to the Constitution as a source for authority when frustrating a popularly elected government, he or she is alleged to be appealing to constraints imposed by the people upon themselves.[18]

The impulse to seek a democratically respectable justification for the practice of judicial review as this is conducted in the United States—and this strategy is likely to be adopted in other democracies when rights are entrenched—is one which is readily understandable. Moreover, alternative approaches lack credibility, for no convincing reasons have been provided to show why a body of elderly unaccountable individuals should be able to overrule the judgment of a popularly elected government and do so, moreover, "in a way that is not subject to 'correction' by ordinary lawmaking processes." Nevertheless, Ely tells us, the claim that by upholding a constitution a court is merely supporting the considered judgments of the people (against those they actually manifest in the midst of political struggle and conflict) carries little of the weight that is placed upon it. In the first place, even if we concede that each one of the rights embodied in a constitution reflects the considered views of a majority of those who voted for or against its ratification, it remains unclear why, in the name of democracy, a contemporary majority should consider itself bound by "the voice of people who have been dead for a century or two." Also, we may well ask those who support judicial review to confront Jennings's point that such rights may become a considerable burden, imposing an inappropriate constraint. Second, in delineating the scope of the protection offered by a constitution, a court must presumably be bound by the wishes of the majority responsible for its ratification, but because of the open-textured wording of many listed rights, it is unclear how this goal can be accomplished. As examples of rights which are not easy to comprehend in a way which is limited to the language of the constitutional text and whatever help can be provided by legislative history, Ely cites the United States First Amendment prohibition of congressional laws abridging freedom of speech, the United States Eighth Amendment's prohibition of "cruel and unusual punishments," and the United States Fourteenth Amendment's provision that no state shall "deprive any person of life, liberty, or property, without due process of law."[19] He argues that is is impossible to interpret the contemporary significance of these rights without reaching for sources beyond the language of the United States Constitution itself; moreover, that it is impossible to say what the intentions of the framers would have been had they confronted modern circumstances. Thus, Ely concludes, whatever legitimation may be gained for the practice of judicial review through an appeal to the notion that courts merely impose the wishes of the people upon themselves is lost because of "the impossibility of clause-bound interpretivism."

JOHN HART ELY'S FUNCTIONALISM

In the light of this analysis, Ely poses the following questions: Do we have to accept the conclusion that the practice of judicial review as this has evolved in the United States is incompatible with the theory of representative democracy, the underlying legitimating ideology of the system of government? If not, how is the claim of the Supreme Court to overrule the expressed wishes of representative legislatures reconcilable with the democratic commitment to majority rule?

In responding to the first question, Ely points out that if we follow the lead of some of the more fashionable contemporary theorists of the United States Constitution, we must conclude that the practice of judicial activism is simply undemocratic. The problem, as he sees it, can be traced to a quite unacceptable conception of legal authority which he attributes to Alexander Bickel. The latter is alleged to argue that because the Supreme Court is the least dangerous branch of the United States system of government, in that the Court responds to initiatives taken elsewhere and lacks the power to plan or implement policy programs of its own, it can be trusted more readily than the legislature or executive. Consequently, it is appropriate for the Supreme Court to presume to act as the guardian of fundamental values, for it can be relied upon not to make unacceptable demands on other branches of government. In terms of Bickel's view of judicial impotence, all supporters of the Court have to provide, if they hope to justify the practice of review, is a way of establishing "which values, among adequately neutral and general ones, qualify as sufficiently important or fundamental or whathaveyou to be vindicated by the court against other values affirmed by legislative acts."[20] Seen in this light, the American practice of judicial review is appropriate and reconcilable with a democratic commitment, because some values are so fundamental that their endorsement may be removed from the arena of politics. Thus, in articulating and defending these values, the Court is not frustrating the people but merely forcing them to reflect on what they truly believe to be important.

Ely is very unhappy with this approach because there does not seem to be any clear criteria in terms of which judges can identify core values. As he points out, it cannot be that they conduct opinion polls or consult widely for, if so, courts would merely duplicate the work of legislatures. Judges have sought for objectivity in natural law, neutral principles, or reason but without much success, because each of these strategies fails to generate agreement as soon as we get beyond a purely abstract level of discourse. Few philosophers agree about the alleged content of natural law, the acceptable list of neutral principles, or the correct ethical theory. The result of this failure, Ely tells us, is that we have to fall back on personal judgment. Nor do modern commentators help. Ely claims that Harry Wellington and Ronald Dworkin, who both seek to identify fundamental community values—so long as they do not reflect bias, prejudice, or serve as rationalizations—launder the list; and that Laurence Tribe articulates traditional values at such a level of abstraction that they are made to come out right. Thus, Ely concludes, the quest to identify core community values is most appropriately conducted through normal democratic channels and courts have no special claim to accomplish this task in a sat-isfactory way.[21]

What we need, then, if we are to successfully defend the practice of ju-dicial review, is a fresh approach. Ely offers an alternative which com-bines the insights of Meiklejohn and Hayek, arguing that the questions (a) whether the opportunity to participate in the political process by which values are appropriately identified and accommodated, or the questions (b) whether the opportunity to share in the accommodations those processes have reached has been unduly constricted, are more ap-propriate considerations for judicial authorities to determine than the question of which substantive values are unusually important or funda-mental. He argues that the advantage of this focus arises out of the fact that judges would not be required to state their own values but would only claim authority to ensure that everyone else has a fair opportunity to express theirs. Thus the interventions of a review court would be sup-portive of the democratic commitment rather than subversive of it.

If we are to follow Ely's suggestions, we can identify two legitimate strategies which a review court may pursue. The first arises out of the re-sponsibility for opening the participation process by which accommoda-tions are made, which establishes the court as a guardian of political liberties. Thus it would be appropriate for it to interpret freedom of speech broadly (going well beyond "clause-bound interpretivism") to in-clude the range of associated liberties presupposed by the ideal of full, equal citizen participation in the political process (such as, the right to as-semble in public places, to travel freely, to hear the views of influential speakers who may include those who seek to visit from other countries, to gain access to important media, to stand for office, and to have one's vote in elections counted equally). In each of these areas, the court would be confronted with hard cases and will have to make judgments that may be controversial. Nevertheless, its claim to authority would be deferential insofar as it demonstrates a willingness to maintain complete impartial-ity, so that the liberties it affords are in no way related to the points of view—the values—expressed by the citizens who enjoy the court's pro-tection. The second strategy involves a revision of the classical liberal ideal of equality before the law. The intuitive idea is clear enough: those who make the value accommodation on behalf of a community should not be permitted to target the goods chosen in such a way that some groups are systematically excluded from the benefits or so that some gain disproportionate advantages. How a court is to exercise its authority to achieve this is, however, more controversial.

I turn now to make good my claim that functionalism provides an inad-equate framework for resolving the dichotomy between rival claims of le-

gal and democratic authority. The difficulty is that Ely's claim to have
offered a way forward beyond positivism, so that we can combine both legal and democratic sources of authority without generating a legitimation
crisis, is not persuasive. Put simply, it is difficult to see how judicial opinions can be reached in hard cases which do not rest on an accommodation
of competing values made by judges themselves for, whether a court
imposes upon a legislature to open the policy-making process ensuring
that it is more democratic or whether it simply claims to be making sure
that everyone is entitled to enjoy the benefits of collective decisions, difficult value judgments have to be made. Let me consider each of Ely's strategies in turn.

First, opening the policy-making processes. The impossibility of
"process-bound interpretivism" is manifest even in the line of cases taken
from United States experience which Ely seems most confident he can account for—namely, those involving the First Amendment protection of
freedom of speech. Clearly, an interpretation of the amendment along
Meiklejohnian lines, holding that its purpose is to facilitate the functioning of open, effective democratic discussion, has initial plausibility. It
is an obvious prerequisite for democratic accountability that everything
that people need to hear in order to exercise popular sovereignty ought to
be communicated and disseminated. What is not as obvious is how this
goal can best be realized; moreover, as a consequence of this ambiguity,
the argument from democracy which Ely relies upon (in interpreting the
amendment) provides insufficient guidance. This can be illustrated by a
consideration of some of the hard questions which will have to be faced,
some of which we have already considered in earlier chapters. May a parliament authorize an agency to regulate the market place of ideas so as to
ensure that every group with a significant point of view has a chance to
put it? If we answer affirmatively, here, it could mean that when a line of
argument has already been well stated, it may have to be censored in order that others can obtain a hearing. Would we wish to allow for this? If
so, we can see how regulations such as those which place limitations on
the amount that can be spent on advertising candidates during elections,
or those which restrict how much money any single person or organization can donate for political causes, could be compatible with a respect for
liberty. If not, what is to be done about these equity problems? Another
difficulty a court relying on the argument for democracy will encounter is
deciding how much information citizens need to have to exercise the ballot effectively. Does freedom of speech entail a right to be informed? Suppose a city's radio stations choose to play music, excluding all news and
public affairs commentary, or that one of them proposes to editorialize
strongly in favor of a candidate for office, refusing access to his rivals,
should—or may—the appointed regulatory agency or tribunal impose on
the media in response? As we have seen, the United States Supreme

Court relied on Meiklejohn when it ruled that the Federal Communications Commission could regulate broadcasting in the name of fairness, that it had a legitimate brief to ensure that every group with a significant contribution to make to public debate had a chance to put its view. What the court has since realized, however, is that such a ruling commits it heavily to reviewing the commission's administration of the media to ensure that a proper accommodation of the competing values (that is, fairness versus autonomy) is made.

The central difficulty with the Meiklejohnian interpretation of freedom of speech is that by focusing on systemic needs—recommending freedom because it helps to produce an informed electorate—his argument is couched in the language of a policy analysis. In such a discussion the problem identified is to select an appropriate means to a chosen end and to balance the cost of that strategy against alternatives. Thus, theorists such as Ely, who use Meiklejohn's interpretation, inevitably face the problem of balancing priorities; for if we justify a freedom by arguing that it is a means to some special good, we must not be surprised if an accommodation has to be made when other significant goods are in conflict. But it is precisely this task of establishing priorities which Ely wishes the court to stand clear of.

These difficulties are in fact manifest in the very case that Ely discusses to illustrate the potency of his Meiklejohnian interpretation of the First Amendment. In *Cohen v. California*, the United States Supreme Court reverses the conviction of a young man who paraded in a jacket which had "Fuck the Draft" written upon it. Ely tells us that the Court correctly notices that any harm (of shock or offense) the protest gave rise to flows entirely from the content of the message (that is, the meaning of the words expressed); and he deduces from this that the court's judgment holding that Cohen's communication is protected speech is well-founded.[22] However, it is difficult to see how we can accept this conclusion if we are required to proceed using only the functionalist theory Ely provides (that is, arguing that the point of the First Amendment is to ensure that the channels of political communication are clear); for, in terms of this suggested framework, we must surely ask whether Cohen's sentiments about the draft make any serious contribution to political debate. When we do confront this issue, we must notice that at the time of his protest, most citizens already knew that large numbers of young men strongly disapproved of the draft. Thus, it is hard to see what information the passing citizens, exposed to Cohen's gesture of defiance, are supposed to learn that is relevant to their exercise of the ballot. Surely, then, given the very slight contribution to public debate of Cohen's "Fuck the Draft" statement, it is in order for a government (protecting the sensitivities of those who may be shocked or offended by his chosen words) to require that he make his feelings known in a less harmful manner. At the very least, it is difficult to see how Ely can avoid committing the Court to this kind of weighing of the competing interests. Nor can this process be distinguished from policy-making.

I turn now to examine Ely's second strategy, that of ensuring that everyone benefits from collective decisions. What Ely must show in attempting to accomplish this objective is how a review court can avoid imposing on the policy-making process when it seeks to ensure that no restrictions are placed on any identified category of citizens which prevent them from benefiting equally in the fruits of existing policies.

In responding to his question, Ely could require that all laws be general (so that they affect everyone equally). Such a holding, however, would make government impossible, for distinctions clearly have to be made between categories of persons whenever social life is regulated (for example, the requirement that all taxis carry a fire extinguisher distinguishes the category "taxi-owner" from the more general category "car owner"). And most of us would not always find a specific reference of this kind anomalous.

Not surprisingly, then, Ely tries to develop a less restrictive test for identifying what may be described as suspect categories. In posing the problem in this way, he is clearly influenced by F. A. Hayek whose conception of the rule of law is based on the notion that, in most circumstances, governments ought to be prevented from making distinctions between citizens.[23] What is interesting is that Ely elects to provide a less restrictive test of what is to count as suspect. Thus, he does not follow Hayek in trying to outlaw all attempts at redistributing wealth and any move by governmental agencies to exclude individuals from participating in any economic or social activity. (Thus, in terms of Hayek's test, if the category taxi-driver is used as the basis for discriminating, a regulative agency may not prevent people from becoming taxi-drivers.) One suspects that Ely's reluctance to follow Hayek results from the fact that he is more of an egalitarian and less committed to the ideal that individuals should not be coerced by governments, but of course he is not free to admit that value commitments of this kind influence his judgment. In any event, the test Ely recommends is that a review court may legitimately examine legislative intent invalidating regulations when these are based on a desire to exclude some targeted group from a benefit otherwise offered to the public.

Apart from the issue of why his rather than, say, Hayek's recommended test should be embraced, Ely must allow that the notion of a suspect legislative motive is full of ambiguity; further, that this standard is even less clear if we take omissions into account. (For example, suppose that a taxi service is required to install and carry fire extinguishers in its cars but a limousine service is not. How is a review court to decide whether the favoritism shown here is, or is not, the result of a suspect motive?) What Ely cannot admit, although it is clearly the case, is that a review court operating with such an ambiguous standard will end up second-guessing representative policy-makers.

I conclude from this brief discussion that Ely's approach, if followed conscientiously, will result in such a narrow reading of the First Amendment and the "equal protection" clause of the Fourteenth Amendment that much of what liberals hope to achieve by entrenching such rights would be lost. This consequence, the failure of "process-bound interpretivism," forces a legitimation problem because we are left to choose between embracing democratic authority (accepting some doctrine of parliamentary supremacy) or allowing that judges may frustrate the realization of the values affirmed by legislative acts. Neither of these options seems appealing. Most of us are disillusioned with the fruits of parliamentary government but we would also allow that, if we politicize courts, there is little reason for hoping that judges will produce a better accommodation of values than, for example, the members of a committee of cabinet. Furthermore, we acknowledge that courts are clumsy instruments for policy-making in that their mistakes cannot easily be corrected.

Faced with this dilemma, then, most of us would be inclined to prefer democratic to legal claims to authority, and we would see more merit in the British Westminister model of democratic government than in the model exemplified by the United State's division of power and practice of judicial review. However, there are a growing number of theorists who are exploring yet another alternative in terms of which judicial review can be more satisfactorily legitimized. As I noted in the Introduction, this orientation takes its inspiration from John Rawls's influential *A Theory of Justice* but has been given jurisprudential shape by Ronald Dworkin, who has provided a critique of Hart's positivism, a theory of adjudication, and many illustrative commentaries on the work of the United States Supreme Court. In what follows, I will try to present and defend what I take to be the core of good sense reflected in this tradition.

THE WAY FORWARD

Courts are not representative, nor do they consult; furthermore, judges cannot claim any special expertise which uniquely equips them to evaluate programs. Thus, so long as a review court is viewed as just one more influential force within the political process, it will most likely lose its identity and, consequently, will not achieve an independent claim to authority, becoming nothing more potent than a second chamber of review and succumbing to the superior claims of elected officials to identify community feelings, needs, and passions. One clue, then, in finding an adequate theory of constitutional adjudication is to seek out the ways in which and areas of life where a review court can claim to be the most appropriate decision-making body—that is, when the skills of leaders trained to bargain on behalf of those they represent are not likely to produce a desirable result. What we need to show is why even those who are strongly committed democrats should be glad to recognize legal authority—that it does not contest the legitimate claims of democratically elected parliaments to make collective decisions about policy.

A good place to begin identifying this area of authority is with John Stuart Mill's concern that governments may be tempted to pursue collective goals in ways which impose special burdens on particular individuals, restricting their autonomy illegitimately or treating them unfairly. This worry is, of course, not unique to Mill but lies at the very foundation of all liberal approaches to politics. Indeed, one way of interpreting the liberal conception of the rule of law (a minimum commitment to natural law which all liberals share) is to emphasize the individualism which it embodies. What liberals require is that rulers articulate their wishes in clearly recognizable rules and that they be held bound by them. Thus, if they wish to alter the behavior of citizens, they are required to proceed in formal ways, establishing clear criteria for what is to count as a valid rule of the system. The ideal reflected is that individuals should be aware of their rights and must be allowed to act in light of them even when they are contemplating a bad action. Thus, even if we concede that the only rights which individuals may claim are those established through statutes passed by a properly constituted parliament (and many liberals would be prepared to recognize other rights besides these), as liberals committed to "the rule of law," we would hold that at the very minimum a government must be bound by its promulgations and that particular individuals should be able to claim authority or immunities in light of them. Further, that in establishing procedures for adjudication so that authoritative decisions are made about what is required by law, the independence of judges from political authorities must be guaranteed. This notion that individual citizens may rely on law and the judicial process to protect them from arbitrary government is also reflected in well-established principles and ideals such as *nulla poena sine lege*, the procedural protections against self-incrimination, and the notion that an individual when acquitted after being charged with a crime should not be subject to double jeopardy.[24]

Individualism is also reflected in the ideal of autonomy, which informs the liberal conception of political rights. What is meant by a right is that, far from begging for appropriate responses from a government, individual citizens affected by given policies in ways deleterious to their special interests (when these are protected as a right) or their enjoyment of liberties may assert a claim through the courts with some confidence that it will be upheld. Liberals disagree about what interests need to be protected as a matter of right, and some seek to keep the authority of courts to an essential minimum. As we have seen, Ely argues that a review court's responsibility is fulfilled when it ensures that the processes of democratic accountability remain open and governments do not discriminate in anomalous ways. Its responsibility is to prevent, as far as possible (but within the limits of the discretion allowed for in the law), a majority from tyrannizing a minority or from changing the rules in a way which enables it to avoid future accountability.

In seeking out an independent responsibility on which to ground judicial claims to review the work of a democratically elected legislature, Ely certainly succeeds in pointing legal theory in the right direction. However, as I have suggested in reviewing his treatment of freedom of speech and equality, his position is implausibly restrictive, for it does not allow us to reach the kinds of resolution in hard cases we feel most comfortable with. A much more adequate orientation would take Ely's concerns as its point of departure but interpret these ideals in a broader way which, besides the argument from the functional prerequisites of democracy which Ely uses, draws on the central humanist values. In terms of this approach we would try to give content to notions such as "respect for persons" and "dignity," and we may well recognize rights—such as the right not to be tortured or treated cruelly and the right to privacy—which are deliberately excluded by Ely.

Once we see that legal authority is based on the argument that it is necessary to recognize and protect the fundamental interests of particular individuals, we can also see that it draws upon a quite distinct realm of moral discourse from that which may be appropriate in a legislature. For, a court exercising legal authority is not concerned with aggregating the common good after considering the many competing claims of contending forces in society but with matters of entitlement. As I have said, there may be competing theories of how we can best identify what is due to an individual in the name of justice; and when a legal claim is based on a listed constitutionally protected right, it will not always be easy to reach a consensus about what entitlements flow as a result of it. However, in the light of the above analysis we can identify good, relevant arguments as those which are grounded in an appeal to a neutral principle. And where two competing principles can be cited, we can identify a good argument as one which reaches for a further level of abstraction, seeking out a theory of justice in terms of which accommodations can be made consistently. Utilitarian arguments which appeal to conceptions of the public interest will, of course, often be used by judges, but when this is the case the distinctive legal claim to authority will usually be weak, for a court (in the light of our commitment to democratic accountability) is an inappropriate body for policy-making. Thus, when judges do determine how the public interest can best be pursued, they must proceed reluctantly, referring matters back to the legislature or seeking authorization (perhaps assuming in the light of convention, that because the latter is silent they have been delegated in an indirect way). Moreover, while it is legitimate for a court to frustrate a parliament in the name of justice, when convincing arguments of principle can be found in support of a judgment that a specific individual is entitled to a benefit or liberty, it is never legitimate for a court to overrule a parliamentary judgment on the ground of a disagreement over matters of policy.

I have already discussed the manner in which Rawlsian liberals attempt to reach some consensus about which interests need to be recognized as a matter of right. The central task is to identify the coordinating principles of justice and then to deduce the rights which anyone committed to those principles would hope to see recognized. If we can reach some consensus over the basic critical principles which must be acknowledged within our critical morality, the problem of grounding legal authority can be confronted in a fruitful way. Whenever judges seek to restrain representative parliaments, we would require, first, that there is scope for the exercise of judicial discretion and, second (in exercising that discretion), that neutral principles accepted as binding should be determining. Both these requirements place considerable limitations on the authority which judges can legitimately claim in a democracy, yet allow for judicial review in a way that is compatible with the notion that those who make policy should be representative.

Consider, first, the issue of discretion. Here, I have in mind a distinction sometimes made between the political program of liberalism (the commitment to pursue goals such as welfare, a high level of minimum wages, full employment, the protection of the national heritage, and so on) and the theory of legal adjudication which may be inspired by it. The Rawlsian approach outlined provides a theory of political morality in terms of which we can identify fundamental goals (for example, maximizing the position of those who are worst off). As Rawlsian liberals, we would hope to live in a social system in which a reasonable level of justice had been achieved and would be committed to pursuing the goal of realizing as great a degree of fairness in the distribution of benefits and burdens as possible. It does not follow, however, that because we accept Rawls's conception of justice, we suppose that judges are free to impose our liberal political theory (as though Rawls were some sort of Philosopher King). What is required before judges may intervene in the name of a liberal ideal is some constitutional license for review. Thus, a judge may only resort to his or her articulated liberal political morality when interpreting specifically listed rights embodied in a constitution or when the statutes applicable to a case under adjudication are vague. And it would be improper for him or her to impose judgments without regard to the conventions (relating to judicial deference) which have been accepted as binding in any particular system. Moreover, if a Rawlsian liberal were asked to draw up a constitutional framework, he or she would be consistent in showing a healthy democratic distrust of elderly unaccountable judges, and there is no reason why he or she should allow judges to follow the precept "anything compatible with Rawls's theory goes." Indeed, he or she would see that the drawing up of constitutional provisions requires us to delineate those goals (identified in the light of the Rawlsian liberal program) which are most appropriately pursued through the mechanism of parliamentary government and would only seek to entrench those rights which it would be foolish to suppose a legislature would support conscientiously. Moreover, because some judgments involving "justice" are so broad-ranging, it is clear that very severe limits would have to be imposed by responsible framers of a democratic constitution on the discretion afforded to legal authorities, for otherwise democratic accountability would be vitiated. (For example, in the light of a Rawlsian analysis, we may deduce that a just society is one which aims at maximizing the circumstances of its worst off members, and we may consequently condemn as unjust a government's budget which fails to contribute to the elimination of unemployment or to increasing the welfare available to the unemployed – supposing that the worst off category in society are those unemployed. But if we allowed a court to declare such a budget invalid, how much authority would be left to the democratically elected parliament which endorsed it?) Thus, in framing constitutional provisions we would, as democrats, be wary of allowing too much scope for the exercise of judicial authority. Indeed, I would suggest (although I cannot argue that point here) that most of the so-called "welfare rights" have no place in a properly constituted democratic system, for objectives such as the achievement of substantive social justice are far better left to be pursued by way of the democratic process than by way of a judicial declaration. This does not of course mean that when a constitution is silent, judges should be indifferent to justice. It does mean that they can only make use of what they take (and argue) to be the most enlightened political theory as a guide in resolving disputes in circumstances where it is clearly appropriate for judges to use their own discretion in resolving a problem case.

The second limitation of legal authority I have listed is equally important. Although the requirement that judges act in a neutral way is compatible with a considerable amount of judicial intervention, in the light of it, we may hold that it is always inappropriate for a judge to cite his own or public prejudices in justifying a finding; further, we may force our judges to acknowledge an obligation to co-ordinate a series of judgments in a principled way.

CONCLUDING REMARKS

I set out to review two competing traditions of jurisprudence in contemporary liberal theory: functionalism, which places great faith in the efficacy of democratic decision-making procedures; and one which is more distrustful (although not to the depths of the pessimism evidenced in the work of libertarians such as F. A. Hayek and Robert Nozick). I have suggested that by clarifying the issues and frankly confronting the question of how claims to legal authority can be reconciled with a commitment to democracy, functionalists like John Hart Ely and Meiklejohn have pointed legal theorists in the right direction. Nevertheless, by carefully reviewing Ely's work, I was able to expose certain weaknesses in the orientation. Primarily, the problem which functionalism seems to treat badly is that of accommodating a commitment to take political rights seriously. For, when a bill of rights has been entrenched, courts have a duty of review thrust upon them and neither the "clause-bound interpretivism" of traditional positivism, or the "process-bound interpretivism" recommended by Ely seem to offer an adequate guide for adjudication when courts are confronted with hard cases.

One response to the failure of functionalism to come to grips with the concept of a political right is to abandon the model of judicial review instanced in the practices characteristic of the United States' system of government. In terms of this view, we should resist the temptation to entrench rights, leaving policy-making in the hands of democratically elected parliaments. Against this suggestion I have argued, first, that attempts to evade the issue of "rights" in this way are misconceived because there are very good reasons for distrusting even democratically elected governments, and we are confronted today (at least in the United States and the United Kingdom) with something of a legitimation problem which can only be solved by way of a recognition of distinctively legal sources of authority. Second, that in pursuing a more adequate theory of adjudication, the work of Ronald Dworkin provides a defensible and fruitful point of departure.

10

General Conclusion

Theoretical approaches dealing with hard cases, in which we must choose between the liberty to communicate and other competing values, usually embrace some form of functionalism. The classical utilitarian approach involves reaching that balance with the best chance of realizing the general good, resisting any claim that the freedom to communicate can be claimed as a right. This kind of pure balancing has the advantage of simplicity and flexibility, allowing us to reach solutions to problem cases in a way which accommodates all competing interests. Unfortunately, it leaves us without any concept of a moral right and is, consequently, incapable of accounting for the special weight most of us are inclined to place on the protection of freedom. For this reason many utilitarians have abandoned the pure balancing strategy, preferring some form of rule-utilitarianism. J. S. Mill's essay *On Liberty* provides a model for such an approach. In terms of it, we distinguish freedom of speech as a fundamental political principle (Mill's liberty principle embraces more than speech and is, consequently, more difficult to defend than a commitment to a principle with a narrower scope), and we hold that our commitment to this principle must be an absolute one. Thus, no balancing is allowed for in cases when freedom is in conflict with some competing conception of the general interest. Balancing problems occur for the Millean functionalist only when free speech is in conflict with some other fundamental principle, such as the principle that individuals be afforded a fair trial before they are punished for committing a crime. The problem with this approach is that it tries to have things both ways. What we are offered is a conception of rights which tells us that some interests of individuals are so fundamental that they must not be balanced in the ordinary way, as required by the classical utilitarian approach, but we are left with no guidance about what is to count as "a fundamental political principle" or about how to resolve cases when such principles are in conflict. Thus, when two individuals make conflicting claims which they demand as a right (for example, the claim of a journalist to communicate freely versus the right of an individual not to have his life placed in jeopardy or to have a fair trial or to vindicate his reputation or to enjoy privacy), we are offered no rule upon which to base our judgment.

I have developed an approach which attempts to avoid these obvious defects. On the account of what it means to make a rights claim which I provided, once we can establish some interest as a right, our claim to have it afforded must take priority over competing considerations. For example, if we claim someone has a right to a fair trial, this commits us to the absolutist view that such a trial should be afforded before that person is punished and that, if such a trial cannot be afforded because of some pressing competing interest, the person in question must be let go free. To this extent my orientation is similar to rule-utilitarianism. However, it differs from Millean liberalism in that a feature of my conception of a right is that the rights individuals may claim cannot come into conflict. Rights are determined by reference to extremely abstract basic political principles such as the commitment to treat individuals with equal concern and to respect their dignity as persons. No balancing of competing rights claims is allowed, for, whenever two or more persons make incompatible claims to have some interest afforded as a right, we are able to determine in the light of our articulated coordinating principles whose claim, if any, has legitimacy.

I demonstrated these advantages of an egalitarian deontological approach by reviewing two kinds of policy dilemma involving freedom of speech. The first involved circumstances when an individual was claiming some interest as a right (for example, the right to gain access to a particular forum or to be afforded an opportunity to reply to a critic) when, in securing it to him or her, a government was forced to impose on the autonomy of the press. The second involved circumstances when there was a conflict between the public interest and press autonomy. My claim is to have shown that a Rawlsian approach provides a framework which enables us to avoid certain anomalies associated with more popular functionalist approaches.

I

The strengths of the orientation I adopted are reflected in the way we were able to achieve flexibility in dealing with a variety of problems while retaining a strong commitment to the notion that individuals have a moral right to speak which must be respected. The framework is also comprehensive and coherent, enabling us to apply a common set of principles to all categories of speech and sections of the media. (I exclude the case of advertising, which is legitimately subjected to stricter regulation than other forms of communication on the grounds that it does not properly qualify as "speech.") Finally, the approach illuminates our strongest intuitions about the circumstances in which it seems legitimate to regulate the media, as well as those when it would be illegitimate; and we were able to achieve this result without having to resort to the implausible scarcity rationale adopted in most conventional orientations.

Flexibility was achieved in a number of ways: First, in defining the protected area of liberty for the purpose of delineating the profile of our right to speak, I drew on the Kantian ethical ideal of personal autonomy. In this regard, I held that before a speaker could expect his communication to be protected as a moral right, he must show clearly that he intended to appeal to the considered judgment of his audience; and that circumstantial factors such as whether there would be time for the audience to reflect or hear other points of view would be relevant in determining whether a claim were established as a moral right. With this conception of what is to count as protected speech I was able to define the area of editorial discretion more narrowly than is usual in liberal approaches, so as to allow access to all public forums. I was also able to hold that commercial advertising and some abusive speech could not qualify as forms of communication which should be treated as part of our protected liberty. Another advantage derived from my Kantian interpretation of what the right to communication includes is that I was able to determine the weight that claims to editorial autonomy could carry in specific circumstances. A speaker is at his strongest in claiming autonomy when someone wishes to impose a point of view upon him. In this regard, I argued that we should not tolerate policies which impose messages forcing speakers to convey points of view which they do not wish to disseminate, and I also supported the supposition that bias is best corrected by encouraging a plurality of outlets. A speaker is at his weakest in claiming autonomy when he is trying to monopolize a forum to prevent others from communicating with a given audience. In this regard, I suggested that editorial autonomy does not extend over adjacent forums, particularly advertising space or time (except in the special circumstances I outlined). I was also able to argue that the good faith of an editor (justifying his claim to autonomy) is exhibited by a willingness to correct acknowledged errors when these have harmed an individual by bringing his or her reputation into question, and that when there is genuine disagreement we may require that a reasonable opportunity for a person under attack to reply be afforded. Second, because the ideal of equality in concern and respect for others was taken as the coordinating value, I was able to treat liberty as a residual right which could only be claimed when all other rights which individuals establish (by reference to this coordinating value) had been afforded. Thus, I was able to advocate that some fairness standards, specifically the right to reply when personally attacked or misrepresented, be imposed even though this involved restricting the liberty of speakers.

Third, when a category of speech causes a nuisance or when regulation seems clearly in the public interest, I allowed for an accommodation of the competing interests so long as there is no discrimination on the basis of message content and the regulations restraining speakers fall short of a complete banning. This latter strategy enabled me to provide a way of resolving the dilemmas posed by the cases of broadcast and offensive speech which offered clear advantages over the balancing recommended by functionalists.

I said that one test for a theory was whether a large number of our intuitive judgments could be accommodated. How successful was the approach in dealing with hard cases? My discussion of some of the more important policy dilemmas shows that a Rawlsian deontological approach allows us to reach a large number of judgments which conform, by and large, with well-established conventional opinion. For example, I was able to hold the line against government intrusion in the name of editorial autonomy while allowing for limited access rights in special circumstances. As I showed in comparing *Miami Herald v. Tornillo* and *Red Lion v. FCC*, we would have been unhappy about the implications had we consistently applied the principles of absolute autonomy established in the former to the domain of broadcast speech and, yet, equally unhappy about applying the functionalist arguments used in the *Red Lion Broadcasting* case in dealing with the print media. My approach, while drawing back from both judgments, enabled us to reach a common ground which nevertheless accommodated a concern for fairness (in recognizing that individuals have a moral right to reply when personally attacked) and a respect for autonomy (treated as a residual right). Neither a Lockean deontological approach nor a functionalist approach could serve as well.

Where I felt most unsure of the guidance provided by my coordinating theory was in dealing with cases in which individuals had been embarrassed by a communication. Intuitively it seems clear to me that the outrage we feel when the private affairs of individuals are discussed on the media, often for no more obvious reason than that an editor supposes that the public's prurient interest in the affairs of others is insatiable, is justified. Yet I held back from allowing that such an individual ought to be afforded a right of action to obtain damages as amelioration for this harm. One of my reasons for this was that I saw the harm as analogous to the psychological suffering individuals experience when they are accused of wrong-doing or when they are placed in a false light, and to the harm they suffer when offended by what others do or say. There are good reasons why our taking offense at the behavior of others should not be regarded as a sufficient justification for restricting liberty. As for the law of defamation, there are so many circumstances in which we would hesitate about allowing for damages that it is difficult to hold that mental suffering should always be avoided or ameliorated. Finally, given the many circumstances in which we are scrutinized by others, it is very difficult and implausible to hold that there is a moral right to control how we are presented to others. For these reasons, I was forced to delineate our moral right not to suffer unnecessary or unfair embarrassment in a way that many would regard as too restrictive. In compensation the orientation offered consistency. Also, when we look at the present state of defamation and privacy law and at some of the proposals put forward for change, we find that alternative orientations have many more difficulties accommodating the competing values in an intuitively satisfying and consistent way.

II

It may be useful, finally, to list the problems which a deontological framework of the kind I recommend seems well-suited to resolve:

1. *The problem of combining flexibility in handling hard cases with a commitment to take freedom of speech seriously as a right.*

In utilitarian ethical theory this problem is reflected in the effort which some writers take to distinguish "rule utilitarianism" from "act utilitarianism." The reasons for this is that if too many exceptions are allowed in applying a rule to cases, or if the force which the rule carries in a given set of circumstances is indeterminate, the point of recognizing a rule (such as the rule that Congress may not censor speech) may be lost.

As I tried to show when discussing the conflict between the public interest and speaker or press autonomy, Rawlsian liberalism provides a framework which allows for a significant amount of balancing. As examples, I looked at cases when speech causes a nuisance because it is offensive or when people make competing claims to use the same forum (as is sometimes the case in broadcasting and when assemblies make use of streets and parks). And I showed how these conflicts could be resolved by allowing for the imposition of regulations, so long as they fell short of a complete ban of the speech in question—for example, by requiring that certain forms of communication take place in private or by regulating the use of streets so as to accommodate demonstrators as well as commuters. Where Rawlsian liberalism offers advantages over functionalism is that it more easily preserves the distinction between recognizing a commitment to liberty as a general rule of thumb reminding policy-makers to be cautious (for example, the rule that parliament should have very good reasons when restricting speech) and recognizing freedom of speech as a fundamental political principle. In the latter case, our commitment marks the point at which individuals have special claims which ought to be accommodated or afforded even at considerable social cost. Further, I claimed that we can most forcefully legitimate imposing such a limitation on the authority governments enjoy to pursue the general good by comprehending this commitment, to individual autonomy, in light of an understanding of the requirements of justice.

2. *Problems which arise because functionalist arguments are usually inconclusive.*

The issues here arise because the tasks of defining "speech," of justifying our right to freedom of speech, and of setting the priority between our enjoyment of it and other competing interests are all interrelated. Functionalists find it more difficult than Rawlsian liberals to provide clear guidance because, for the former, all three tasks are accomplished by deciding whether and to what extent a defined realm of freedom is likely to produce good consequences. Thus, what is delineated as the category of protected speech for functionalists depends very much on the general utilitarian reasons we have for thinking liberty important, and the weight we attach to our principle will be determined by the same considerations. But this leads to indeterminancy. (For example, if we suppose that freedom of speech is a necessary prerequisite for democratic accountability, then we have a good reason for protecting political speech as a category, but we would have no warrant for holding that offensive or obscene speech should be protected. Further, the weight which we place on the free speech principle, protecting our conception of political speech, when there is a conflict with some competing consideration—say that of affording justice when an individual is being accused of a crime, is determined by this consideration. Thus, we may hold that freedom is generally of less importance than justice. However, circumstances may bring us to revise this judgment in dealing with cases when a trial is likely to be of great political significance.)

Rawlsian liberalism avoids this kind of indeterminancy by providing clear criteria delineating when a communication falls into the protected category "speech" and a way of resolving conflicts when competing rights claims are made. This is what I demonstrated in Part Two.

3. *The problem of delineating the protected liberty.*

Here the most significant anomaly reflected in current policy is the different treatment afforded to the broadcast media in both the United Kingdom and the United States. The main justification given for this is that there is a scarcity of outlets for potential broadcasters which is not the case with other communicators. But this rationale is no longer plausible. Another area of current debate where definitional problems have been significant relates to the proposals which have been made for reforming the law of defamation. Functionalists wish to allow for vigorous and open public discussion but they also wish to protect individuals who may be vulnerable.

I showed that the Rawlsian approach, by allowing for individuals to claim a right of reply when personally attacked, allowed us to recommend plausible changes in the law of defamation; and that it also provided a way of accommodating the difficult broadcasting cases when we would be inclined to impose standards in the name of fairness within a comprehensive general theory, without leading to results which are intuitively unacceptable.

4. *The problem of justifying judicial review and of developing an adequate theory of adjudication.*

The most significant advantage which an absolutist deontological approach has over functionalism as a liberal theory is that it provides a way of accounting for legal authority. Functionalist writers have, of course, provided us with arguments legitimating judicial review but, as I hope should be clear from my discussion in chapter 9, even the most plausible functionalist account (that provided by Ely) is less satisfactory than the orientation derived from Rawlsian liberalism and developed into a jurisprudential theory by Dworkin.

III

Last, it is worth reiterating that in contrasting Rawlsian with functionalist liberalism, my purpose was not to show in any conclusive way that the latter is inadequate as the basis for a liberal theory. Rather I wished to draw attention to the advantages which follow once the Rawlsian alternative is accepted; more specifically, that it offers us a distinct alternative, carrying implications which differ from even the most sophisticated functionalist theory. Nor had I hoped to produce novel policy positions in the light of my chosen Rawlsian approach. The idea was to see whether, once we reconceptualize communications policy issues using a deontological approach, we would find ourselves committed to policy choices far removed from our considered intuitive sense of how cases should be resolved. In fact, as my discussion has shown, Rawlsian liberalism accommodates our intuitive judgments at least as well as functionalism, and it also provides a better understanding of why we require governments to respect freedom of speech.

Notes

Introduction

1. For a short introduction see Peter Singer, *Practical Ethics* (Cambridge: Cambridge University Press, 1979), pp. 8–14; also R. M. Hare, *The Language of Morals* (Oxford: Oxford University Press, 1952), pp. 175–79; and Hare, *Freedom and Reason* (Oxford: Oxford University Press, 1963), pp. 30–50; Kurt Baier, *The Moral Point of View* (Ithaca, N.Y.: Cornell University Press, 1958), ch. 8; Immanuel Kant's views are most forcefully presented in his *Groundwork of Metaphysics and Morals*.
2. On this point see Ronald Dworkin, *Taking Rights Seriously* (London: Duckworth, 1977), ch. 7, pp. 184–206; John Rawls, *A Theory of Justice* (Oxford: Oxford University Press, 1973), pp. 161–83.
3. Rawls, *A Theory of Justice*, pp. 30–31.
4. Dworkin, *Taking Rights Seriously*, pp. 169–70.
5. On the idea of "reflective equilibrium," see Dworkin, *Taking Rights Seriously*, pp. 159–68; Rawls, *A Theory of Justice*, pp. 49 ff. For discussion see Norman Daniels, "Wide Reflective Equilibrium and Theory Acceptance in Ethics," *The Journal of Philosophy* 76, (1979):256–82; and Philip Pettit, *Judging Justice* (Routledge & Kegan Paul, 1980), pp. 31–42.
6. The clearest account of "polyarchy" is Robert A. Dahl, *Polyarchy* (New Haven, Conn.: Yale University Press, 1971), ch. 1; see also, *A Preface to Democratic Theory* (Chicago: University of Chicago Press, 1956), pp. 63 ff. for Dahl's assessment of the extent to which the United States realizes the standards of "polyarchy," see "On Removing Certain Impediments to Democracy in the United States," *Political Science Quarterly* 92, no. 1 (Spring 1977):1–20.

PART ONE

Chapter 1

1. On utilitarian ethics, see J. J. Smart "An Outline of a System of Ethics" in J. Smart and B. Williams, eds., *Utilitarianism: For and Against* (Cambridge: Cambridge University Press, 1973); and more generally, R. B. Brandt, *Ethical Theory* (Englewood Cliffs, N.J.: Prentice-Hall, 1959); D. Lyons, *The Forms and Limits of Utilitarianism* (Oxford: Oxford University Press, 1968). Anthony Quinton has provided a useful historical account in *Utilitarian Ethics* (London: Macmillan, 1973).
2. The quotation is taken from John Stuart Mill, *Three Essays: On Liberty, Representative Government, The Subjection of Women* (Oxford: Oxford University Press, 1960), p. 15.
3. P. Devlin, *The Enforcement of Morals* (Oxford: Oxford University Press, 1965), pp. 1–25.
4. *Whitney v. California* 274 U.S. (1927) 376–77; quoted by Thomas Emerson, *The System of Freedom of Expression* (New York: Random House, 1970) pp. 106–7.

5. Emerson, *The System of Freedom of Expression*. The quotations are from p. 7 of his earlier essay, *Towards a General Theory of the First Amendment* (New York: Random House, 1963), where his arguments justifying the recognition of a right to liberty are stated most forcefully (see pp. 1–16).

6. See Sean MacBride, *Many Voices One World* (Report by the International Commission for the Study of Communication Problems, UNESCO, 1980).

7. See H. J. Eysenck, *Race, Intelligence and Education* (London: Temple-Smith, 1971); for a survey of relevant literature see Christopher Jencks, *Inequality* (New York: Allen Lane, 1973).

8. H. J. McCloskey, "Liberty of Expression: Its Grounds and Limits," *Inquiry* 13 (1970):227 ff.

9. For a discussion of this problem see Richard Wollheim, "A Paradox in the Theory of Democracy," in Peter Laslett and W. G. Runciman, eds., *Philosophy, Politics and Society*, Second Series, (Oxford: Blackwell, 1962), pp. 71–87.

10. J. S. Mill, *On Representative Government*, in *Three Essays*, pp. 324–29; J. A. Schumpeter, *Capitalism, Socialism and Democracy* (London: Allen & Unwin, 1970), p. 269.

11. This is essentially Wollheim's argument. For critical comment see Brian Barry, *Political Argument* (London: Routledge & Kegan Paul, 1965), pp. 293–94.

12. David Lyons has recently put forward a new interpretation of Mill's liberalism which provides a framework for the development of a new form of "indirect" utilitarianism; see his "Mill's Theory of Morality," *Nous* 10 (1976):101–20. This position has been explored and developed by John Gray in his recent *Mill on Liberty: A Defence* (London: Routledge & Kegan Paul, 1983), and by Fred R. Berger, *Happiness, Justice and Freedom: The Moral Philosophy of John Stuart Mill* (Berkeley: University of California Press, 1984). See also John Gray, "Indirect Utility and Fundamental Rights," in Ellen Frankel Paul, Fred D. Miller and Jeffery Paul, eds., *Human Rights* (Oxford: Blackwell, 1984), pp. 73–91.

13. Frederick Schauer, *Free Speech: A Philosophical Enquiry* (Cambridge: Cambridge University Press, 1982). My discussion follows my review of this book in *Australian Journal of Philosophy* 62, no. 1 (1984):82–84.

14. Ibid., p. 168 and p. 205.

15. Indeed, his most fundamental argument is a poorly documented notion of consent: he argues that those who founded the democratic system in the United States had no intention of allowing Congress to govern without supervision by the people. But his case is flawed by the fact that the system is one of representative democracy in which the majority of people do not make complex policy choices. This is a point which is made with some force by R. Bevier, "Press Access Rights," *California Law Review* 68:507. See also Leonard W. Levy, *Legacy of Suppression: Freedom of Speech and Press in Early American History* (Cambridge, Mass.: Harvard University Press, 1960) for an account of U.S. history which contradicts Meiklejohn's assumptions. Levy claims: "The evidence drawn particularly from the period 1776 to 1791 indicates that the generation that framed the first state declaration of rights and the First Amendment was hardly as libertarian as we have traditionally assumed. They did not intend to give free rein to criticism of the government that might be deemed seditious libel, although the concept of seditious libel was—and still is—the principal basis of muzzling political dissent. There is even reason to believe that the Bill of Rights was more the chance product of political expediency on all sides than of principled commitment to personal liberties." (Taken from the Preface, p. vi).

16. Alexander Meiklejohn, *Political Freedom* (New York: Oxford University Press, 1965), p. 27.

17. Meiklejohn's orientation has been strongly supported by Thomas Scanlon in his article "A Theory of Freedom of Expression," in R. Dworkin, ed., *Philosophy of Law* (Oxford: Oxford University Press, 1977). What the latter provides is a philosophical rather than historical defense of the commitment to self-government by appealing to the Kantian liberal tradition. Scanlon argues that governments may not disturb the processes of public debate by preventing people from exposure to controversial ideas because "the powers of the state are limited to those that citizens could recognise while still regarding themselves as equal, autonomous rational agents" (p. 160). Scanlon discusses

Meiklejohn's influence on his work in "Freedom of Expression and the Categories of Expression," *University of Pittsburgh Law Review* 40 (1979): 519–24.

18. The potentially narrow category of protected speech allowed for within his theory is something which worried Meiklejohn, and in 1961 he wrote a paper in which he claims that an established right to freedom of communication should protect "all forms of thought within the range of human communications" from which the voter derives the knowledge, intelligence, and sensitivity to human values with which to make sound and objective judgments (Alexander Meiklejohn, "The First Amendment is an Absolute," *Supreme Court Review*, 1961). It is, however, one thing for Meiklejohn to articulate liberal sentiments and quite another to justify them, and it is not surprising that some of his disciples have reached a quite different conclusion (see particularly Robert Bork, "Neutral Principles: Some First Amendment Problems," *Indiana Law Journal* 47, no. 1 (1979). For discussion, see Kent Greenawalt, "Speech and Crime," *American Bar Foundation Research Journal* No. 4 (1980):733 ff.

19. Scanlon's formulation (see note 17 above) avoids these difficulties because, in terms of his revision, authorities may not presume to make judgments balancing the harm caused by speech against any good consequences it may also have, so long as the harm results indirectly by way of persuasion. Scanlon has had second thoughts about this in his "Freedom of Expression and the Categories of Expression."

20. Dworkin does not mention Meiklejohn, but it is clearly the latter's argument which is reflected in the reasoning of the press representatives he has in mind in, "Is the Press Losing the First Amendment?" *New York Review of Books* 27, No. 19, (1980):49–57. Also, see his comments in the Introduction to Dworkin, ed., *Philosophy of Law*.

21. *United States v. Progressive* 467 F. Supp. 990 (1979); *Herbert v. Landau* 441 U.S. 153, 60 L.ed. 2d 115 (1979); *United States v. Snepp* 100 Sp. Ct. 763 (1980).

22. *New York Times v. Sullivan* 376 U.S. 254 (1964).

Chapter 2

1. For Justice Black's views see his concurring opinion in *Cox v. Louisiana* 379 U.S. 559 (1965), and the interview "Justice Black and the First Amendment 'Absolutes': A Public Interview," *New York University Law Review* 37, no. 549 (1962):557–58.

2. Schauer, *Free Speech: A Philosophical Enquiry*, elaborates on the idea that "free speech" is "defined not by what it is, but by what it does," pp. 91 ff.

3. Thomas Scanlon, "A Theory of Freedom of Expression," in Dworkin, ed., *The Philosophy of Law*, at p. 161. Scanlon has come to question this principle: see "Freedom of Expression and the Categories of Expression."

4. This is a point Scanlon makes with some force against himself. See, "Freedom of Expression and the Categories of Expression," pp. 530 ff.

5. Rawls, *A Theory of Justice*, pp. 204 ff.

6. The recent UNESCO, MacBride Report, *Many Voices One World* (1980) reflects this way of thinking.

7. Dworkin, *Taking Rights Seriously*, p. 271. See his chapter 12, "What Rights do we Have?" for a more general development of this point.

8. Ibid., pp. 272–73.

9. Bruce A. Ackerman, *Social Justice and the Liberal State* (New Haven, Conn.: Yale University Press, 1980).

10. Ibid., at p. 11. But see Dworkin's criticism of these principles because they do not include any egalitarian commitment, in "What Liberalism Isn't," *New York Review of Books*, January 20, 1983. While Dworkin is correct to stress the importance of an egalitarian commitment in liberalism (see also his discussion of Mill in *Taking Rights Seriously*, pp. 236 ff.), I do not agree that the principle of neutrality is as formal as he claims. Any distributive principles which may be suggested will inevitably embrace a theory of value, and the neutrality principle can be used to question the allocation it allows for. We can ask why one person's contribution should be rewarded more than someone else's, questioning the assumptions embodied in the value theory. (For example, the notion that an allocation is justified if it results from processes which reflect the prices which people freely choose to pay for services and commodities assumes a market theory of

value. But would we be acting in a neutral way if we allow this evaluation of the worth of individual contributions?) For discussion and commentary on this point, see my *Marxism and Individualism* (Oxford: Blackwell, 1981), pp. 168 ff.

11. Dworkin's approach is made most explicit in his discussion of the Williams Report; see "Is there a Right to Pornography?" *Oxford Journal of Legal Studies* 1, No. 2 (1981): 177 ff.

12. H. L. A. Hart, *Law, Liberty and Morality* (Oxford: Oxford University Press, 1963), pp. 20 ff.

13. Hart's most comprehensive discussion of the concept of a right is "Bentham on Legal Rights," in A. W. B. Simpson, ed., *Oxford Essays in Jurisprudence*, Second Series (Oxford: Oxford University Press, 1971). His "Are There any Natural Rights?" *Philosophical Review* 69 (1972):535–45, is still useful. The best review of the recent literature on "rights" is by Rex Martin and James W. Nickel in the *American Philosophical Quarterly* 17 (1980):14.

14. Hart makes this observation in "Bentham on Legal Rights," p. 197.

15. Hart, "Are There Any Natural Rights?" in Anthony Quinton, ed., *Political Philosophy* (Oxford: Oxford University Press, 1967), p. 62.

16. In his "The Basic Liberties and their Priority", (in Sterling M. McMurrin, ed., *The Tanner Lectures on Human Values*, vol. III, Cambridge University Press, 1982, pp. 3–87) Rawls presents an argument along the lines I develop below. Here, he works out in greater detail than *A Theory of Justice* an answer to the issue of the kinds of liberties his negotiators would regard as fundamental, and he also has a great deal to say about freedom of speech. Although I had not read his lecture at the time of writing, I have decided to urge readers to attend to Rawl's own statement, rather than to revise my own. On why it is useful to focus on 'freedom of speech' as a distinct liberty, see Schauer, *Free Speech: A Philosophical Enquiry*, pp. 5–7.

17. For a different view, see Robert F. Ladenson, *A Philosophy of Free Expression* (Totowa, N.J.: Rowman & Littlefield, 1983). Ladenson argues that Rawlsian negotiators would be convinced by Mill's arguments in chapters 2 and 3 of *On Liberty*. See pp. 30–39.

18. See *A Theory of Justice*, pp. 207 ff.

PART TWO

1. See the references cited in note 1, chapter 2.

Chapter 3

1. *Avin v. Rutgers* 385 F.2d 151 (3rd Cir. 1967); cert. denied, 390 U.S. 920 (1968).

2. *Miami Herald Publishing v. Tornillo* 418 U.S. 241; 41 L.Ed. 2d 730 (1974); and *Red Lion Broadcasting v. FCC* 395 U.S. 367; 23 L.Ed. 2d 371 (1969).

3. Federal Communications Commission, "Fairness Doctrine and Public Interest Standards," *Federal Register* 39, No. 139 (1974):Sect. III, pp. 26380 ff.

4. *Lehman v. City of Shaker Heights* 418 U.S. 241 (1974).

5. Ibid. (41 L.Ed. 2d 770 at p. 778).

6. Benno C. Schmidt, Jr., *Freedom of the Press v. Public Access* (New York: Praeger, 1977), ch. 7, pp. 87–102.

7. Brennan, dissenting opinion in *Lehman v. City of Shaker Heights*. Actually Blackmun's opinion did not gain the support of a majority. The court was evenly divided (4–4). Surprisingly, Justice Douglas cast his vote with Blackmun but for completely different reasons from those cited in the latter's opinion. Douglas claimed that bus commuters are a captive audience and that they have a right to privacy which is violated by political advertising. This argument does not carry much weight, however, for whatever privacy interest is likely to be violated by political advertising is equally vulnerable to commercial advertising. The consideration serves only to justify imposing a total ban on advertising in buses, rather than a partial exclusion of only political messages.

8. In the United Kingdom, no political advertising is allowed. Neither the IBA nor the BBC may carry political messages of less than five minutes. The rationale behind this is that election periods are a time for considered reflection and that spot advertising is, allegedly, not conducive to this.

9. I do not wish to imply that those who promote their own business activities by on-site advertising have opened a forum. If the tobacco company was simply using the wall to advertise its own commodity and activities, it could legitimately exclude others.

10. See particularly, *United States v. Lorain Journal*, 342 U.S. 143 (1951), and *Klor's v. Broadway Hale Stores*, 359 U.S. 207 (1959). For discussion see Schmidt, *Freedom of the Press v. Public Access*, pp. 47–51.

11. The case of liquor advertisements in bars can be accommodated as an on-site communication. See note 9 above.

12. *Business Executives' Movement for Vietnam Peace v. FCC* and the companion case, *Columbia Broadcasting System v. Democratic National Committee* 412 U.S. 94 (1973); my quotation is at pp. 124–25.

13. Communications Act 1970 (47 U.S.C., S. 302 a). The phrase is borrowed from a statute regulating railroads and grain elevators. For commentary on the act, see Schmidt, *Freedom of the Press v. Public Access*, ch. 9.

14. *Red Lion Broadcasting v. FCC* 23 L.Ed. 2d 371 at p. 338.

15. See Schmidt, *Freedom of the Press v. Public Access*, pp. 133–35.

16. It is worth noting that the *Red Lion Broadcasting v. FCC* judgment embraces Meiklejohn's interpretation of the First Amendment with less reservation than in earlier cases. In other cases an appeal to audience interests had always been made in order to protect the press. Thus, in *New York Times v. Sullivan*, the argument is put that if the press is to serve effectively, it must be free from the impact of libel law when discussing the character or actions of a public official. In the *Red Lion Broadcasting* case, in contrast, the audience interest is put forward as a reason for imposing upon broadcast stations.

17. It is worth noting with regard to this second problem that counsel for the broadcasters had argued that the imposition of "fairness standards" produced an inhibiting effect on public debate by encouraging self-censorship, but the point was dismissed as "at best speculative." Nevertheless, Justice White conceded that "if experience with the administration of these doctrines indicates that they have the net effect of reducing rather than enhancing the volume and quality of coverage, there will be time enough to reconsider the constitutional implications." Perhaps, then, if we follow Justice White's reasoning, the time may have come to abandon *Red Lion Broadcasting v. FCC*, for the Court has now acknowledged that the implementation of "fairness" standards can inhibit the airing of controversy by broadcasters. This recognition is made in *Miami Herald Publishing v. Tornillo* by Chief Justice Burger.

18. Jerome Barron, *Freedom of the Press for Whom?* (Bloomington: University of Indiana Press, 1973); "Access to the Press—A New First Amendment Right," *Harvard Law Review* 80 (1967): 1641 ff.; "An Emerging First Amendment Right of Access to the Media?" *George Washington Law Review* 37 (1969):487 ff.

19. Prof. Barron (who acted as counsel for Tornillo) drew attention to the similarity of the issues raised by *Red Lion Broadcasting v. FCC* and Tornillo's case. But despite this, not one of the three justices who wrote an opinion (not even Justice White!) took trouble to distinguish the two cases.

20. The evidence is presented in Barron, *Freedom of the Press for Whom?* pp. 335–39, citing U.S. figures.

21. *Miami Herald Publishing v. Tornillo* 41 L.Ed. 2d 730 at p. 740.

22. *In Re Kay* 464 F.2d 142 (Cal. 1970), quoted and cited by Franklyn S. Haiman, ed., *Freedom of Speech* (Lincolnwood, Ill.: National Textbook Company, 1976) at p. 74.

Chapter 4

1. Schauer, *Free Speech: A Philosophical Enquiry*, p. 171.

2. *New York Times v. Sullivan* 11 L.Ed. 2d. at p. 705.

3. *Coleman v. Maclennan* 78 Kan. at 724, quoted by Justice Brennan in his judgment for the Supreme Court in *New York Times v. Sullivan* 11 L.Ed. 2d., at p. 707.

4. Butt's case was dealt with in the same opinion as Walker's: 388 U.S. 130 (1967); *Time v. Hill* 385 U.S. 374 (1967); *Gertz v. Welsh* 94 S. Ct. 2997 (1974).

5. *Carol Burnett v. National Enquirer* (unreported). Burnett claimed that the newspaper defamed her in a gossip column item in 1976, in which it was alleged that she had had a

drunken run-in with Henry Kissinger in a Washington restaurant. The jury awarded $1.6 million in damages. See the *New York Times*, March 26, p. 19, col. 1.

6. *Herbert v. Landau* 441 U.S. 152 (1979).

7. *Street v. NBC*. This case was reported in the *Media Law Reporter*, May 1982.

8. *Firestone v. Time* 424 U.S. 448 (1976). The notion of a "public figure" has been narrowly drawn: see Don R. Pember, *Mass Media Law*, 2d ed. (Dubuque, Iowa: Wm. C. Brown, 1981), pp. 173–82. The Supreme Court has ruled that unless someone occupies a position in society of "persuasive power and influence" he or she must thrust himself or herself into the public arena to influence the resolution of an important social issue before he or she can be regarded as a "public figure." Emphasis is placed on whether someone has voluntarily sought out pubicity and on whether the context in which such public standing has arisen involves a matter of legitimate public interest. A messy divorce, for example, would not count as a matter of legitimate public interest.

9. Faulks Report, *Committee on Defamation* (London, HMSO, Cmnd. 5909, 1975), at p. 617.

10. The best known case where this two-level standard is articulated is *Chaplinski v. New Hampshire* 315 U.S. 568 (1942). For critical commentary on the idea that only some forms of speech are protected by the First Amendment, see Harry Kalven, Jr.'s "The New York Times Case: A Note on 'The Central Meaning of the First Amendment,' " *Supreme Court Review* (1964):191 ff.

11. On this point see Harry Kalven, Jr, *The Negro and the First Amendment* (Chicago: University of Chicago Press, 1966). In these lectures Kalven demonstrates the impact which a social movement can have on the development of the law.

12. See particularly, *Lewis v. The Daily Telegraph*, and *Lewis v. Associated Newspapers*, in which awards were made of over £100,000 in each case to the same plaintiff, (1964) A.C. 234. The awards were set aside by the Court of Appeal and the House of Lords. See Justice, *The Law of the Press* (1965), pp. 25–26; and for notes on this and other cases see Appendix III, pp. 50–52 at the end of the Report.

13. Justice, *The Law of the Press* (1965), p. 26.

14. The Justice group's suggestions were embodied in a private member's bill and presented to the British parliament for debate. This plea for a qualified privilege for the press is echoed by the Australian Law Reform Commission in their initial Discussion Paper, No. 1, *Defamation, Options for Reform*, p. 8. The Commission suggests that monetary damages be replaced by a "right of reply," and that a publisher be afforded a defense to general damages when he can prove that, "after making all reasonable inquiries and on reasonable grounds he believed the matter to be true, and provided he had afforded the defamed person a full and adequate right of reply."

15. The Faulk Committee discuss the work of *Justice* in paras. 211–15. Its assessment of the bias of the press representatives is shared by Zelman Cowen, *Individual Liberty and the Law* (Calcutta: Eastern Law House, 1977), pp. 64 ff. See also Lord Lloyd, "The Law and the Press," *Current Legal Problems* 43, (1966):55 ff.

16. Quoted by the *Committee on Defamation* at p. 54. Lord Goodman, Review of "Wicked, Wicked Libels," *New Statesman* (March 31, 1972), p. 426. Charles Winstow, editor of the British *Evening Standard*, has a different opinion. In his view the law of libel inhibits reporting on the following matters of legitimate public interest: local government corruption, shoddy work on public work contracts, city stories about dubious concerns and advice to sell shares, criticism of the fitness for office of public figures, and the connection of public figures with criminals. Winstow's statement was made in 1972, and he is quoted by Colin R. Munro, *Television and Censorship* (Westmead: Saxon House, 1979), p. 79.

17. Australian Law Reform Commission, *Unfair Publication* (Report No. 11, Australian Government, 1979) pp. 22–23 and pp. 91–92.

18. *Committee on Defamation*, paras. 211–15.

19. The Australian Law Reform Commission draws attention to the issues relating to the dilemma faced by radio broadcasters who wish to allow others rights of access to their station. See *Unfair Publication* (Report No. 11, Australian Government, 1979) para. 169, p. 90, and para. 172, pp. 91–92.

20. The New South Wales Defamation Act (1974) takes this into account by allowing for an extension of the defense of partial justification. S. 16 provides, in effect, that where the plaintiff sues on one (or some) only of a group of imputations contained in the publica-

tion complained about, the defendant may rely on the substantial truth of the imputa-
tion(s) not sued upon if, in that context, the imputation complained of does not further
injure the plaintiff's reputation.

21. This rule was supported by the Younger Committee in the United Kingdom on the
grounds that an unscrupulous complainant might use the council as a testing ground
for legal action. On the other hand, the Annan Committee are highly critical of the arrangement. They write: "Our conclusion was that the waiver was an unjustifiable interference with individual rights. Complainants should not have to choose between public
vindication and legal redress. They are entitled in some cases to both" (p. 59). This judgment would be easier to support if reforms of the law of defamation along the lines I recommend were to be implemented—an unlikely prospect.

22. On the functioning of the Press Council, see the McGregor Report: *Royal Commission on
the Press* (HMSO, Cmnd. 6810, 1977), p. 187, para. 19, 18; and the Younger Committee,
Report of the Committee on Privacy (HMSO, Cmnd. 5012, 1972), para. 45, p. 13.

23. See p. 59, para. 6.17.

24. For an account of "right of reply" in the U.S., see Pember, *Mass Media Law*, pp. 467-68.

Chapter 5

1. The definition of "privacy" which seems to have had the most influence is that of
Warren and Brandeis who talk about "a right to be let alone," which they link with the
notion of an "inviolate personality." Another influential attempt at definition is that of
A. F. Westin, who talks about our privacy interests "as the claims of individuals, groups
or institutions to determine for themselves when, how and to what extent information
about them is to be communicated to others." See, S. D. Warren and L. D. Brandeis,
"The Right to Privacy," *Harvard Law Review* IV, No. 5 (December 1890-91):pp. 193-220;
and A. F. Westin, *Privacy and Freedom* (New York: Atheneum, 1967), p. 7.

2. William L. Prosser, "Privacy," *California Law Review* 48 (1960):383.

3. In the United States, the Supreme Court has recognized "the right to control one's
body" as a privacy interest, and because of this, it declared certain state statutes proscribing abortion to be unconstitutional. See *Roe v. Wade* 410 U.S. 113 (1973).

4. This is a point which is made most forcefully in C. Fried, "Privacy," *Yale Law Journal* 77,
No. 3 (1967/68):475-93.

5. Kenneth Younger (Chairman), *Report of the Committee on Privacy* (presented to the U.K.
Parliament, July 1972) Cmnd. 5012 at p. 24.

6. On this point see Emerson, *The System of Freedom of Expression*, p. 557.

7. See the list provided in the Australian Law Reform Commission Report, *Unfair Publications*, para. 247, p. 133.

8. This is a point which is made with some force by Lord Denning in *Woodward v. Hutchins*
(1977) 1 W.L.R. 760.

9. J. J. Thomson, "The Right to Privacy," *Philosophy and Public Affairs* 4, No. 4 (1975):
295-314.

10. For a discussion of promising along these lines, see A. I. Meldon, *Rights and Persons* (Oxford: Blackwell, 1977), pp. 32-56.

11. See Arthur Miller, *Assault on Privacy* (Ann Arbor: University of Michigan Press, 1971),
for a lively account of privacy violations in the United States.

12. Some surreptitious surveillance involves a very indirect violation of privacy. For example, it is now possible to trace people's contacts and transactions over a period by
compiling a list of the contact numbers dialed on their telephone or by looking over their
record with their bankcard agency. These forms of surveillance involve no intrusion nor
do they affront dignity, yet we do think of this snooping as an infringement of privacy
primarily because a person is not normally conscious that the trail they leave will be followed and is, consequently, often unaware of the image of himself or herself that will be
constructed. In this sense, then, these forms of surveillance violate our interest in
controlling the way we are presented to others. I do not think we have any right to prevent these forms of investigation when the only information used is already a part of the
public record, but there are grounds for moral disapproval—we can say that such surveillance is a bad practice.

13. See Frank J. Donner, *The Age of Surveillance* (New York: Knopf, 1980), pp. 214-19.

14. Ibid., at p. 217. Donner cites Hugh Sidey, "L.B.J., Hoover and Personal Spying," *Time*, Feb. 10, 1975; and Bill Moyers, *Newsweek*, March 10, 1975, as authority for this claim.
15. See Harry Kalven, Jr.'s lecture, "Anonymity, Privacy, and Freedom of Association," in *The Negro and the First Amendment*, pp. 65–121.
16. Zelman Cowen, *The Private Man* (The Boyer lectures, Australian Broadcasting Commission, 1969), pp. 9 ff.
17. The idea that political liberty should have priority among our values is stated most forcefully by John Rawls, *A Theory of Justice*, pp. 226 ff. For criticism, see R. Miller, "Rawls and Marxism," *Philosophy and Public Affairs* 3, No. 2 (1974):167–91.
18. For an important example, see the discussion of terrorism in *Intelligence and Security*, Royal Commission Report to the Australian Parliament (4th Report, Paper no. 248, 1977), pp. 34–67.
19. Younger Committee, *Report on Privacy*, para. 163, p. 48.

Chapter 6

1. The case which the Australian Law Reform Commission cite (*Unfair Publication*, p. 120) in which a journalist's involvement with "another man" was a matter of comment in the media seems to be typical. If the complainants in this case are the radio personality Claudia Wright and Dr. John Helmer (I suspect that they are), I fail to see why the commisson should question the Press Council's ruling that the woman concerned was a public figure. In Ms. Wright's case, her private relationships were clearly relevant to her public role as she frequently discussed sexual morality and personal relationships on her program. Anyone who enters into public debate as a critic or supporter of prevailing morality must expect that his or her own behavior will be a matter of interest to others.
2. Surveillance devices are described by the Younger Committee, *Report on Privacy*, pp. 154–56; the examples are presented on pp. 156–57.
3. *Dietemann v. Time, Inc.* 449 F.2d 245 U.S. 352 (1971). This case is discussed by Floyd Abrams, "The Press, Privacy and the Constitution," *The New York Times*, Aug. 21, 1977, sec. 6.
4. *McCall v. Courier Journal* 4 M.L.Rept. 2337 (1979) affd. 6 M.L.Rept. 1112 (1980). My account is taken from the summary in Don Pember, *Mass Media Law*, 2d ed. (Dubuque, Iowa: Wm. C. Brown, 1981) pp. 239–40.
5. *Onassis v. Gallela* 487 L.F.2d 986 (1973).
6. Quoted by Australian Law Reform Commission, *Unfair Publication*, p. 120
7. Younger Committee, *Report on Privacy*, p. 47.
8. These points were put to the Younger Committee by press representatives. See *Report on Privacy*, para. 174 p. 51.
9. Report of the United Kingdom meeting of Justice, *The Law and the Press* (1965).
10. *Pell v. Procumier* 94 S. Ct. 2800 (1974), and *Saxbe v. Washington Post* 94 S. Ct. 2811 (1974).
11. Warren and Brandeis, "The Right to Privacy."
12. Younger Committee, *Report on Privacy*, p. 37.
13. Proceedings before the Family Court in Australia may not be reported. The situation will soon be changed as a bill has been introduced into the parliament which will allow reporting so long as the names of the people involved in the cases are not disclosed. See *Age*, Oct. 21, 1981, p. 1.
14. Emerson, *A System of Freedom of Expression*, p. 557.

Chapter 7

1. See the Race Relations Act, 1976.
2. See Scanlon, "A Theory of Freedom of Expression."
3. Mill, *On Liberty* in *Three Essays*, p. 120.
4. Patrick Devlin, *The Enforcement of Morals* (Oxford: Oxford University Press, 1965).
5. H. L. A. Hart, *Law, Liberty and Morality* (London: Oxford University Press, 1967): Joel Feinberg, " 'Harmless Immoralities' and Offensive Nuisances," in *Rights, Justice, and the Bounds of Liberty* (Princeton, N.J.: Princeton University Press, 1980) pp. 69–109.
6. Hart, *Law, Liberty and Morality*, p. 43.
7. Ibid., at p. 47.

8. In what follows, I comment on Feinberg's paper "Harmless Immoralities." His most recent work, now published by Oxford University Press, was not available to me.

9. In reaching this conclusion, I have benefited from Anthony Ellis, "Offense and the Liberal Conception of Law," *Philosophy and Public Affairs* (1984), pp. 1–23.

10. In practice, stations which aim at a mass audience are keen to ensure that they do not cause offense and can be relied upon to self-regulate.

11. *Chaplinski v. New Hampshire* 315 U.S. 568 (1942).

12. See Emerson, *A System of Freedom of Expression*, pp. 314, 338.

13. Ibid., pp. 313 ff.

14. In the United Kingdom, section 5 of the Public Order Act (1936) as amended by the Race Relations Act (1976) makes it an offense for any person in a public place, or at any public meeting, to use threatening, abusive, or insulting words or behavior or to distribute or display any writing, sign, or visible representation which is threatening, abusive, or insulting with intent to provoke a breach of the peace or whereby a breach of the peace is likely to be occasioned. The Race Relations Act (1976) itself makes it a crime to communicate in a way which is likely to stir up hatred against any section of the public distinguished by color, race, or ethnic or national origins, or citizenship.

15. In the first five years after the passing of the U.K. Race Relations Act (1976), fourteen people were prosecuted under section 6. Nine of these were white and five colored. Michael Malalik (known as Michael X), a flamboyant Black Power leader was given twelve months' imprisonment as a result of an inflammatory speech. See Barry Cox, *Civil Liberties in Britain* (Harmondsworth: Penguin Special, 1975), pp. 248–49.

16. For an account of one significant conflict, see Justice Scarman, *Report on the Disturbances in Red Lion Square, London 1974*, Cmnd 5919, HMSO 1975.

17. *Milk Wagon Drivers Local 753 v. Meadowmoor Dairies* 312 U.S. 287 (1941). A good account of this case is provided by Emerson, *A System of Freedom of Expression*, pp. 314 ff. I have benefitted from his discussion of the "hostile audience" problem.

18. Among the more important cases reflecting a change in the attitude of the United States Supreme Court since the Meadowmoor Dairies case are: *Terminiello v. Chicago* 337 U.S. (1949); *Feiner v. New York* 340 U.S. 315 (1951); *Edwards v. South Carolina* 372 U.S. 229 (1963); *Cox v. Louisiana* 379 U.S. 536 (1965); *Gregory v. City of Chicago* 394 U.S. 111 (1969).

19. The Scarman Report, *Disturbances in Red Lion Square*, provides a useful account of these events.

20. Ibid., pp. 6–7.

21. Emerson, *A System of Freedom of Expression*, concludes his review of the cases with this observation: "Generally speaking, the effect of the Supreme Court decisions in this area has been to support the system of freedom of expression. But many issues remain and many of the principles are undeveloped" (p. 327).

22. *Edwards v. South Carolina* 372 U.S. 229 (1963).

23. For a statement of the law in the United States which takes *Edwards v. South Carolina* as a reversal of *Feiner v. New York* and extracts some of the more important cases, see Franklyn S. Haiman, ed., *Freedom of Speech* (Skokie, Ill.: Natonal Textbook Co., 1976) ch. 2.

24. This point is made forcefully by Justice Black in his dissenting opinion in *Feiner v. New York* 340 U.S. 315 (1951). Dissenting Opinion, at p. 323.

25. See H. Street, *Freedom, the Individual and Law* (Harmondsworth: Penguin Books, 1977), p. 49.

26. In the United Kingdom, The Public Order Act (1936) empowers a chief officer of police to impose conditions on marchers and even, in some circumstances, provided the local authorities and home secretary consent, to prohibit classes of procession for a period of three months.

27. See note 14 above.

28. For a useful account of police discretion to clear a highway when demonstrators cause an obstruction, see Geoffery A. Flick, *Civil Liberties in Australia* (Melbourne: Law Book Company, 1981) pp. 94–99.

29. Permit systems are not very useful in practice. As Justice Scarman points out in *Disorders in Red Lion Square*, if a large meeting or a march is going to be held, local authorities will almost certainly learn of this even if no notice is given. The police already have the power to instruct marchers as to the route they must take and have power, at their dis-

cretion, to prevent hostile groups from coming into physical contact. The need for additional powers is, therefore, superfluous.

Chapter 8

1. On the fragility of the "scarcity rationale" for regulating broadcasters, see Bruce M. Owen, *Economics and Freedom of Expression* (Cambridge, Mass., Ballinger, 1975) pp. 102–8; but especially Ithiel de Sola Pool, *On Free Speech in an Electronic Age: Technologies of Freedom* (Cambridge, Mass.: Harvard University Press, 1983), pp. 113–16 and 152 ff.
2. De Sola Pool, *Technologies of Freedom*, is an informative recent history of the modern media.
3. The installation of recorders by consumers seeking to achieve greater flexibility in viewing and listening times is another factor which is helping to encourage fee-for-service programing. Thus, video outlets already offer such a service and it is clear that there is a big demand for it.
4. It is interesting to note that because broadcasters are limited in the amount of advertising they can deliver, the competition between major companies seeking to obtain advertising revenue is not vicious. The leading company can only take that proportion of the advertising revenue it can successfully carry and must often leave enough and as good to its competitors.
5. In reaching this judgment I have been influenced by de Sola Pool, *Technologies of Freedom*. He is optimistic that, in the long term, cable systems will be able to "create for video the kind of diversity and choice that exists in print." But he warns that a major issue "for the 1980s and 1990s will be how to prevent cable casters from seeking the advantage of becoming publishing monopolists in their communities, controlling both the conduit and its contents" (see p. 172).
6. For a good statement of this view, see Tim Rowse, "Culture and Democracy: The Economists and the Performing Arts," in *Media Interventions* (Leichhardt, N.S.W.: Intervention Publications, Sept. 1981), pp. 25–44.
7. See the Annan Committee Report, *On the Future of Broadcasting* (HMSO, Cmnd 6753, 1977), pp. 125–27, for a discussion of the BBC's income.
8. In the United Kingdom, the IBA has ruled that television stations must not show more than 5 ½ hrs of overseas material during peak time (6:30PM to 10:30PM) in a week and that 86 percent of the material broadcast should be British-made. The BBC has a rule that only 14 percent of the total output in any given year will be imported from the United States, and it encourages programers to use British materials. (See Colin R. Munro, *Television, Censorship and the Law*, pp. 39 ff. and p. 48).
9. In the United Kingdom, the charter of the BBC and the *Independent Broadcasting Authority Act* (1973) set out as a general obligation that each of the authorities has a duty to broadcast its services as a means of "disseminating information, education and entertainment," and this has been interpreted as requiring a wide range of subject matter and balance in the kinds of service which each must provide. The IBA is also obliged to ensure that "a sufficient amount of time in the programs is given to news and news features" (sec. 4, 1b). It has met this latter obligation by ensuring that all companies show certain mandated programs. These latter include the news and usually the most important current affairs programs, documentaries, and educational programs (see Munro, *Television, Censorship and the Law*, p. 48).
10. In the United Kingdom, the BBC is required to refrain from expressing its own opinion on current affairs or matters of public policy and sec. 4 (2) of the *Independent Broadcasting Authority Act* imposes a similar obligation on the IBA, which must ensure that stations do not propagate the opinions of its members or officers, program contractors and any directors or officers thereof, or anyone with a controlling interest in a program company. Munro comments: "Whereas it is only the [BBC's] own opinion that is disallowed . . . a large number of individuals are caught by Section 4 (2), with some anomalous results" (p. 36).
11. Both the BBC and the IBA operate a form of classification of the suitability of programs, and both have agreed that materials deemed unsuitable for family viewing should not be shown before 9 PM.

12. It was only in 1972 that the BBC's monopoly over radio broadcasting was broken.
13. The relationship between the governors and the managers of the BBC is discussed by Munro, *Television, Censorship and the Law*, op. cit., pp. 16–19. He concludes that "despite some blurring of respective functions, the gubernatorial influence on program matters in general remains small."
14. In the United Kingdom, there has been and is full consultation between the major broadcasters and political parties regarding the coverage of general elections. Indeed, prior to 1974, the parties insisted: (a) that they hold a right of veto over the speakers who are chosen to present their case on the broadcast media, (b) that they be consulted on which constituencies would be given attention, (c) that the booking of all speakers be done through national party headquarters, and (d) that there should be no live discussion in front of audiences. These restrictions have now disappeared, but broadcasters are still very deferential to politicians, and conventions relating to equal treatment for political broadcasting are well-respected. See Munro, *Television, Censorship and the Law*, p. 145.
15. The best review of U.S. practice in this regard is Schmidt, *Freedom of the Press v. Public Access*, pp. 137–39 and pp. 157–59.
16. Annan Committee, *Future of Broadcasting*, para. 17.10, p. 269.
17. Ibid., para. 17.12
18. Ibid.
19. *NBC v. FCC* 516 F.2d 1101 (1974)
20. *Office of Communication of United Church of Christ v. FCC* 425 F.2d 543 (D.C.Cir. 1969).
21. On this point see Schmidt, *Freedom of the Press v. Public Access*, pp. 188–89.
22. See Pember, *Mass Media Law*, from which I have taken these figures. He tells us that a West Coast television station won a "fairness doctrine" hearing which cost the broadcaster $20,000 to defend [p. 465].

Chapter 9

1. Robert Nozick argues that the only legitimate function of the state is to protect rights. Thus, he would disallow most of the activities I have listed. See *Anarchy, State and Utopia* (Oxford: Blackwell, 1973). This view is highly unrealistic and has little support. F. A. Hayek, for example, concedes that the state will have to intervene to provide goods and services whose benefits cannot be restricted to those who pay but are inevitably general, such as the protection of environmental resources or the making provision for an adequate national defense, the conduct of foreign policy, and the provision of energy. Moreover, he thinks it should act to ensure that those in severe need are provided for. See *The Constitution of Liberty* (London: Routledge & Kegan Paul, 1952) pp. 285 ff.
2. It may be argued that I have left out of account at least one other major liberal tradition. Thus, Gerald Gaus in *The Modern Liberal Theory of Man* (London: Croom Helm, 1983) identifies a distinct idealistic tradition which he calls "modern liberal." Although I concede that most contemporary liberal writers argue positively that liberal principles are compatible with and supportive of the highest humanist ideals, I do not accept that any significant writer holds that it is the goal of realizing our true nature (rather than, say, the demands of justice, a conception of general utility, or the fear of despotism) which provides the most persuasive supporting argument for recognizing such principles.
3. Hayek favors democracy because it allows for peaceful change, is less likely to violate core liberties than other forms of government, and raises the level of political education (*The Constitution of Liberty*, pp. 107–9). Nevertheless, he distinguishes liberalism as a "doctrine about what the law ought to be" from democracy as "a doctrine about the manner of determining what will be law," and he thinks it likely that democratically elected governments, like other governments, will succumb to the temptation to act in illiberal ways (ibid., pp. 103 ff.). Cf. the views of John Hart Ely, *Democracy and Distrust* (Cambridge, Mass.: Harvard University Press, 1980), discussed below, who argues that the United States Supreme Court should be concerned with process (with the manner of determining the law) and Congress should determine policy.
4. W. Ivor Jennings, *The Law and the Constitution*, 3rd ed. (London: University of London Press, 1943), p. 59.

5. Ibid., p. 139. Jennings' views on fundamental rights are stated on pp. 237 ff.
6. For an extended treatment of the process of abdication in the United States, see Theodore J. Levi, *The End of Liberalism*, 2nd ed. (New York: Norton, 1979), esp. ch. 5. Levi observes that after the New Deal, "Although Congress continued to possess the lawmaking authority, it delegated that authority increasingly in statute after statute to an agency in the Executive Branch or to the president, who had the power to sub-delegate . . ." and that "ultimately, delegation was recognized for what it really was— administrative legislation" (p. 274). And he argues that this process allows organized groups to dominate the policy-making process.
7. J. S. Mill, *Representative Government* in *Three Essays* (Oxford: Oxford University Press, 1975), pp. 226 ff.
8. On the presidency, see Robert Dahl, *Pluralist Democracy in the United States*, 3rd ed. (Chicago: Rand McNally, 1967), ch. 13, esp. pp. 170-79. On the British parliament see, generally, Bernard Crick, *The Reform of Parliament* (London: Weidenfeld & Nicolson, 1964), and John P. Mackintosh, *The British Cabinet*, 3rd ed. (London: Stevens, 1977). First published in 1968. For critical comment of Crick's thesis, see Ronald Butt, *The Power of Parliament* (London: Constable, 1967).
9. This is the central thesis of Levi, who, in *The End of Liberalism*, includes a number of care-fully researched case studies focused on the United States system to illustrate the point. What the demise of parliamentary responsibility seems sometimes to give rise to, in his view, is the phenomenon of "clientelism"—agencies charged with responsibility for regulating an area of social and economic life become captives of the interest groups they are supposed to impose upon in the general interest.
10. See Charles Lindblom, *Politics and Markets* (New York: Basic Books, 1977), pp. 266-72.
11. Ibid., p. 41. The evidence in other democracies is more reassuring.
12. They would probably enjoy an even greater advantage in systems where there was no competition, and this is often overlooked by those who seem to think that because lib-eral systems do not work perfectly other systems would be better.
13. See Frank J. Donner, *The Age of Surveillance* (New York: Knopf, 1980), which describes abuse of authority by the FBI and United States military intelligence agencies. Levi (*End of Liberalism*) tells us that "Between 1966 and 1976, court records show that the FBI in Chicago alone paid $2.5 million to recruit more than 5,000 spies to inform on Chicago area residents and organizations. The FBI files themselves reveal that the Trotskyist So-cialist Workers Party, although composed of only 3,500 members by the FBI's own gen-erous count, had been infiltrated by over 300 paid informants placed by the CIA and other agencies in the same political party" (pp. 276-77).
14. On jury vetting, see David Leigh, *The Frontiers of Secrecy* (London: Junction Books, 1980), pp. 154 ff. On the more general civil liberty problems, see Patricia Hewitt, *The Abuse of Power: Civil Liberties in the United Kingdom* (Oxford: Martin Robertson, 1982).
15. Levi, *End of Liberalism*, provides a summary of what he takes to be four major defects; Lindblom provides a negative appraisal in his presidential address, "Another State of Mind," to the American Political Science Association (1981), in which he emphasizes the importance of cultural manipulation—something I have not mentioned—(*American Political Science Review* 76, (1982); and Dahl lists a number of problems in his *Dilemmas of Pluralist Democracy* (New Haven, Conn.: Yale University Press, 1983), pp. 40-54.
16. Ely, *Democracy and Distrust*, pp. 1-9.
17. Ibid., p. 8.
18. It is not clear how widely held this view is among American writers. Ely tells us that its lineage stretches back to Alexander Hamilton's Federalist 78 and Chief Justice Marshall's opinion in *Marbury v. Madison*, and that it also lies at the core of the constitu-tional adjudication of Mr. Justice Black.
19. Ely argues that history can be of very little help (apart from providing a dictionary of the meaning of words at the time of ratification) in interpreting these provisions, because the processes for establishing a constitution or amending it involve many millions of voters each of whom would have different conceptions of what they support; thus, the views of the few politicians who initiate or draft the relevant clauses cannot be accepted as authoritative (ibid. pp. 17 ff.).
20. Quoted by Ely, ibid., p. 71, from Alexander Bickel, *The Least Dangerous Branch* (1962), p. 55.

21. Ibid., pp. 65–69.
22. Ibid., p. 114.
23. Hayek, *Constitution of Liberty*, pp. 209–10.
24. Strictly interpreted, *nulla poena sine lege* requires no punishment without a statute. However, in the common-law tradition this requirement is dropped, and all that is required is that legal obligations be clear.

)

References

Abrams, Floyd. "The Press Privacy and the Constitution." *The New York Times*, Aug. 21, 1977, sec. 6.

Ackerman, Bruce A., *Social Justice and the Liberal State*. New Haven, Conn.: Yale University Press, 1980.

Australia, Law Reform Commission. *Defamation, Options for Reform*. Discussion Paper no. 1.

_____. Unfair Publications. Report No. 11, 1979.

Australia, Parliament. *Report of the Royal Commission on Intelligence and Security*. 4th Report, Paper 248, 1977.

Baier, Kurt. *The Moral Point of View*. Ithaca, N.Y.: Cornell University Press, 1958.

Barron, Jerome. *Freedom of the Press for Whom?* Bloomington: Indiana University Press, 1973.

_____. "Access to the Press – A New First Amendment Right." *Harvard Law Review* 80 (1967): 1641 ff.

_____. "An Emerging First Amendment Right of Access to the Media." *George Washington Law Review* 37 (1969): 487 ff.

Barry, Brian. *Political Argument*. London: Routledge & Kegan Paul, 1965.

Berger, Fred R. *Happiness, Justice and Freedom: The Moral Philosophy of John Stuart Mill*. Berkeley: University of California Press, 1984.

Bevier, R. "Press Access Rights." *California Law Review* 68: 507 ff.

Bork, Robert. "Neutral Principles, Some First Amendment Problems." *Indiana Law Journal* 47, no. 1 (1979).

Brandt, R. B. *Ethical Theory*. Englewood Cliffs, N.J.: Prentice-Hall, 1959.

Butt, Ronald. *The Power of Parliament*. London: Constable, 1967.

Cowen, Zelman. *The Private Man*. The Boyer Lectures, Australian Broadcasting Commission, 1969.

_____. *Individual Liberty and the Law*. Calcutta: Eastern Law House, 1977.

Cox, Barry. *Civil Liberties in Britain*. Harmondsworth: Penguin Special, 1975.

Crick, Bernard. *The Reform of Parliament*. London, Weidenfeld & Nicolson, 1964.

Dahl, Robert. *A Preface to Democratic Theory*. Chicago: University of Chicago Press, 1956.

_____. *Pluralist Democracy in the United States*. Chicago: Rand McNally, 1967.

_____. *Polyarchy*. New Haven, Conn.: Yale University Press, 1971.

_____. "On Removing Certain Impediments to Democracy in the United States." *Political Science Quarterly* 92, no. 1 (Spring 1977): 1–20.

_____. *Dilemmas of Pluralist Democracy*. New Haven, Conn.: Yale University Press, 1983.

Daniels, Norman. "Wide Reflective Equilibrium and Theory Acceptance in Ethics." *The Journal of Philosophy* 76 (1979).

Devlin, Patrick. *The Enforcement of Morals*. Oxford: Oxford University Press, 1965.

Donner, Frank J. *The Age of Surveillance*. New York: Knopf, 1980.

Dworkin, Ronald. *Taking Rights Seriously*. London: Duckworth, 1977.

_____. Introduction to Dworkin, ed., *Philosophy of Law*. Oxford: Oxford University Press, 1977.

_____. "Is the Press Losing the First Amendment?" *New York Review of Books*, 27, no. 19 (1980): 49–57.

_____. "Is there a Right to Pornography?" *Oxford Journal of Legal Studies* 1, no. 2 (1981): 177 ff.

_____. "What Liberalism Isn't," *New York Review of Books*. Jan. 20, 1983.

Ellis, Anthony. "Offense and the Liberal Conception of Law." *Philosophy and Public Affairs* 13, no. 1 (1984): 1–23.

Ely, John, Hart. *Democracy and Distrust*. Cambridge Mass.: Harvard University Press, 1980.

Emerson, Thomas. *Towards a General Theory of the First Amendment*. New York: Random House, 1963.

_____. *The System of Freedom of Expression*. New York: Random House, 1970.

Feinberg, Joel. "Harmless Immoralities and Offensive Nuisance." *Rights, Justice, and the Bounds of Liberty*. Princeton, N.J.: Princeton University Press, 1980.

Flick, Geoffrey A. *Civil Liberties in Australia*. Melbourne: Law Book Company, 1981.

Fried, Charles. "Privacy." *Yale Law Journal* 77, no. 3 (1967/68): 475–93.

Gaus, Gerald. *The Modern Liberal Theory of Man*. London: Croom Helm, 1983.

Gray, John. *Mill on Liberty: A Defense*. London: Routledge & Kegan Paul, 1983.

_____. "Indirect Utility and Fundamental Rights." In Ellen Frankel Paul, Fred D. Miller, and Jeffery Paul, eds., *Human Rights*. Oxford: Blackwell, 1984.

Federal Communications Commission. "Fairness Doctrine and Public Interest Standards." *Federal Register* 39, no. 139 (1974).

Goodman (Lord). "Wicked, Wicked Libels." *New Statesman*, March 31, 1972, p. 426.

Greenawalt, Kent. "Speech and Crime." *American Bar Foundation Research Journal* no. 4 (1980):733 ff.

Haiman, Franklyn S., ed. *Freedom of Speech*. Skokie, Ill.: National Textbook Company, 1976.

_____. *Speech and Law in a Free Society*. Chicago: University of Chicago Press, 1982.

Hare, R. M., *Freedom & Reason*. Oxford: Oxford University Press, 1963.

_____. *The Language of Morals*. Oxford: Oxford University Press, 1952.

Hart, H. L. A. *Law, Liberty and Morality.* London: Oxford University Press, 1963.

————. "Bentham on Legal Rights," in A. W. B. Simpson ed., *Oxford Essays in Jurisprudence,* Second Series. Oxford: Oxford University Press, 1971.

————. "Are there any Natural Rights?" *Philosophical Review* 69 (1972): 535–45.

Hayek, F. A. *The Constitution of Liberty.* London: Routledge & Kegan Paul, 1952.

Hewitt, Patricia. *The Abuse of Power: Civil Liberties in the United Kingdom.* Oxford: Martin Robertson, 1982.

Jencks, Christopher. *Inequality.* New York: Allen Lane, 1973.

Jennings, Ivor W. *The Law and the Constitution.* London: University of London Press, 3rd ed., 1943.

Justice. *The Law and the Press.* London, 1965.

Kalven, Harry, Jr. *The Negro and the First Amendment.* Chicago: University of Chicago Press, 1966.

————. "The New York Times Case: A Note on the Central Meaning of the First Amendment." *Supreme Court Review* (1964):191 ff.

Kant, Immanual. *Groundwork of Metaphysics and Morals.* Translated by H. J. Paton. New York: Harper and Row, 1956.

Ladenson, Robert F. *A Philosophy of Free Expression.* Totowa, N.J.: Rowman & Littlefield, 1983.

Leigh, David. *The Frontiers of Secrecy.* London: Junction Books, 1980.

Levi, Theodore J. *The End of Liberalism,* 2d ed. New York: Norton, 1979.

Levy, Leonard W. *Legacy of Suppression: Freedom of Speech and the Press in Early American History.* Cambridge, Mass.: Harvard University Press, 1960.

Lindblom, Charles. *Politics and Markets.* New York: Basic Books, 1977.

————. "Another State of Mind." *American Political Science Review* 76 (1982).

Lloyd (Lord). "The Law and the Press." *Current Legal Problems* 43 (1966):55 ff.

Lyons, David. *The Forms and Limits of Utilitarianism.* Oxford: Oxford University Press, 1968.

————. "Mill's Theory of Morality." *Nous* 10 (1976):101–20.

MacBride, Sean (Chairman). *Many Voices One World.* UNESCO, 1980.

Mackintosh, John P. *The British Cabinet,* 3rd ed. London: Stevens, 1977.

McCloskey, H. J. "Liberty of Expression its Grounds and Limits." *Inquiry* 13 (1970).

Meiklejohn, Alexander. *Political Freedom.* New York: Oxford University Press, 1965.

————. "The First Amendment is an Absolute." *Supreme Court Review.* 1961.

Meldon, A. I. *Rights and Persons.* Oxford: Blackwell, 1977.

Mill, John Stuart. *Three Essays: On Liberty, Representative Government, The Subjection of Women.* Oxford: Oxford University Press, 1960.

Miller, Arthur. *Assault on Privacy.* Ann Arbor: University of Michigan Press, 1971.

Miller, Richard W. "Rawls and Marxism." *Philosophy and Public Affairs* 3, no. 2 (1974):167–91.

Munro, Colin R. *Television and Censorship.* Westmead: Saxon House, 1979.

Nozick, Robert. *Anarchy, State and Utopia.* Oxford: Blackwell, 1973.

Owen, Bruce M. *Economics and Freedom of Expression.* Cambridge, Mass.: Ballinger, 1975.

Pember, Don, R. *Mass Media Law,* 2d ed. Dubuque, Iowa: Wm. C. Brown, 1981.

Pettit, Philip. *Judging Justice.* London: Routledge & Kegan Paul, 1980.

Pool, Ithiel de Sola. *On Free Speech in an Electronic Age: Technologies of Freedom.* Cambridge, Mass.: Harvard University Press, 1983.

Prosser, William L. "Privacy." *California Law Review* 48 (1960):383 ff.

Quinton, Anthony. *Utilitarian Ethics.* London: Macmillan, 1973.

Rawls, John. A Theory of Justice. Oxford: Oxford University Press, 1973. "The Basic Liberties and their Priority" in Sterling M. McCurrin, ed., The Tanner Lectures on Human Values, Vol. III. Cambridge: Cambridge University Press, 1982.

Scanlon, Thomas. "A Theory of Freedom of Expression." In R. Dworkin, ed. Philosophy of Law. Oxford: Oxford University Press, 1977.

_____. "Freedom of Expression and the Categories of Expression." *University of Pittsburgh Law Review* 40 (1979):519-24.

Schauer, Frederick. *Free Speech: A Philosophical Enquiry.* Cambridge: Cambridge University Press, 1982.

Schmidt, Benno C., Jr. *Freedom of the Press v. Public Access.* New York: Praeger, 1977.

Schumpeter, J. A. *Capitalism, Socialism and Democracy.* London: Allen & Unwin, 1970.

Singer, Peter. *Practical Ethics.* Cambridge: Cambridge University Press, 1979.

Smart, J. J., and Williams, B., eds. *Utilitarianism: For and Against.* Cambridge: Cambridge University Press, 1973.

Street, H. *Freedom: The Individual and the Law.* Harmondsworth: Penguin Books, 1977.

Thomson, Judith J. "The Right to Privacy." *Philosophy and Public Affairs* 4, no. 4 (1975):295-314.

Tucker, D. F. B. *Marxism and Individualism.* Oxford: Blackwell, 1981.

_____. Review of Schauer, *Free Speech: A Philosophical Enquiry, Australian Journal of Philosophy* 62, no. 1 (1984):82-84.

United Kingdom, Parliament. *Report of the Committee on Privacy* (Younger, Chairman). Cmnd. 5012, 1972.

_____. *Report of the Committee on Defamation* (Faulks, Chairman). Cmnd. 5909, 1975.

_____. *Report on the Disturbances in Red Lion Square* (Scarman). Cmnd. 5919, 1975.

_____. *Report of the Royal Commission on the Future of Broadcasting* (Annan, Chairman). Cmnd. 6753, 1977.

_____. *Report of the Royal Commission on the Press.* (McGregor, Chairman). Cmnd. 6810, 1977.

Warren, S. D., and Brandeis, L. D. "The Right to Privacy." *Harvard Law Review* 4, No. 5 (December 1890-91):193-220.

Western, A. F. *Privacy and Freedom.* New York: Atheneum, 1967.

Wollheim, Richard. "A Paradox in the Theory of Democracy." In Peter Laslett and W. G. Runciman, eds. *Philosophy, Politics and Society,* Second Series. Oxford: Blackwell, 1962.

Index

Abrams, Floyd, 197 *n.* 3
access right to a forum, 66–67, 69–70, 72–76; to information, 122–23, *See also* Advertising
Ackerman, Bruce M., 43–44, 193 *n.* 9
advertising, 37–39, 68–69, 149–50; access to media, 73, 75, 200 *n.* 4; on-site, 194 *n.* 9; political, 70–72, 194 *n.* 8
Annan, *See* United Kingdom: Committee on Broadcasting
Associated Press v. Walker, 87, 195 *n.* 4
Australian Law Reform Commission, 92–93, 196 *n.* 17, 19, 197 *n.* 7, 198 *n.* 1, 6
Avins v. Rutgers Law Review, 66–68, 194 *n.* 1

Baier, Kurt, 191 (Introduction) *n.* 1
Barron, Jerome, 63; 195 *n.* 18, 19
Bentham, Jeremy, 11–12
Berger, Fred R., 192 *n.* 12
Bevier, R., 192 *n.* 15
Black, Hugo (Justice), 33; 58–59, 136, 193 *n.* 1, 199 *n.* 24
Blackmun, Harry (Justice), 70–71, 194 *n.* 7
Bork, Robert, 193 *n.* 18
Brandeis, Louis D., 123, 197 *n.* 1, 198 *n.* 11
Brandt, R. B., 191 (ch. 1) *n.* 1
Brennan, William (Justice), 71, 86–87, 91
British Broadcasting Corporation, 99, 121, 152, 154–55, 194 *n.* 8, 200 *n.* 7; local content rule, 200 *n.* 8:

neutrality, 155, 159–60, 200 *n.* 10; public interest standards, 200 *n.* 9
broadcasting, special treatment of, 77–83; new technologies, 150; public, 151–56, public interest standards, 152–53, 157–58, (in U.S.) 161–62, (in U.K.), 200 *n.* 9, 10; scarcity of spectrum, 67, 79, 148–50, 153, 200 *n.* 1
Burger, Warren E. (Chief Justice), 5, 33, 76–77, 80–81, 123
Business Executives Movement for Vietnam Peace v. FCC, 76–77, 195 *n.* 12
Butt, Ronald, 201 *n.* 8

Carol Burnett v. National Enquirer, 90, 195 *n.* 5
Chaplinsky v. New Hampshire, 139, 199 *n.* 11
Cohen v. California, 175
Coleman v. Maclennan, 86–87, 195 *n.* 3
Columbia Broadcasting System v. Democratic National Committee, 195 *n.* 12
Cowen, Zelman, 111, 196 *n.* 15, 198 *n.* 16
Cox v. Louisiana, 193 *n.* 1, 199 *n.* 18
Crick, Bernard, 202 *n.* 8
Curtis Publishing v. Butts, 87–88, 195 *n.* 4

Dahl, Robert, 168, 191 *n.* 6, 202 *n.* 8, 15
defamation and right of reply, 54; case for reform of law, 84–93; First Amendment, 85–89, 90–91; group libel, 140–41

deontological approach, 1, 3–4; defamation, 93–100; defining speech, 35–37; freedom of speech, 39–42, 48–52; judicial review, 164, 178–82; offense problem, 134–36; privacy, 105–14; strengths listed, 184–89

De Sola Pool, Ithiel, 200 *n*. 1, 2, 5

Devlin, Patrick (Lord), 13–4, 129–32, 198 (ch. 7) *n*. 4

Dietemann v. Time, 117–8, 198 *n*. 3

Donner, Frank, 197 *n*. 13, 202 *n*. 13

Douglas, William (Justice), 194 *n*. 7

Duncan v. Jones, 146

Dworkin, Ronald, 172, 177, 182, 194 *n*. 11; concept of rights based theory, 3–4, 193 *n*. 7; critical morality, 44–45; criticism of functionalism, 27–30; liberalism, 41, 193 *n*. 10; newsman's privilege, 28–30; reflective equilibrium, 5, 191 *n*. 5

editorial autonomy, 66–67, 72–76; over advertising, 74; fairness, 83

Edwards v. South Carolina, 144, 198 *n*. 18, 22, 23

Ellis, Anthony, 199 *n*. 9

Ely, John Hart, 170–177, 182, 201 *n*. 3, 202 *n*. 16, 17, 18, 19

Emerson, Thomas, 1, 197 *n*. 6, 198 (ch. 5) *n*. 14, 199 *n*. 12, 17, 21; abusive insults, 139; definition of speech, 20; indirect utilitarianism, 20–21; justification of freedom of speech, 15, 191 *n*. 5; privacy, 125

fairness, standards, 77–79, 195 *n*. 17; basic principles, 83

Faulks, *See* United Kingdom: Committee on Defamation

Feinberg, Joel, 129, 132–34, 198 (ch. 7) *n*. 5

Firestone v. Time, 196 *n*. 8

First Amendment, United States, 5, 34, 122–23, 174–76; *See also* Defamation, Fairness standards

Flick, Geoffery, 199 *n*. 28

free speech, as residual right, 52, 53–54, 101; balancing approach to, 21–24; competing rights, 50–55; justification of, 39–42; Meiklejohn's approach to, 26–27; Rawlsian

approach to, 34–37, 50–52

Fried, Charles, 197 *n*. 4

functionalism, defined, 1; judicial review, 164, 171–77, 189; Meiklejohnian functionalism, 24–30; offense problem, 128–34; privacy, 104–105; *Red Lion Broadcasting* case, 78–79; utilitarianism, 12–21

Gaus, Geral, 201 *n*. 2

Gertz v. Welsh, 87, 89, 90, 195 *n*. 4

Goodman, Arnold (Lord), 92, 196 *n*. 16

Gray, John, 192 *n*. 12

Greenawalt, Kent, 193 *n*. 18

Gregory v. City of Chicago, 144, 199 *n*. 18

Haiman, Franklyn S., 199 *n*. 23

harassment, by hostile audience, 82, 141–47; by journalists, 120–1

Hare, Richard, 191 *n*. 1

Harlan, John (Justice), 88–89

Hart, H. L. A., concept of a right, 45–47, 194 *n*. 13, 14, 15; critical morality, 44–45, 194 *n*. 12; judicial review, 166; offense problem 129–32

Hayek, F. A., 176, 182, 201 *n*. 1, 3, 203 *n*. 23

Herbert v. Landau, 28, 193 *n*. 21

Herwitt, Patricia, 202 *n*. 14

Independent Broadcasting Authority (U.K.), 99, 194 *n*. 8

Jennings, Ivor (Sir), 165–66, 202 *n*. 4

judicial review. *See* Rights, Functionalism, Deontological approach

Justice (U.K.), 91–93, 121, 196 *n*. 12, 13, 14, 198 *n*. 9

Kalven, Harry, 196 *n*. 11, 198 *n*. 15

Kant, Immanuel, 3, 50, 191 *n*. 1

legal positivism, 165–66; judicial review, 169–71

Lehman v. City of Shaker Heights, 70–71, 194 *n*. 4

Leigh, David, 202 *n*. 14

Levi, Theodore J., 202 *n*. 6, 15

Levy, Leonard W., 191 *n*. 15

liberalism, and free speech, 9; assumed circumstances of justice, 47–48;

competing theories evaluated, 59–63; equality, 42; Lockean, 31–34, 60; Rawlsian, 33–42; utilitarian, 10–18

Lindblom, Charles, 168, 202 *n.* 10, 15

Lyons, David, 18, 191 (ch. 2) *n.* 1, 192 *n.* 12

MacBride, Sean, 62–63, 192 *n.* 6, 193 *n.* 6

Mackintosh, John P., 202 *n.* 8

McCall v. Courier Journal, 117–18, 198 (ch. 6) *n.* 4

McCloskey, John, 17, 192 *n.* 8

media imperialism, 15–16, 62–63

Meiklejohn, Alexander, 24–30, 39–40, 49, 79, 192 *n.* 16; defamation law, 85–86; definition of speech, 26–27, 192 *n.* 18

Meldon, A. I., 197 *n.* 10

Miami Herald Publishing v. Tornillo, 80–83, 194 *n.* 2

Milk Wagon Drivers' Local 753 v. Meadowmoor Dairies, 142 199 *n.* 17

Mill, James, 10

Mill, John Stuart; democracy, 17–18, 167, 202 *n.* 7; freedom of speech, 21; harm principle, 12, 19; indirect utilitarianism, 18–19; Kantian humanism, 51; offense problem, 128–29, 134, 198 (ch. 7) *n.* 3

On Liberty, 1, 12–18, 178, 183, 191 *n.* 2 (ch. 1)

Miller, Arthur, 197 *n.* 11

Munro, Colin R., 200 *n.* 8, 9, 10; 201 *n.* 13

NBC v. FCC, 201 *n.* 19

newsman's privilege, 28–30, 122

New York Times v. Sullivan, 29, 85–87, 91, 193 *n.* 22

Nozick, Robert, 182, 201 *n.* 1

offense problem, 128–36; demonstrations, 136–47

Office of Communication of the United Church of Christ v. FCC, 200 *n.* 20

Onassis v. Gallela, 120, 198 *n.* 5

Owen, Bruce M., 200 *n.* 1

Pell v. Procumier, 122–23, 198 *n.* 10

Pember, Don R., 196 *n.* 8, 197 *n.* 24, 201 *n.* 22

personal attacks, and compensation, 84–85, 95–97; right of reply to, 97–99; in U.S., 100

privacy, 54–55, 101–104, 197 *n.* 1; control over personal facts, 106–107; harassment, 120–22; human dignity, 113–14; intrusion, 116–20; personal autonomy, 103; right not to be deceived, 107–110; right to political liberty, 110–12; surveillance, 118–20, 198 *n.* 2; unwanted publicity, 123–25; U.S. law, 125

Prosser, William L., 102, 197 *n.* 2

Quinton, Anthony, 190 (ch. 1) *n.* 1

Rawls, John, characteristics of approach, 3–5, 33–34, 39–41, 42–43, 194 *n.* 16; Kantian ideal, 39; liberty principle, 48; priority of rights, 4, 112, 190 *n.* 2, 198 *n.* 17

Red Lion Broadcasting v. FCC, 78–79, 194 *n.* 2

reflective equilibrium, 5–7, 191 *n.* 5

rights, conceptions of, 45–47; identifying rights, 42–45, 47, 52–55; judicial review, 163–66, 171–81; to assemble, 137, 142–47; *See also* Access, Deontological approach, Free speech, Privacy

Roe v. Wade, 197 *n.* 3

Rowse, Tim, 200 *n.* 6

Saxbe v. Washington Post, 198 n. 10

Schauer, Frederick, 22–24, 85, 193 *n.* 2, 195 *n.* 1

Schmidt, Benno C., 194 *n.* 6, 195 *n.* 10, 201 *n.* 15, 21

Schumpeter, Joseph, 17, 192 *n.* 10

Singer, Peter, 191 *n.* 1

Smart, J. J., 191 (ch. 1) *n.* 1

Street v. NBC, 90, 196 *n.* 7

Supreme Court (U.S.), 5–6, 140, 142, 145–46, 195 *n.* 8, 199 *n.* 18, 21

Terminiello v. Chicago, 199 *n.* 18

Time v. Hill, 87–88, 195 *n.* 4

Thomson, Judith J., 197 *n.* 9

United Kingdom, Parliament: Commission on the Future of Broadcasting, 77; Commission on the Press, 197 *n.* 22; Committee on Defamation, 90–91, 92, 95, 196 *n.* 15; Committee on Privacy, 103, 116, 121, 123–24, 196 *n.* 21, 22, 198 *n.* 7, 8, 12, 19; Race Relations Act, 127, 140, 191 *n.* 1, 199 *n.* 14, 15; Public Order Act, 199 *n.* 14, 26

United States v. Progressive, 28, 193 *n.* 21
United States v. Snepp, 29, 193 *n.* 21
utilitarianism. *See also* Functionalism 11–24, 51

Warren, Samuel D., 123, 197 *n.* 1, 198 *n.* 11
Westin, A. F., 197 *n.* 1
White, Byron (Justice), 78–79, 195 *n.* 19
Winstow, Charles, 196 *n.* 16
Wollheim, Richard, 192 *n.* 9
Woodward v. Hutchins, 197 *n.* 8

Younger. *See* United Kingdom: *Committee on Privacy*